AMERICAN CHARACTERISTICS

BOOKS BY THORNTON WILDER

NOVELS

The Cabala
The Bridge of San Luis Rey
The Woman of Andros
Heaven's My Destination
The Ides of March
The Eighth Day
Theophilus North

COLLECTIONS OF SHORT PLAYS

The Angel That Troubled the Waters
The Long Christmas Dinner

PLAYS

Our Town
The Merchant of Yonkers
The Skin of Our Teeth
The Alcestiad, *with a Satyr Play,*
The Drunken Sisters

COLLECTION OF LONG PLAYS

Three Plays:
Our Town
The Skin of Our Teeth
The Matchmaker

ESSAYS

American Characteristics

American Characteristics

AND OTHER ESSAYS

Thornton Wilder

EDITED BY DONALD GALLUP

Foreword by Isabel Wilder

1817

HARPER & ROW, PUBLISHERS

NEW YORK, HAGERSTOWN, SAN FRANCISCO

LONDON

Copyright acknowledgments appear on page 297.

FIRST EDITION

Designer: Sidney Feinberg

Library of Congress Cataloging in Publication Data

Wilder, Thornton Niven, 1897–1975.
    American characteristics and other essays.
    I. Title.
PS3545.I345A79   809   79–1692
ISBN 0–06–014639–7

---

79 80 81 82 83 10 9 8 7 6 5 4 3 2 1

CONTENTS

EDITOR'S NOTE

The source for each essay is given in a note at the foot of its first page. The text is presented as there written, typed, or printed, except that errors have been corrected without comment and some (mostly minor) changes have been made in the interest of uniformity. (The omission of one paragraph—at the end of the first research paper on Lope de Vega—is explained in a footnote.)

The collective title for the three Norton lectures is adapted from that announced by the author for the series, "The American Characteristics of Classical American Literature" (see page 9).

FOREWORD

It is not as scholar nor critic that I have been asked to make a contribution to this book of my brother's essays. My rôle is to supply some facts and gather a sheaf of memories apropos of the various works listed in the table of contents.

More than once I have heard Thornton say: "The hardest thing for me as a writer is to put down one declarative sentence after another."

The essay is a literary form composed of one declarative sentence after another declarative sentence after another. . . . A collection of essays is a showcase of these grammar-riddled statements; the purpose in the progression from colon to semicolon, from dependent to independent clause to final period is to instruct, interest, convince, or, hopefully, delight the reader.

Before my brother had learned that it was hard to write essays he could toss off definitive statements for his fourth-grade English assignments with the speed of light: "Vulcan was the god of goldsmiths, ironsmiths, leadsmiths, silver-smiths, and Mrs. Smiths—there, now I'm out of breath."

His difficulty with the declarative sentence is easily explained: when he had something to say he instinctively burst into dialogue or telling stories. The dramatist is protected from his audience by the theater's proscenium arch or by curtains and pools of light, his words pronounced by other lips than his. The novelist functions under the disguise of omniscience, manipulating imaginary characters through a fictional cosmos of his own design, and binding them all together between the covers of a book.

The essayist? The essayist has no need of architectural devices or artistic subterfuges. Clothed in the emperor's raiment and armed with the limitless uses of the declarative sentence, he addresses the world in his own voice. But he does move about under many names: historian, lawyer, philosopher, scientist, pedagogue, scholar, man of letters, man of the church. The essayist is also the confessor. For him to speak is for us to learn who he is, what he thinks and believes, and how he spends his talent and his years.

As I glance over the table of contents of this collection of my brother's essays I see a faint outline for a biography, the self-story that he would never, never have written in the first-person singular.

The table of contents does not march forward chronologically. Greenwich precision time is suspended while the hour and the minute hands mark words rather than numbers. High noon, for instance, reads congeniality. The half-hour, associated subject matter. Something called "ideas" and "contrast for balance" fills the quarter-hour spaces. Furthermore, I, the commentator, use the table of contents as though it were a map and saunter or hurry over some paths to find a greener pasture in which to linger.

Thornton came to the essay from teaching, the public-lecture platform, and the theater. The lecture and the essay would seem to be blood-brothers. He made them into cousins who offered to each other hospitality and familial intimacies at weddings and funerals. Thornton, a writer first, insisted that what he put down to be set on the page in print for the reader was different from what he wrote to be spoken from the podium—the person there, his voice filling every corner of the auditorium.

Most of the selections in this volume were prepared for the reader, alone with a book of printed pages. The most conspicuous examples of lectures transformed into essays are the three first items, sheltered under the title "American Characteristics."

These two words in this particular connotation give me a visual image of the Stars and Stripes billowing in the breeze high above Thornton's head. Thornton Wilder, Patriot. And he *was* a patriot, although his first novel was laid in modern Rome, shadowed by the gods of antiquity; his second had the setting of Lima, Peru, of long ago; and the third, published in 1930 when the Great Depression was raging, was laid on a small island off the coast of Greece, B.C. The critics and editors of the journals of the new Left and their readers raised a storm of protest, poured scorn and ill will upon Thornton for dallying in beauty and nostalgic comfort while our country was a starving shambles.

In 1953 when *Time* magazine had a Wilder cover story—with no collusion on my part—the portrait on the cover had him posed three-quarter face against the American flag drawn in colored chalk on a school blackboard. A quote from the text reads: ". . . he has written some of the most authentic Americana of his time. . . ." Later in the article Thornton is quoted from an interview: "I am the only American of my generation who did not 'go' to Paris."

No, he didn't go to Paris and he didn't write about America until his fourth novel because, as he explained when challenged, "I didn't know enough about it." The earlier books were written out of his vast reading from early youth in library reading rooms. Crisscrossing the United States on several lecture tours after the success of the earlier novels gave him the material he needed to write *Heaven's My Destination.* Then some American-based one-act plays followed by *Our Town* finally gave him full citizenship.

The invitation from Harvard University to fill the one-year

guest appointment as the Charles Eliot Norton Professor of Poetry, 1950–51, came at the right moment for Thornton. He had recovered from the experience of serving three years in World War II—much of the time overseas—and had adjusted to the lingering disillusionment of the still agitated world. His fifth novel, *The Ides of March,* had come out and been well received, an important factor in giving him confidence again as a writer. He had had an active and exciting summer at the Goethe Convocation at Aspen, Colorado. The *hommage* he gave to the great German poet is one of the essays in this volume. A few days after delivering his own contribution he was on the platform again, standing side by side with Dr. Albert Schweitzer, translating his oration, sentence by sentence, German into English. The same drama had occurred a few days earlier when Thornton stood at the side of the distinguished Spanish man of letters Ortega y Gasset and translated *his* tribute.

My brother returned to his study in Hamden eager to start preparing the Norton lectures. He had his subject, American Characteristics; he had a cast as if he were going into rehearsal with a new play: Thoreau, Melville, Emily Dickinson, Poe, and Whitman. He knew that eyebrows would be raised if he, a stranger from Connecticut, denied Emerson a full lecture in his own name, but had decided that his subject for a possible sixth lecture would be not Emerson but Nathaniel Hawthorne.

Thornton was prepared for the cross-questioning, and even the reprimand, but when the first lecture came he was not prepared to learn that the little old lady near the front row was the great-grandniece of Ralph Waldo Emerson. She came each time. He buttered the crumbs which he had ready to give, for Emerson's name came up frequently in relation to the main topic and to the other personages involved, but even buttered crumbs did not begin to approximate the banquet it would have been pleasant to give with all his heart. He met the

great-grandniece several times; she was always cordial and
friendly—even a bit flowery—but Thornton always felt that
she never truly forgave him.

The three Norton essays reprinted here are from the series
of five. Only some notes for the other two survive and they
are not sufficient to be put together—"transformed" from
lecture to essay—either for this collection or for use by the
Harvard University Press to make a book uniform with the
dozens of other Norton lectures.

For the writer who hesitates as to what form to use in
presenting his material there is the old, old, almost flip remark, "Content takes care of form." It is good advice on an
easily understood level. Certainly the essay mold is the only
one my brother could have used, and in spite of his impatience
with the declarative sentence he had tamed it in one sense and
found a few tricks and wiles to make its restrictions more
interesting to him. What helped him, also, to put down those
one-after-another sentences was his enthusiasm. He cared for
and believed deeply in what he was saying. "Toward an
American Language" is packed with ideas—and facts—yet it
is not heavy; it also gives a picture and is almost storytelling.

The same qualities surround the essay "The American
Loneliness" while it concentrates on the figure of Thoreau—
he is seen plain in a fresh light. Here becomes apparent Thornton's increasing lack of sympathy for Emerson. Emerson had
had his great success; today his fulsome, insistent optimism
sounds hollow. His truths seem often like pretension and his
didacticism is hard to accept. It was all this that upset Thornton
and tended to blind him to what is still valid in Emerson today
—the shoe pinched.

Thornton inherited the tendency to didacticism from our
father (and prep-school mastering nurtured it), while our father got it from his father and "sainted" mother. My brother
was an early riser, I a late one. He had the habit of slipping
notes under my door. One day when he was well along with

the text of the five Norton lectures this is what one note said:

REMIND ME TO REMEMBER NOT TO BE DIDACTIC.

From childhood Thornton was a hero worshipper (and advised the young to go out and become the same). A hero and a heroine are saluted in these pages. The essay "Goethe and World Literature" is his *hommage* to Goethe, companion from his sixteenth year when he heard our mother read (she attended German classes at the university so that she could "keep up" with her children):

Kennst du das Land wo die Zitronen blüh'n?

The cadence and glow of that poem caught and held his imagination. Open on his bedside table the day he died was a heavily annotated copy of a German edition of the *Conversations with Eckermann.*

The heroine of his literary life was Mme. de Sévigné. He used to say: "She's one of the treasures of France!" His gratitude to her for the delight and ever refreshing surprises she brought him as he read and reread her letters is recorded here in the essay "On Reading the Great Letter Writers."

These two extraordinary people were important influences in his life.

Another extraordinary woman with whom he shared a rare friendship as well as mutual interest in literature was Gertrude Stein. It was a very different kind of relationship indeed—two people living and breathing on earth and visible to each other. The influences were more immediate and direct, with an exchange of ideas and convictions that flowed in several directions of the compass. The introductions he wrote for three of her books over a span of more than eleven years were acts of love, love that encompassed appreciation of the works and the friend. "She is such a laughing person," he would say. "Not enough people know that about her." And he would regale us with stories of outings, one special saga of the hilarious time they had seeing a performance of *Pinafore*. In her reading of each and every book that was available, Gertrude Stein had devoured scores of volumes about the sea and, most apropos to the Gilbert and Sullivan operetta, many about the British Navy.

Other friendships are marked here by tributes: Chauncey Brewster Tinker, a revered and loved teacher over decade after decade at Yale; Thornton had looked up to him as an undergraduate and matured to be accepted as an equal. My brother had met Frederick J. E. Woodbridge, distinguished savant, on several occasions at the Century, and was honored to be asked to write the tribute of the American Academy of Arts and Letters. Thomas Mann, Thornton had met only briefly at a number of events; but the stories and novels by the great German had illuminated countless hours of his reading life.

The almost giddy, saucy tidbit that combines Thornton's sincere regard and liking for "Bébé" Bérard helps balance the load of the formal eulogies. We were having tea with Alice Toklas the day of Bérard's funeral. She greeted us with the news that some of the mourners would be stopping by for a cup of tea—or a wee drop—to tell her about the ceremony. Afterward Thornton rushed me back to the hotel in order to get to his desk. That evening the declarative sentences fell into place with startling ease as he recorded other people's reports of the service.

My brother's 1957 speech-essay in the huge Paulus Church in Frankfurt, "Culture in a Democracy," aroused a good deal of controversy. In fact, in some segments of the conservative factions of the university and among the city officials it blew up into a small scandal that reached across the Channel to London and incited T. S. Eliot to rise and defend himself.

This was the last formal lecture Thornton expected ever to make. He wanted to say something, but although he knew his message was strong he had no wish to offend or anger anyone.

His "message" was far from new: after two shattering wars it would seem impossible that anyone had to be warned that changes were ahead. Thornton's message was the simple fact that in a democracy there is no room for what he calls the "myth" holding that inherited privilege is sacred, that a right is carried on from father to son with no allowance made for the individual's character or talents, that privilege of birth rests with the few—the most elite—who rule over all the rest of us.

As soon as he could get away after the formal festivities of the occasion in 1957, Thornton sent me a cable:

IT IS OVER. I FEEL TEN YEARS YOUNGER ALREADY.

A very important part of Thornton's life was, of course, the theater. The section headed "On Drama and the Theater" draws together six different aspects of that complex world. Listed first is an introduction to Sophocles's *Oedipus the King,* from the Golden Age of Greece. Thornton's background for undertaking such a responsibility stemmed from his years of lecturing at the University of Chicago.

Centuries later by the calendar is George Bernard Shaw, always a challenging figure as man, critic, playwright, pamphleteer—particularly so for a younger American playwright-novelist to cogitate over.

Thornton himself is represented by three prefaces to his own works and two essays on the theater. There is also a valuable introduction to the play *Jacob's Dream* by a Viennese literary personality of note, Richard Beer-Hofmann.

Besides the enthusiasms that came and went, my brother was always carrying along at least two continuing serious projects. One of these absorbing preoccupations was dating the plays of Lope de Vega, the leading dramatist of Spain's golden age of conquest and literature that ran currently with the grandeur of the Elizabethan Age in England. The two papers printed in the Appendix are a scholar's work.

The other continuing interest was James Joyce. I remember well how Thornton came to write the first essay listed, "James Joyce, 1882–1941." The telephone rang, the blind ring of any phone. I answered. "Long distance for Mr. Thornton Wilder." He was at home and took the receiver. James Joyce had died. The editor of *Poetry,* the Chicago magazine founded by Harriet Monroe, was calling. The next issue was ready to go to press. Would Mr. Wilder write a memorial, a tribute? The press would be held for a few days—a week if necessary. Thornton had been working on *Finnegans Wake* when the call interrupted him. He pulled out some sheets of the lined paper punched for notebooks that he used and started. And as with the writing of the Bébé Bérard piece, the pesky declarative sentences fell into place.

"Joyce and the Modern Novel" was written thirteen years later, in 1954. Thornton's fascination with *Finnegans Wake* continued for another ten years. "Giordano Bruno's Last Meal," printed in the Appendix, is a report of a tiny portion of the passionate search to find the heart of the matter, from which Thornton finally succeeded in tearing himself away. It was at first a gradual falling behind; astonished sometimes at the muck and the rubbish, which seemed to come in larger and larger barrels, he began to find himself bored. He was, of course, only one of an army of passionate diggers whose progress would be reported from here and there, with false alarms of a light ahead spotted in Dublin, Paris, Zürich, Farmington, London, and New York. The world was so large, but so was the army, and Thornton decided he would not be missed. He gave away some of the books that were essential for the digger; he put away the bulging notebooks and all the untidy loose papers. He was almost seventy at the time, suddenly free to rediscover some of his former interests—though music had never been neglected for *Finnegans Wake*—and free to explore new ideas. Through a geologist friend his imagination had been fired by Carbon-14 and the plates under the floor of the ocean.

However, I did feel sad the time he said: "I wasted all those hours!" "That's not fair, Thornton. Oh, you forget how much you enjoyed yourself! And when I came upon you bent over that old falling-apart copy of *Finnegan,* I knew you were doing exactly what you wanted to do. Be fair."

He admitted he had enjoyed the chase for years. But he had stayed in the running too long. "I didn't know then that life was so short."

ISABEL WILDER
New Haven, Connecticut
February 1979

AMERICAN

CHARACTERISTICS

TOWARD AN AMERICAN LANGUAGE

I

No, here they are. . . . Last night I had the lecturer's vocational nightmare: I dreamed that I had lost my notes.

Since this is a series of lectures concerning American characteristics, I must be sure to offer these young people an American lecture.

Is there a difference?

Bronson Alcott (in 1856) claimed that the lecture is an American invention. If so, it was also invented independently in Europe. Discourses have been delivered in all times and ages; but the lecture as we understand it, the secularization of the sermon and the popularization of the academic address, is probably a product of the middle-class mind. The Swiss have a passion for lectures. Conrad Ferdinand Meyer said that if the citizens of Zürich were required to make a choice between going to Heaven or going to a lecture about Heaven they would hesitate only a moment.

Yet there is a wide difference between an Old-World and a New-World lecture, and the difference arises from those American characteristics which are precisely the subject of these lectures.

A revision of Thornton Wilder's first Charles Eliot Norton lecture at Harvard, 1950. Published, with deletions, in *The Atlantic Monthly* for July 1952, it was subsequently reworked by the author, the deletions restored, and further additions and corrections made. The copy-text for the present publication is a paste-up of the *Atlantic* printing, with typed and manuscript insertions, among the Thornton Wilder papers in the Collection of American Literature, Beinecke Rare Book and Manuscript Library, Yale University (hereafter cited as YCAL).

Emerson, describing the requirements for lectures in the Lyceums of his day, said:

There are no stiff conventions that prescribe a method, a style, a limited quotation of books and an exact respect to certain books, persons, or opinions.

There's the crux: no respect.

An American is insubmissive, lonely, self-educating, and polite. His politeness conceals his slowness to adopt any ideas which he does not feel that he has produced himself. It all goes back to the fundamental problem of an American's relation to authority, and related to it is the American's reluctance to concede that there is an essential truth, or a thing true in essence.

For centuries—over there—kings were held to be invested with an essential authority. The child born into a royal cradle, be he nonentity or genius, was held to be, for mysterious and unsearchable reasons, the ruler of his people (May he live forever! May God take particular pains to save him, rather than you and me!) and held the royal authority.

Tradition commanded us to revere our fathers, not because they took the trouble to beget us and to pay our board in our earlier years, but because they wielded a paternal authority. America is now rapidly becoming a matriarchy and fathers are bewildered to discover that they are no longer accorded any such magical sway.

For Americans there is no inherent and essential authority accruing to the elderly, either. Thoreau said:

Practically, the old have no very important advice to give to the young. Their own experience has been so partial, and their lives have been such miserable failures, for private reasons, as they must believe. . . . I have lived some thirty years on this planet, and I have yet to hear the first syllable of valuable or even earnest advice from my seniors.

The same indocility holds in the intellectual life. In Europe the **Herr** Professor *and* **Cher Maître** *and the knighted scholar and the*

Member of the Royal Academy of . . . have enjoyed a distinction above and beyond their learning and wisdom. What better illustration of it than the fact that in Germany—in the good old days—no one less than a full professor could be invited to a dinner in society at which a full professor was present? To be sure, a mere Professor Extraordinarius might become a full professor next Tuesday, but on Monday he was still lacking the mystical qualification, the Mana. He was not salonfähig; *like a dog, he was not* hausrein.

American universities are still filled with vestigial Old-World elements. Our academic world is in labor trying to bring forth its first American university. There is still present among us many a tacit allusion to a state of grace enjoyed by authorities. From time to time we professors become aware that twentieth-century students are not completely sensible of this grace. The situation is far more serious: a student's mind goes blank when authority and tradition are invoked, so seldom does he confront them outside the classroom. Many an apparently stupid student is merely a student who has been browbeaten, has been stupefied, by being overwhelmed with too much of the unarguable, unanswerable, unexaminable. The intellectual life has been presented to him as a realm in which man is not free.

In the Old World a lecture tended to be a discourse in which an Authority dispensed a fragment of the Truth. Naturally I am not talking of informative lectures—"Recent Theories on the Origin of the Nebulae"; "Silversmiths in Eighteenth-Century New England"— which are inherently reading matter, and are so delivered: but of lectures in fields where every listener can be assumed to have formed or to be forming his own opinion. When Queen Victoria, accustomed to the discretion of Melbourne and Disraeli, complained that Gladstone addressed her as though she were a public meeting; when in impatience we hear ourselves saying, "Please don't lecture to me!" what is meant is: "Kindly remember that I am a free agent. Everything you say must be passed upon by the only authority I recognize—my own judgment." An American lecture is a discourse in which a man declares what is true for him. This does not mean that Americans are skeptical. Every American has a large predisposition to believe that there is a truth for him and that he is in the process of laying hold of it. He is building his own house of thought and he rejoices in seeing that someone else is also abuilding. Such houses can never be alike—begun in infancy and constructed with the diversity which is the diversity of every human life.

So I must remember to maintain the tone of a personal deposition. I may make as many generalizations as I wish, and as emphatically; but I must not slip into that other tone (how easy when one is tired; how tempting when one is insecure) of one in privileged relation to those august abstractions—tradition and authority.

MR. ARCHIBALD MACLEISH: Ladies and gentlemen: The Committee charged with the selection of . . .

My good friend, our admired poet, is introducing me. During the introduction of a lecturer in America everyone suppresses a smile: the introducer, the audience, and the lecturer.

This introduction is a form, a convention; it is very Old-World. To Americans conventions are amusing. They have attended many lectures; they have heard many a clarification and many an ineptitude. They have suffered often. Yet on every occasion they have heard the obligatory words: ". . . we have the pleasure of . . . it is a particular privilege to have with us this evening . . ."

Americans more and more find conventions amusing. It is amusing (and it is beginning to make us uncomfortable) that all letters must begin with the word "Dear." Hostesses are becoming impatient at writing ". . . request the pleasure of. . . ." They telephone or telegraph.

The audience is not in evening dress, but Archie MacLeish and I are. That is a convention. We explain it as being a "courtesy to the audience," but this audience which has just kindly hustled over from its dormitories sees through this. They suspect that it is an attempt to dress me in a little essential authority. What do I do next week when I must talk on Thoreau, who said, "Beware of all enterprises that require new clothes, and not rather a new wearer of clothes"?

The chief thing to remember about conventions is that they are soothing. They whisper that life has its repetitions, its recurring demonstrations that all is well—happy thought, that life with all its menace, its irruptions of antagonism and hatred, can be partially tamed, civilized by the pretense that everyone to whom one addresses a letter is dear and that every dinner guest is a pleasure. Densely populated countries—in Europe, but above all in Asia—develop a veritable network of these forms; but Americans feel little need of them. They even distrust them; they think that civilization can advance better without fictions.

Time was when one had to flatter the tyrant by telling him how kind he was; one reminded him that he was Serenissimus *and* Merced *and* Euer Gnaden, *and that as a Majesty he was certainly gracious—as one says to a snarling dog: "Good, good Fido."*

Americans do not ask that life present a soothing face. Even if they are in a contented situation they do not hope that life will continue to furnish them More of the Same. They are neither fretful nor giddy, but they are always ready for Something Different. In Europe everyone is attentive and pleased during ceremonial and secular ritual and these conventions of courtesy; in America people shuffle their feet, clear their throats, and size up the audience.

Archie is introducing me just right. He is telling them that I am a very hard-working fellow and that I travel about a good deal exhibiting curiosity.

THE AUDIENCE applauds.
MYSELF: Mr. MacLeish, ladies and gentlemen: In 1874, Charles Eliot Norton wrote his friend John Ruskin . . .

Another convention.

The French do this kind of thing superlatively well. They manage in an opening paragraph to allude to the auspices which furnished the occasion, to thank the authorities which invited them, to hint at their own unworthiness, to announce their subject, and to introduce a graceful joke.

But I am an American before Americans and immediately some-thing goes wrong. The fact that I am happy to have received their invitation now comes into collision with my obligation to say that I am happy. And at once an air of unreality enters the auditorium. It is not a chill; it is not a skepticism; but it is a disappointment. Convention demands that I say it, but the moment I have said it, it is spoiled.

These young men and women are near enough to their childhood to remember their agony when, on leaving a party, they knew that they had to say to their hostess: "I had a very good time." A certain number of children always manage to say: "My mother told me to tell you I had a very good time."

Here we are plunged into the heart of a basic American characteris-tic.

If you have to do a thing, you have lost your freedom. If you have to say a thing, you have lost your sincerity. If you have to love your parent, wife, child, or cousin, you begin to be estranged from them already. If you have to go into the Army . . . if you have to study Shakespeare . . .

Life, life, life is full of things one has to do; and if you have a passion for spontaneity, how do you convert What You Have To Do into The Thing You Choose To Do?

That is one of the most exciting things about being an American and about watching American life: how an American will succeed in converting Necessity into Volition. It is a very beautiful thing and it is new; and it is closely related to our problem of authority.

I hurried over this formal salutation as best I could. There lay several months ahead during which I could show in other ways that I was happy to be among them. Most Americans solve this problem without the slightest difficulty by a resort to humor. Much American humor is precisely the resolution of the conflict between obligation and spontaneity. But we cannot all call upon that happy national gift when most we need it.

In January 1874, Charles Eliot Norton wrote to his friend John Ruskin: "I want to be made a professor in the University here"; and five months later he was writing to Thomas Carlyle that one of his aims would be

> to quicken—so far as may be—in the youth of a land barren of visible memorials of former times the sense of connection with the past . . . and of gratitude for the efforts and labors of . . . former generations.

I then went on to announce that the subject for my lectures was "The American Characteristics of Classical American Literature" and that this first lecture dealt with the American Language, and that I did not mean the use of new words and idioms, nor did I mean slang or incorrectness. I meant the result of an omnipresent subtle pressure which writers and speakers in the United States were exerting on the mother tongue—within the bounds of syntactical correctness—in order to transform an old island language into a new continental one. And I proposed to show that this was not a recent effort but that the group of great writers whose major works appeared about a hundred years ago were deeply engaged in this task.

In about a quarter of an hour I am going to examine with you one of the most famous pages in American literature—the first direct view of the White Whale in *Moby Dick.* Our study of this page will not be primarily a literary one, but an attempt to discover these American modes of seeing and feeling—characteristics born of a nation's history and geography before they are characteristics of style.

So first let us review some of these elements of history and geography that had a part in forming the American.

When I think of those who founded this country I soon find myself thinking of *those who did not come.*

Of those who *almost* came.

I think of those conversations in East Anglia, the Thames Valley, in Somersetshire—conversations which probably took

place after dark and with long pauses between the exchanges:
"Farmer Wilkins, will ye go with us?" "Brother Hawkins,
will ye remove with us?"

And the same questions were to be put in Dutch, in the
Moravian dialect, in Gaelic. . . .

Who came? Who didn't come?

It was not, for many years, a flight from persecution or from
want. At most, for the first generations from England, it was
a flight from the shadow of a persecution. And it was not until
many generations afterward that the travelers could be said to
have come in the assurance that they would find an easier life.

Those who came were a selection of a selection in Europe.
But to say that it was a selection is not to say that it was an elite.
Here was the bigot, the fanatic, the dreamer, the utopian, the
misfit, the adventurer, the criminal. By the middle of the
eighteenth century the phrase was already current: "He has
skipped to America."

They all had one thing in common.

Their sense of identity did not derive from their relation to
their environment. The meaning which their lives had for
them was inner and individual. They did not need to be supported, framed, consoled, by the known, the habitual, the
loved—by the ancestral village, town, river, field, horizon; by
family, kin, neighbors, church and state; by the air, sky, and
water that they knew.

The independent.

Independence is a momentum. Scarcely had the first settler
made a clearing and founded a settlement than the more independent began pushing further back into the wilderness. The
phrase became proverbial: "If you can see the smoke from
your neighbor's chimney, you're too near."

These separatists broke away from church at home, but
separatism is a momentum. New religions were formed over
and over again. Ousted clergymen went off into the woods
with portions of their contentious flocks, there to cut down

more trees and raise new churches. When Cotton Mather went to what is now Rhode Island, he said that there had probably never been so many sects worshiping side by side in so small an area.

These were the men and women who were most irritably susceptible to any of the pressures which society and social opinion can bring.

I have recently read George Santayana's *Character and Opinion in the United States*. In it I find:

> The discovery of the new world exercised a sort of selection among the inhabitants of Europe. All the colonists, except the Negroes, were voluntary exiles. The fortunate, the deeply rooted, and the lazy remained at home; the wilder instincts or dissatisfactions of the others tempted them beyond the horizon. The American is accordingly the most adventurous, or the descendant of the most adventurous of Europeans. . . . Such a temperament is, of course, not maintained by inheritance [but by] social contagion and pressure.

A mentality so constituted will experience in a certain way and will shape its language—in this case, reshape an inherited language—to serve as instrument of its perception.

The Americans who removed to this country, then, during its first century and a half had these characteristics in common. The conditions under which they lived and the institutions which they created engraved these characteristics still more deeply into their natures.

However:

However:

Those basic characteristics have had to suffer violent opposition. It is still a question whether many of them may survive.

The force and prestige of the original traits remained, however. One has the feeling that their expression—personal, social, and literary—has been driven underground. Perhaps they are so powerful that they will yet be able to furnish a framework—a religion, a social thought, and an art—within which an entire continent can understand itself as unity and as growth. That was the hope frequently voiced by the great writers of the middle of the last century and it was accompanied by a great fear that it might not obtain; for they saw very clearly that the European modes, however fruitful for Europeans, could no longer serve the American people.

There have been no American writers of equal magnitude since their time—nor any comparable leaders, philosophers, or artists. There have been enormous activity and many considerable talents.

There are certain clarifications, however, that only great genius can achieve. And since great genius is lacking, we would do well to return to the last occasions on which it spoke.

A number of these writers consciously discussed the problems that arose from being an American. It is rather *how* they lived and thought, however, which will engage our attention. From the point of view of the European an American is nomad in relation to place, disattached in relation to time, lonely in relation to society, and insubmissive to circumstance, destiny, or God. It is difficult to be an American because there is as yet no code, grammar, decalogue by which to orient oneself. Americans are still engaged in inventing what it is to be an American. That is at once an exhilarating and a painful occupation. All about us we see the lives that have been shattered by it—not least those lives that have tried to resolve the problem by the European patterns.

These writers have not been chosen because they were exemplary citizens, but each was incontestably American and each illustrates dramatically one or more ways of converting an American difficulty into an American triumph. Each of them was what the man in the street would call "ill"—his word for it would be "cracked"; but their illness, if such it was, should throw light on a disequilibrium of the psyche which follows on the American condition.

As they were all writers, our study of them will be primarily a literary one, and will bear upon the language in which they wrote.

The American space-sense, the American time-sense, the American sense of personal identity are not those of Europeans—and, in particular, not those of the English. The English language was molded to express the English experience of life. The literature written in that language is one of the greatest glories of the entire human adventure. That achievement went hand in hand with the comparable achievement of forging the language which conveyed so accurately their senses of space, time, and identity. Those senses are not ours and the American people and American writers have long been engaged in reshaping the inherited language to express our modes of apprehension.

Paul Valéry—playing—once inserted four minus signs into Pascal's most famous sentence.

Pascal had said that the eternal silence of infinite space filled him with fright (*"le silence éternel des espaces infinies m'effraie"*). Valéry restated it by saying that the intermittent racket of our little neighborhood reassures us (*"le vacarme des petits coins où nous vivons nous rassure"*).

Laughter.

There lies a great difference between Europeans and Americans. Try as he will, the American cannot find any such soothing support in his social or natural surroundings. The racket in which he lives is greater than any European *vacarme*—not because it is noisier (any European city is noisier than an American city), but because of the disparity of things which press upon his attention.

The disparity arises because he is not deeply connected with any of them. And his inability to find any reassurance in this turbulence of unrelated phenomena which is his environment is increased by his unprecedented and peculiarly American consciousness of multitude and distance and magnitude. An American is differently *surrounded*.

It all goes back to the problem of identity.

Where does the American derive his confidence that— among so many millions—he is *one,* and that his being *one* is supported and justified? A European's environment is so pervasive, so dense, so habitual, that it whispers to him that he is all right where he is; he is at home and irreplaceable. His at-homeness is related to the concrete things about him.

Gertrude Stein used to quote in this connection a phrase from the Mother Goose rhymes: " 'I am I,' said the little old lady, 'because my dog knows me.' "

"I am I," says the European, "because the immemorial repetitions of my country's way of life surround me. I know them and they know me."

An American can have no such stabilizing relation to any one place, nor to any one community, nor to any one moment in time.

Americans are disconnected. They are exposed to all place and all time. No place nor group nor moment can say to them: We were waiting for you; it is right for you to be here. Place and time are, for them, negative until they act upon them, until they bring them into being.

Illustrations of this disconnection? Illustrations of so omnipresent a condition will scarcely persuade those who have not long observed it in themselves and in those about them; but:

Europeans have long been struck with consternation at our inability to place emphasis on the concrete aspect of things. Taking tea with a friend in London, I am told that I must return to dine and go to the opera.

"All right," I say, "I'll hurry home and change my clothes."

"What?"

"I say: I'll go back to the hotel and change my clothes."

"Home! *Home!* How can you Americans keep calling a hotel home?"

Because a home is not an edifice, but an interior and transportable adjustment. In Chicago—in the good old days—my friends used to change their apartment on the first of May. They were not discontented with the old one; they simply liked to impress their homemaking faculty on some new rooms.

More and more farmers of the Middle West are ending their days in Southern California and Florida. After fifty years of hard work in Iowa they do not find it strange to live, to die, and to be buried among palms.

This unrelatedness to place goes so deep that, in an Old-World sense, America can have no shrines. For us it is not *where* genius lived that is important. If Mount Vernon and Monticello were not so beautiful in themselves and relatively accessible, would so many of us visit them? What difficulties private individuals have had—in rich America—to save the Whitman and Poe houses.

Americans are abstract. They are disconnected. They have a relation, but it is to everywhere, to everybody, and to always.

That is not new, but it is very un-European.

It is difficult, but it is exhilarating. It shatters many lives; it inspirits others.

There are those countries of Europe, each shut in on itself by borders immemorially defended; each shut in with its own loved hills, streams, towns, and roads; each with the monuments of its past continually renewing the memory of its history; each with its language—not a self-evident thing, as natural as breathing, but a thing rendered assertive and objective because beyond the borders were all those *others* speaking no less assertively a deplorable gibberish; shut in with the absorbing repetitions of customs and long-molded manners; shut in with its convulsions which themselves had the character of repetitions. Shut in, above all, with the memories of old oppressions and with the memories of the long, bloody revolts against old oppressions, against Authorities and Powers—

once awe-inspiring, but now hollow as the bugaboos of infancy—still vestigially present, however, as disavowed menaces and seductions, invitations to escape from the burdens of freedom *(Führer! Duce! Kommissar!).*

How close together they live, in each nation, how shoulder to shoulder!—not only by reason of the density of population, but because of a sort of psychic consanguinity—another aftermath of feudalism. The relation of master and serf is a *hot* relation; it is a bond of either love or hate, as is any relationship which involves command over another's freedom. It is no wonder that the English have developed the stratification of the social classes, of the greatest precision and of the greatest sensitivity to encroachment: overcrowding, centuries long, has resulted in a condition where *Englishmen can hear one another think.* The barriers were rendered necessary to protect them from this steamy intimacy. Modern English plays and novels show us that the English live in anguish because of the indelicacy of their exposure to one another. In France life and conversation and love itself seem to us to be overruled by a network of conventions as intricate as a ballet or a game; just so the Chinese built walls of ceremonial behind which they could hide from the piercing intelligence of their neighbors.

Yet such density is also warming and reassuring.

I am I because my fellow citizens know me.

Americans can find in environment no confirmation of their identity, try as they may. The American gregariousness strikes every European visitor as hollow and strained—the college fraternity ("brothers till death"), the businessmen's clubs ("one for all and all for one"), the febrile cocktail party ("Darling, do call me up; you're my favorite person in the world and I *never* see you").

There is only one way in which an American can feel himself to be in relation to other Americans—when he is united with them in a project, caught up in an idea and propelled with them toward the future. There is no limit to the degree with which an American is imbued with the doctrine of progress. Place and environment are but *décor* to his journey. He lives not on the treasure that lies about him but on the promises of the imagination.

"I am I," he says, "because my plans characterize me." Abstract! Abstract!

Another element entered the American experience which has rendered still more difficult any hope of an American's deriving comfort from environment: he learned to count.

He can count to higher numbers—and realize the multiplicity indicated by the number—than any European. It began with his thinking in distances; it was increased by his reception into this country of the representatives of many nations.

How wide and high was the America to which he came? How many thousands of miles wide and high is a country whose boundaries have not yet been reached? The peoples of Europe knew well the dimensions of their own lands; one's own land is one's norm and scale. Several of these peoples were voyagers and colonizers; their travelers had experience of great distance and vast populations; but concepts of magnitude are not communicable by hearsay. It is amazing the extent to which European literatures are without any sense of the innumerability of the human race—even those literatures which draw so largely on the Bible, which is indeed the book of the myriad. An individual genius—Dante and Cervantes and Goethe—may grasp it, but it is not in Shakespeare, for a joy in the diversity of souls is not the same thing as an awe before the multiplicity of souls. French literature is about Frenchmen, though their names be Britannicus and Le Cid; and Frenchmen are not innumerable. For a century English writers were infatuated with the West Mediterranean people (they felt them to be splendid and damned), but their interest in them did not, to the imagination, increase the population of England or of the earth. Nor was it increased when England came to govern colonies in all parts of the globe; those peoples beyond the sea spoke other tongues and many of them were of another color. How many is many, if the many seem to be deplorably immature and incult? The imagination plays tricks on those who count souls in condescension.

Americans could count and enjoyed counting. They lived under a sense of boundlessness. And every year a greater throng of new faces poured into their harbors, paused, and streamed westward. And each one was one. To this day, in American thinking, a crowd of ten thousand is not a homogeneous mass of that number, but is one and one and one . . . up to ten thousand.

Billions have lived and died, billions will live and die; and this every American knows—knows in that realm beyond learning, knows in his bones. American literature of the great age is filled with the grasp of this dimension; it is in Whitman's oft-derided catalogues, in Poe's "Eureka," in Melville's resort to myth, in Emily Dickinson's lyrics. It is not in Thoreau and Emerson, and its absence is all the more conspicuous when they are writing under the influence of the Sanskrit scriptures, where the realization abounds.

This knowledge is now in every American and in his glance. And there as everywhere it never ceases to call into question one's grasp on one's own identity.

Fortunately, for several generations the American had the Bible. The Bible, like the Sanskrit scriptures, is one long contemplation of the situation of the one in the innumerable and it sternly forbids its readers to draw any relief from what lies about them. Its characters hang suspended upon the promises of the imagination; for generations most Americans were named after them. Those (one and one and one . . .) to whom destiny has extended a promise and a plan have this consolation, that they feel themselves to be irreplaceable. Each one is a bundle of projects.

It would seem as though I were about to say that the Americans are unworldly, spiritual natures like the Hindu initiates for whom the earth is but an illusion or like the saints engrossed only in intangibles ("I count nothing my own save my harp"; "Here on earth have we no abiding place albeit we seek one to come"). No, for them concrete things concretely exist, so solidly that these things do not exhale a deep emotion nor invite it. How seldom in American literature—outside of Europeanizing epigenous writers like Washington Irving—does one find such effusions as "Dear Tree, beneath which so often I played as a child," or "Newburgh, rising in glorious serenity above the lordly Hudson, would that once again I could tread thy steep streets. . . ." Americans do not readily animate things; their tireless animation is active elsewhere, in the future.

This is the disconnection from place; the disconnection from time is no less radical.

II

Now to search in a great page of *Moby Dick* for the literary and stylistic reflections of these characteristics.

The Melville of *Moby Dick,* the most widely admired work in American literature, is a notably interesting example for our study. Melville was not only writing within the tradition of English literature: he was writing very bookishly and stylishly indeed. No doubt he was conscious that the vogue for his books was beginning to be greater in England than in America; *Moby Dick* was first published in London. Under the mounting emotion of composition Melville's "Americanism" erupted in spite of himself. It can be seen progressively manifesting itself. The first eleven pages of the novel are the worst kind of English English—that is to say, the English of the contemporary New York literary cliques. There are many pages in *Moby Dick* which betray the insecurity of a writer thirty-one years old who has launched upon a mighty subject; but the page from which I am about to quote is completely successful and its success has been achieved through the presence within it of elements inherent in the nation's adventure.

The following pages will appear to some to be an excursion into that French pedagogical practice called the "explication de texte." *It is not; there is no space here for those patient ramifications, nor is it my aim to explore this passage in and for itself. Yet I often regret the ready disparagement expressed by so many American educators of a method which seems to me to arise from the never failing French respect for* métier. *One of our professors in discussing it said to me that "a flower under a microscope ceases to be a flower"—a view which belongs rather to Thoreau's ecstasy-before-nature view than to Goethe's awe-before-nature. I have always felt—again with Goethe—that works of art are also works of nature and like the works of nature afford, under probing, new reaches of wonder. The American depreciation of the* explication de texte *may proceed from a characteristic that I shall discuss later, namely that Americans have a tendency to be far more interested in wholes than in parts.*

The passage I am about to read is from Chapter 133. It affords us our first direct view of the White Whale; it is probably the most delayed entrance of a star in all literature—in my edition it is on page 538.*

During the reading of this page I wish you to ask yourself a number of questions: What is its *movement* and where have you heard it before? Does its rhythm and ordering of phrase recall to you the Bible of 1611? or Elizabethan drama? or Sir Thomas Browne? Or does it seem to you to sound like a prose translation or adaptation of an epic poem? Does it, indeed, seem to be trying to capture in prose the effects peculiar to

---

*EDITOR'S NOTE: Thornton Wilder seems to have used a copy of the edition of *Moby Dick* edited by Luther S. Mansfield and Howard P. Vincent and published in New York by Hendricks House in 1952.

poetry? But, above all, are you aware of any elements that separate it from English literature, the English spirit recounting the English experience of life?

The whale has been sighted, "A hump like a snow-hill!" and the boats of the *Pequod* have started in pursuit.

> Like noiseless nautilus shells, their light prows sped through the sea; but only slowly they neared the foe.

Melville's emotion is gaining on him. The alliterations in *n* and *s* begin to introduce an incantatory tone which will presently be confirmed by constructions employing repetition; but the approach to a state of trance does not prevent his marking the rapidity of the boats with monosyllables, and the dragging slowness—as felt by the whalers—by open vowels.

> As they neared him, the ocean grew still more smooth; seemed drawing a carpet over its waves; seemed a noon-meadow, so serenely it spread. At length the breathless hunter came so nigh his seemingly unsuspecting prey, that his entire dazzling hump was distinctly visible, sliding along the sea as if an isolated thing, and continually set in a revolving ring of finest, fleecy, greenish foam. He saw the vast, involved wrinkles of the slightly projecting head beyond. Before it, far out on the soft Turkish-rugged waters, went the glistening white shadow from his broad, milky forehead, a musical rippling playfully accompanying the shade; and behind, the blue waters interchangeably flowed over into the moving valley of his steady wake; and on either hand bright bubbles arose and danced by his side.

Melville's emotion is under powerful control.

We are approaching a paroxysm of swooning love and shuddering horror, but so far he has mainly presented himself to us All Eyes. The emotion is present, however, in this insistence that everything is serene and in the undulation of the rhythm. Scarcely a noun is offered which is not preceded by one or two adjectives, many of which ("projecting," "soft," "white," "broad," "blue") tell us nothing new. We call this practice a mid-nineteenth-century vice and today children are punished for it. Today such a scene—picture and emotion— would be conveyed with the economy of a telegram. But style is not only the man; it involves also the thought-world of the time, including the writer's effort to alter it. This page is an exercise in flamboyant rhetoric; it is a "purple patch," unashamed. Its triumph issues from the superimposition of novel elements upon a traditional form.

The visual details which Melville has furnished, and which he is about to furnish, are the most brilliant precision, but they do not render the scene objective, nor do they mitigate our awe and terror. The impression is that his eyes are "starting out of his head." Only the greatest authors—and Dante in chief—can thus continue to *see* while they are in a state of transport. Lesser authors relapse into abstract nouns and fashion from them a sort of cloudy "sublime."

> But these were broken again by the light toes of hundreds of gay fowl softly feathering the sea, alternate with their fitful flight; and like to some flagstaff rising from the painted hull of an argosy, the tall but shattered pole of a recent lance projected from the White Whale's back; and at intervals one of the cloud of soft-toed fowls hovering, and to and fro skimming like a canopy over the fish, silently perched and rocked on this pole, the long tail feathers streaming like pennons.
>
> A gentle joyousness—a mighty mildness of repose in swiftness, invested the gliding whale.

At last we have an abstract noun—four of them, and how abstractly dependent upon one another! But Melville's grasp of this visible world is so sure that we can afford a plethora of them. Abstract nouns come naturally to Americans, but they must constantly find an idiosyncratic way of employing them. New-World abstractions are very different from Old-World abstractions; they are not "essences" but generalizations; or, to express it most paradoxically, an American strives to render his abstraction concrete.

> Not the white bull Jupiter swimming away with ravished Europa clinging to his graceful horns; his lovely, leering eyes sideways intent upon the maid; with smooth bewitching fleetness, rippling straight for the nuptial bower in Crete; not Jove, not that great majesty Supreme! did surpass the glorified White Whale as he so divinely swam.

What! These whalefishers are hurrying to their death and the great blasphemer to his retribution and Melville chooses this moment to linger over the behavior of some birds and to insert an elaborated Renaissance vignette?

This beautifully wrought metaphor, though not at all classical in feeling, represents a device we frequently find in Homer. The simile which arises from the presented action begins to lead an independent life of its own; it flowers into details and developments which occasionally disturb and even reverse its relation to its original correlevant. This evocation of Jupiter not only arrests our excitement; it almost cuts us off from direct vision. This would seem to be a flaw, but its justification lies in its relation to time.

There are three times transpiring on this page. There are— as in all narration—the time of the action and the time of the narrative; Ishmael at his desk recalls and re-experiences those events from the past. But the time which is passing in the mind of Ishmael the narrator is invaded by another time which can best be called the timeless. If Melville were writing an adventure story for boys, "Joe Foster, the Young Whaler," it would indeed be lamentable to deflate our excitement at this moment. But in the realm of moral issues and total experience such human tensions are out of place. Older readers know that life is crisis. (Goethe said that the *Iliad* teaches us "that it is our task here on earth to enact Hell daily.") The house burns down and no Joe Foster rushes through the flames to rescue the child from the cradle; the survivors of the wreck turn black and expire upon their raft before Joe Foster appears upon the horizon; the consequences of the lives we have fashioned advance toward us with age and death on their heels. Homer and Melville remove us to a plane of time wherein catastrophe or rescue are mere incidents in a vast pattern.

But these birds and this fragment of mythology have another character. They proceed from another form of excitement. They have about them the hushed, glassy precision of hallucination. For those who come upon them in their place in the vast book they are like the intrusions of a dream and like the irrelevances in a moment of danger. They are that moment when the matador sees the bull dashing toward him and at the same time, out of the corner of his eye, sees that a woman in the second row is wearing three red roses and that her black scarf is being fanned by the wind. The timeless is for a moment identified with the time of all those other people and things that are not caught up in our crisis—the people who pass whistling happily under our hospital window, the people who are held up at a crossing while we drive to a burial—the birds, and the nuptials of Jupiter and Europa.

Whereupon, after this far journey into the timeless, Melville brings us back abruptly to the most concrete level of his story:

On each soft side—coincident with the parted swell, that but once leaving him,

'(The autograph manuscript of *Moby Dick* has been lost. I have no doubt that Melville wrote "laving him." After finishing this novel, something broke in Melville; he lost his concentration. *Pierre* and *The Confidence Man* are on the level of "leaving.")

then flowed so wide away—on each bright side, the whale shed off enticings. No wonder there had been some among the hunters who, namelessly transported and allured by all this

serenity, had ventured to assail it; but had fatally found that
quietude but the vesture of tornadoes.

This is very extravagant writing, indeed, but, as the word
"namelessly" shows, Melville is returning us for a moment to
the symbolic level.

We do not have to think of the Nantucket whalefishers as
subject to throes of aesthetic transport. We may read:

> It is not surprising that some men have been mistaken by the
> apparently serene orderliness of God-in-Nature and, swept up
> into *hubris,* have attempted to blaspheme against it and to set
> themselves up as its antagonists, only to discover that . . .
>
> Yet calm, enticing calm, oh whale! thou glidest on, to all
> who for the first time eye thee, no matter how many in that
> same way thou may'st have bejuggled and destroyed before.

The climax employs the most rhetorical—that is to say, the
most potentially absurd—of all devices: the invocation to an
abstraction, to an insensible or absent being. It is characteristic
of our time, and related to what I was saying about the decline
of our belief in authorities and essences, that few orators can
be heard saying, "Oh, Commonwealth of Massachusetts, per-
severe!" and few poets now address the Evening or Sweet
Days of Childhood.

> And thus, through the serene tranquillities of the tropical
> sea, among waves whose hand-clappings were suspended by
> exceeding rapture, Moby Dick moved on, still withholding
> from sight the full terrors of his submerged trunk, entirely
> hiding the wrenched hideousness of his jaw. But soon the fore
> part of him slowly rose from the water; for an instant his whole
> marbleized body formed a high arch, like Virginia's Natural
> Bridge, and warningly waving his bannered flukes in the air,
> the grand god revealed himself, sounded, and went out of
> sight. Hoveringly halting, and dipping on the wing, the white
> sea-fowls longingly lingered over the agitated pool that he
> left.

There are some literary echoes in this passage, but they are drowned out by an influence that is not of the printed page. I find but one cadence which recalls the Bible: "suspended in exceeding rapture"; and but one reminiscence of Elizabethan, though not Shakespearean, blank verse:

> Yet calm, enticing calm, oh whale! thou gli-
> dest on, to all who for the first time eye thee. . . .

Sir Thomas Browne is never far absent; he has had his part in the evocation of Europa and in him Melville "fatally found that quietude but the vesture of tornadoes." To my ear, however, the movement of this passage is primarily oratorical.

Yet the observation that this passage has the air of being written for declamation does not distinguish it as a work of the New World. De Quincey and Carlyle and Ruskin and Chateaubriand and Victor Hugo and Kierkegaard had all been writing or were about to write prose that took its tone from forensic and pulpit eloquence.

There are three elements in it, however, which indicate that it is written in America:

1.   It contains a number of locutions which reveal the emergence of the American language.

2.   It is directed to a classless society—to Everybody.

3.   It constantly betrays what I have called a certain disconnection in the American mind.

III

Before I enter upon a discussion of the first two of these elements (a discussion of the third as applied to this passage will be found in a later lecture), I wish to return to a consideration of the page as an example of the Grand Style Ornate. That it is a successful example of such a style does not mark it as a product of the New World, but that it is so in 1851 is, from the point of view of English literature, a matter of remark.

Americans were filled with a sense of newness, of vastness, and of challenge.

As Walt Whitman put it:

It almost seems as if a poetry with cosmic and dynamic features of magnitude and limitlessness suitable to the human soul, were never possible before.

And for this big feeling within them they needed to employ a grand style, a swelling rhetoric unabashed. And they needed it at the precise moment that England lost it.

England did not lose it because of any diminution of her exterior or interior greatness. Her exterior greatness had not yet reached its peak; and her interior greatness has never been greater than in our own time. She lost it for two reasons: one, the verbal expression for that greatness had been under employment so long that it had begun to show exhaustion; and, two, the islanders (as I said earlier) had dwelt so long in congested proximity that a heroic view of one another was no longer possible. The mock-heroic had been able to flourish side by side with the heroic in the eighteenth century, but finally it had begun to sap the heroic. British feeling in regard to all that was venerable in their institutions did not decline, but their expression of it became more and more an understatement in public and an affectionate persiflage in private. Poet laureates found it increasingly difficult to celebrate great personages and great events in the lofty language that was called for. English humor of the last half of the nineteenth century was precisely based on the mocking application to daily life of the grandiose diction of the preceding centuries.

But America was not overcrowded, and neither its geography nor its history had been for centuries the subject of literature. The heroic flourished side by side with the mock-heroic, and the mock-heroic itself seemed to be a smiling tribute to the heroic. All of the writers we are considering were highly "bookish" authors and may have been aware of the increasing hollowness of the English grand style (which accompanied an increasing precision and beauty in the description of the homely and intimate), but all advanced unhesitatingly and often into the perilous reaches of ornate eloquence. Boldest of all was Walt Whitman, who saw the necessity of desophisticating himself in order to achieve it. All of them were able to renew the validity of impassioned utterance by availing themselves of a number of novel elements.

The novel element which seems to me to be of least importance was the presence of new words and idioms. There are no examples of this in the page we are studying. "Bejuggled" —which Melville had already employed in *Mardi*—is not in most dictionaries, but "juggled" has a long history on both sides of the Atlantic. But if there are no new words, there are some examples of novel usage.

"The whale shed off enticings." There is little doubt that De Quincey or even Carlyle would have written "shed enticements." "Enticings" will be followed in the next paragraph by "hand-clappings." These verbal nouns based on the present participle are relatively rare in the plural. A number, after losing their dynamic force (paintings, savings, undertakings), have entered common use, and others (understandings, risings, mumblings) are on their way to the same static condition. But we do not say laughings, shoppings, studyings, enticings, or hand-clappings. Melville in *Moby Dick* offers us intertwistings, spurnings, coincidings, imminglings, and even "what lovely leewardings!" I have counted thirty-one of them. The following year, while writing *Pierre,* he will have forgotten his infatuation with plural gerunds and will have set out to create new words in -ness, heightening the abstraction in abstract words. There we find beautifulness, domesticness (twice!), unidentifiableness, and undulatoriness—all deplorable and some of them atrocious.

(Yet genius on wings can confound any of our own theoretical objections. Emily Dickinson wrote:

> 'Tis glory's overtakelessness
> That makes our running poor.

Emily Dickinson, in addition to forging our American language for us, enjoyed many a witches' sabbath with the language, on her own.)

Much of this coinage in Melville is mere huffing and puffing. A young man of thirty-one with barely a high-school education has remarked Shakespeare's bold inventions without having acquired the tact that controlled them. I find the plural gerunds on this page, however, completely successful.

"The whale shed off enticings." As foreigners who are learning our language frequently inform us, we Americans are forever putting prepositions and adverbial particles to new uses. Here the "off" combined with the "enticings" gives the impression of a continuous fulguration. It is not only an expression of vivacity and energy; it reveals our national tendency to restore to the past its once-present life rather than to immobilize it, to bury it under the preterite. In narration this assumed a great importance, for Americans wish to declare that all living things are free—and were free—and the past tenses in narration tend to suggest that we, telling the story from its latter end, see them as "determined" and as the victims of necessity. When we come to discuss the American time-sense and its struggle to reshape the syntax of the English language, we shall see that one of its principal aims has been to give even to the past tenses the feeling of a "continuous present," a door open to the future, a recovery of the we-don't-know-what-will-happen.

On this page we are shown the bull and Europa "rippling straight for the nuptial bower in Crete." Water ripples; tresses ripple. Had we read in a present-day author, English or American, that "Leander rippled straight for Sestos," we would have condemned it as a vulgarity. What saves this phrase from vulgarity is the *gamut of tones* that are juxtaposed in this nineteenth-century page—which brings us to our second consideration.

A novel element in our classics of a century ago is the fact that they were written for a classless society, they were written for everybody. European literature for two and a half centuries had been directed to an audience of cultivation, to an elite —Molière's farces not excepted, Dickens's (imminent) novels not excepted. The assumption on the part of our American writers that they were addressing a total society has since disappeared; we are now in the famous division between the highbrows and the lowbrows; but, given the basic considerations of our American life, such an assumption should constitute the natural function of a much larger part of American writing.

What are the signs that a writer feels himself to be addressing the total community rather than an elite? There are many; I am about to give two, both drawn from the realm of the grand style. It is well to note first, however, that this consideration has nothing to do with whether or not a writer uses long words or erudite allusions. It has nothing to do with a condescension to semi-literacy. The 1611 Bible and the works of Shakespeare are filled with incomprehensible phrases; millions pore over them daily; we read right on, sufficiently nourished by what is intelligible to us.

It is not necessary to remind you that Walt Whitman addressed himself to everyone who could read or be read to.

Listen to Thoreau in *Walden* (and note the forensic tone; there is no surer sign of it than these redundant numerations):

> Simplicity, simplicity, simplicity. I say let your affairs be as two
> or three, and not a hundred or a thousand; instead of a million
> count half a dozen, and keep your accounts on your thumbnail.
> In the midst of this chopping sea of civilized life, such are the

clouds and storms and quicksands and thousand-and-one items
to be allowed for, if he would not founder and go to the
bottom, and not make port, by dead reckoning, and he must
be a great calculator who succeeds. Simplify, simplify. Instead
of three meals . . .

Thoreau is addressing so vast a throng that in his effort to
be heard he has lost control of subjects and verbs—scrupulous
writer though he usually is.

Cultivate poverty like a garden herb, like sage. Do not trouble
yourself much to get new things whether clothes or friends.
. . . Things do not change; we change.

All this is for the farmhand, the blacksmith, and the cook as
well as for the Governor's lady. It is for Ralph Waldo Emerson
as well as for Thoreau's mother, the boardinghouse keeper.

New Englanders have been proverbially inarticulate; but
they could unlock their hearts and throats if they felt the
audience to be sufficiently large. Did not Emily Dickinson say
of her poetry:

> This is my letter to the world
> That never wrote to me?

Her grand style—sunbursts of Handelian rhetoric—invokes a
universe:

> Mine by the right of the white election!
> Mine by the royal seal!

> One dignity delays for all.

> Struck was I, yet not by lightning.

Wherein do these paragraphs from *Moby Dick* reveal the fact
that Melville was addressing an undifferentiated audience?
They are certainly highly "bookish"—what with that elaborated classical allusion, that stylish subjunctive, and their high
percentage of words from the Latin.

First, we observe that elevation and intensity are not solely and inseparably associated with noble images. The sublime does not wear a cothurnus. There are not two doors for words in America, no tradesmen's entrance: all can go in the front door. In the very same sentence in which Melville apostrophizes divinity we are told that God has "bejuggled" many a man. It is a word from the skulduggeries of the country fair and the card game at the livery stable. We remember the horror with which Racine's contemporaries greeted the mention of a dog in tragedy, the protest of the audience against Hugo's use of the humble phrase *"Quelle heure est-il?"* in *Hernani.* Generations of critics deplored the drunken porter in *Macbeth.* What better illustration of the limited gamut of tones available for European full-throated utterance than the observation that so many of the words that describe lofty moods are also words that stem from the designations of social rank, or that run concurrently with them and derive much of their force from connotations of status: "noble" and *"herrlich"* and *"edel"* and *"magnifico"* and *"grande"* and *"soberano"* and "majestic" and even "gentle." The United States is a middle-class nation and has widened and broadened and deepened the concepts of the wide and the broad and the deep without diminishing the concept of the high. We notice that the angelic host of birds that glorify the White Whale have soft toes. Toes, like noses, have not hitherto entered the exalted, the dithyrambic style. This page did not have the drawing room in view.

Second, most European exercises in the sublime, in avoiding the common and humble, avoid the specific. In the tirades of Burke and Carlyle on the French Revolution, in the impassioned visions of De Quincey and Chateaubriand, the noble is associated with a high vagueness. Audiences which are composed of the selected and the cultivated and the *Gebildeten* and the *honnêtes gens* and the *cognoscenti* are not interested in life's diversity; the pressures upon them work toward the formulation of taste and convention and the Rules of the Beautiful and an ever narrowing purity (*i.e.,* economy) in the selection of

detail. But the American public was one and one and one
. . . to an unlimited number. Their taste could never be
codified, for it was overwhelmed by an ever enlarging vision
of the universe and its multifarious character. The bigger the
world is, the *less* you can be content with vagueness. The
catalogues of Walt Whitman, which have displeased so many
immured scholars, are filled with this kind of apprehension.
He hears a runaway slave

> . . . crackling the twigs of the woodpile,
> Through the swung half-door of the kitchen I saw him
>   limpsy and weak, . . .
> The bride unrumples her white dress, the minute-hand
>   of the clock moves slowly,
> The opium-eater reclines with rigid head and just-opened
>   lips. . . .

Whitman can get a million people into his poem by making
sure that not *one* of his twenty is amorphous.

What European poet, reminding us that the sunlight falls on
all alike, would have selected as an illustration the reminder
that it falls upon the "Squirrel in the Himmaleh"—or have
drawn from the thought so chillingly abstract a conclusion as
did Emily Dickinson? ("But not for Compensation—/It holds
as large a Glow/To Squirrel in the Himmaleh/Precisely, as to
you.")

Since the American can find no confirmation of identity
from the environment in which he lives, since he lives exposed
to the awareness of vast distances and innumerable existences,
since he derives from a belief in the future the courage that
animates him, is he not bent on isolating and "fixing" a value
on every existing thing in its relation to a totality, to the All,
to the Everywhere, to the Always? And does that not require
of him a new way of viewing and feeling and describing any
existing thing? And would that not require, in turn, a modifi-
cation of the language?

THE AMERICAN LONELINESS

I

Walking to the auditorium where I am to lecture on Thoreau, I pass Hollis Hall in which he lived as an undergraduate.

I think we can understand why on graduation he changed his name —David Henry became Henry David, peremptorily. Like Emerson before him, he was a scholarship student. During his first year he had one coat—his mother and aunt had made it for him out of green homespun. That year the right students were wearing black. All his life he railed with particular passion against any discrimination that is based on dress. A classmate tells us that, as a student, Thoreau in conversation did not raise his eyes from the ground and that his hands were continually moist. That chapter over, he changed his name.

As I pass Hollis I become uncomfortable; I feel those extraordinary blue eyes not on me, but directed over me, in taciturn reproach. Thoreau set down a portrait of himself and he took pains with its details. He wished it to be known that he was direct, simple, forthright, candid, and uncomplicated. Many have taken him at his word; but no, his life and personality have more important things to tell us.

How hard it is to discuss Thoreau in the presence of the young. Many aspects of his life and thought lie in that sole territory which is inaccessible to young men and women. I never feel an incomprehension on their part when I treat of death or loss or passion; their

The second of the Charles Eliot Norton lectures as printed in *The Atlantic Monthly* for August 1952.

imaginations can extend themselves—by that principle which Goethe called "anticipation"—to such matters. What is difficult is to treat of the slow attrition of the soul by the conduct of life, of our revolt against the workaday—the background of such works as Le Misanthrope *and* Don Quixote. *I must tell these young people, who are hurrying by me, that Thoreau met defeat in his impassioned demands upon Love, Friendship, and Nature; and yet I must tell them that at the same time he was an American who fought some of our battles for us, whose experience we are to follow with a sort of anxious suspense. The rewards we obtain from the contemplation of Thoreau, however, begin their consolatory and inspiriting effect upon us as we move through our forties.*

I wish I were somewhere else.

Ladies and gentlemen:

We were talking last time about how difficult it is to be an American. We spoke of the support which Europeans receive from all those elements we call environment— place, tradition, customs: "I am I because my neighbors know me." Their environment is so thickly woven, so solid, that the growing boy and girl have something to kick against. The American, on the other hand, is at sea—disconnected from place, distrustful of authority, thrown back upon himself.

Here I am again.

And suddenly, as my eyes rest on the upturned faces before me, I am encouraged. It is in many ways a sad story I have to tell. Whenever I think of Thoreau I feel a weight about my heart, a greater weight than descends in thoughts of Poe or Emily Dickinson. Yet all of us here are Americans. My subject is the loneliness that accompanies independence and the uneasiness that accompanies freedom. These experiences are not foreign to anyone here. So forward.

Perceptive visitors to America from Europe are uniformly struck by what they call an "American loneliness" which they

find no less present in that fretful and often hollow gregariousness we talked about last time.

Now there are several forms of this loneliness, and the one
that occurs to us first is the sentimental form. In America the
very word is sentimental and it makes us uncomfortable even
to employ it. Yet we see this kind of loneliness about us
everywhere; like the loneliness which springs from pride, it is
a consequence, a deformation, and a malady of that deeper
form which we are about to discuss. Both proceed from the
fact that the religious ideas current in America are still inadequate to explain the American to himself. The sentimental
loneliness arises from the sense that he is a victim, that he was
slighted when Fortune distributed her gifts (though it is notably prevalent among those who seem to "have everything");
the proud loneliness arises from the sense of boundlessness
which we described as related to the American geography and
is found among those who make boundless moral demands on
themselves and others.

Thoreau illustrates certain American traits connected with
loneliness in an extreme and exaggerated form. He finally lost
his battle—the typical American battle of trying to convert a
loneliness into an enriched and fruitful solitude—but before
he died (at forty-four, murmuring: "It is better some things
should end") he furnished us many a bulletin of the struggle,
many an insight, and many an aid.

Another of the most famous pages in American literature is
that wherein Thoreau gives his reasons for going to live in
solitude at Walden Pond.

> I went to the woods because I wished to live deliberately,
> to front only the essential facts of life, and see if I could not
> learn what it had to teach, and not, when I came to die,
> discover that I had not lived. . . . nor did I wish to practise
> resignation, unless it were quite necessary. . . . if [life] . . .
> proved to be mean, why then to get the whole and genuine
> meanness of it, and publish its meanness to the world; or if it

were sublime, to know it by experience, and be able to give a true account of it in my next excursion.

Thoreau's books are a sort of *cento* of transcriptions and amplifications of entries in his Journal. Here is what he wrote on the third day of his residence at the pond (6 July 1845):

> I wish to meet the facts of life—the vital facts, which are the phenomena or actuality which the Gods meant to show us— face to face, and so I came here. Life! who knows what it is, what it does?

There are several things to notice about these passages: among them, first, that he will put his question as though no one had ever said anything valuable before; and, second, that in order to ask what life is, it is necessary to remove oneself from the human community.

Americans constantly feel that the whole world's thinking has to be done over again. They did not only leave the Old World, they repudiated it. Americans start from scratch. This is revolt indeed. All authority is suspect. And this is boundless presumption. I quoted Whitman's words in our last session ("It almost seems as if a poetry . . . suitable to the human soul were never possible before"). Poe, clutching some mathematics and physics he had acquired during a brief stay at West Point, launched into a description of how the universe came into being, and deduced the nature of God from his theory of the galaxies. He called his work *Eureka* and did not leave us in doubt that he felt that he had succeeded where the greatest minds had failed. Professional astronomers dismiss it with a smile, but we notice that the great French poet Paul Valéry, who occupied himself with mathematics for thirty years, tells us how great a rôle this book played in the growth of his thought. *("L'idée fondamentale de Poe n'en est pas moins une profonde et souveraine idée.")*

Thoreau did some reading at Walden Pond, but it is astonishing how small a part it plays in this central inquiry of his life. He invokes neither the great philosophers nor the founders of religions. Every American is an autodidact; every American feels himself capable of being the founder of his own religion. At the end of the passage I have quoted from the Journal there is an allusion by Thoreau to his reading of the Sanskrit scriptures. It is an ironic jest: "to give a true account of it in my next excursion." He does not believe that our souls return to inhabit other bodies, though billions have reposed in that idea all that they know of hope and courage. He makes a jest of it—fit example, to him, of the uselessness of *other people's* thinking. There is something of this religious and metaphysical pioneer in us all. How often I have heard people say: "No, Mr. Wilder, we don't go to church. My husband and I each have our own religion —here—inside!" What student at the height of a lofty argument has not been heard to cry: "Listen, everybody! My theory is *this* . . ."?

To others this must all seem very deplorable. To Americans it is wearing and costing and often desolating; but such is the situation. The die is cast; and our interest in Thoreau is precisely that we see one of ourselves fighting, struggling, and finally fainting in this inescapable American situation. Thoreau asks, What is life? and he asks it in a world from which any considerable reliance on previous answers is denied him, and through his long inquiry he heard the closing of three doors—doors to great areas of experience on which he counted for aid and illumination, the doors to Love, Friendship, and Nature.

Here are the reverberations of these closing doors:

LOVE (27 October 1851, aged 34):

> The obstacles which the heart meets with are like granite blocks which one alone cannot remove. She who was the

morning light is now neither the morning star nor the evening star. We meet but to find each other further asunder. . . .

FRIENDSHIP (4 March 1856, aged 38):

I had two friends. The one offered me friendship on such terms that I could not accept it, without a sense of degradation. He would not meet me on equal terms, but only to be to some extent my patron. . . . Our relation was one long tragedy. . . .

NATURE: As early as 16 July 1851, Thoreau was saying:

Methinks my present experience is nothing; my past experience is all in all. I think that no experience which I have today comes up to, or is comparable with, the experiences of my boyhood. . . . Formerly, methought, nature developed as I developed, and grew up with me. My life was ecstasy. . . .

II

The story of Thoreau's love is only beginning to be pieced together. The obstacles that separated him from this woman were indeed granite blocks. The expressions he gives to his love in his Journal are often strange "whirling words":

My sister, it is glorious to me that you live! . . . It is morning when I meet thee in a still cool dewy white sun light in the hushed dawn—my young mother—I thy eldest son [lightly crossed through: "thy young father"] . . . whether art thou my mother or my sister—whether am I thy son or thy brother. . . . Others are of my kindred by blood or of my acquaintance but you are part of me. I cannot tell where you leave off and I begin.

In another passage, Journal 1850, he says:

I am as much thy sister as thy brother. Thou art as much my brother as my sister.

We have reason to be surprised that the erotic emotion expresses itself in images borrowed from the family relationships. Yet such a coloring is present elsewhere in our writers of this period, in Whitman, in Melville *(Pierre),* and in Poe. In America the family is the nexus of an unusually powerful ambivalence. On the one hand, the child strains to break away and lead his own life. The young seldom settle down near their parents' home; less and less frequently do the parents end their days in the homes of their children; I have remarked that young people are increasingly eager for the moment when they are no longer financially dependent on their parents. On the other hand, the American—as we were saying— is exceptionally aware of the multitude of the human race; his loneliness is enhanced by his consciousness of those numbers. The family is at once an encroachment on his individualism and a seductive invitation to rejoin the human community at a level where he does not feel himself to be strange. Moreover, individualism has its arrogance. It has long been a tag that every American is king. Royalty marries only royalty. Other people aren't good enough. Thoreau elevates the woman he loves to this kinship. Poe's mother died when he was three; he lived the latter part of his life with his aunt and married his cousin. The blocks of granite which separated Thoreau from this "sister" were not all outside of him. The door of love closed and he never returned to it.

It was the friendship with Ralph Waldo Emerson that Thoreau described as "one long tragedy." The second friend who proved unworthy was William Ellery Channing, who seems to have enjoyed shocking Thoreau with an occasional ribaldry. Tragedy we too can call it, for few men could more have needed friendship, and few have been less ready to accommodate themselves to it. He wrote (11 June 1855):

> What if we feel a yearning to which no breast answers? I walk alone, my heart is full. Feelings impede the current of my

thoughts. I knock on the earth for my friend. I expect to meet
him at every turn; but no friend appears, and perhaps none is
dreaming of me.

Emerson knew that he was incapable of friendship, and the
knowledge caused him some pain—brief pain, for Emerson
had a short way with moral discomfiture; he mounted up into
pink clouds and began to give voice to abstractions. This
woeful triangle skirts the comic. A letter has recently come to
light which gives Channing's view of a friendship with Emerson. Channing wrote to Elizabeth Hoar from New Bedford on
23 December 1856:

> . . . how strange it seemed to hear W[aldo]. lecturing on
> friendship. If he knew all the hearts he has frozen, he might
> better read something on the fall of human hopes. . . . I have
> never parted from him without the bitterest regret, not for
> having parted, but for having come. . . .

Individualism! It is the point of honor of men and nations
in this century. Every nation boasts that it is a nation of individualists and implies that the other nations are composed
of sheep. ("You Americans—you all eat the same things; you
repeat the same slogans; you read the same book of the month;
the very streets in which you live have not even names, but
merely numbers and letters!") Yet no man (and no nation) is
as individualistic as he thinks he is; each is so in one area of
his existence, and the extent to which he is—fortunately!—
conformist in others is not apparent to him. Friendship is not
incompatible with individualism, as the great pages of Mon-
taigne have shown us, but it was incompatible in the lives of
our Concord philosophers. Thousands of schoolchildren were
formerly required to read Emerson's chaotic essay on the
subject. For generations Emerson's style had the power to put
the judgment to sleep, but one wonders what the teachers
made of that farewell address to "our dearest friends": "Who
are you? Unhand me: I will be dependent no more."

Thoreau's inability to come to terms with friendship was aggravated by the vastness of his expectations. To this day many an American is breaking his life on an excessive demand for the perfect, the absolute, and the boundless in realms where it is accorded to few—in love and friendship, for example. The doctrines of moderation and the golden mean may have flourished in Rome and in China (overcrowded and overgoverned countries), but they do not flourish here, save as counsels of despair. The injunction to be content with your lot and in the situation where God has placed you is not an expression of New-World thinking. We do not feel ourselves to be subject to lot and we do not cast God in the rôle of a civil administrator or of a feudal baron.

III

Thoreau goes to the pond, then, to find an answer to the question, What is life? He will not admit other thinkers to his deliberations, and his answer will not reflect any *close* relation with his fellow men. With what frustrated passion, then, he turned to nature. Nature meant primarily the flora and fauna of the Concord River valley, though he made some trips elsewhere. Now that region has no tigers, avalanches, coral vipers, Black Forests, deserts, or volcanoes. Margaret Fuller warned her Concord friends of the dangers of accustoming themselves to a view of nature which omitted both cruelty and grandeur. On his walks Thoreau came upon some malodorous plants (26 June 1852):

> For what purpose has nature made a flower to fill the lowlands with the odor of carrion?

The question seems, to us, both biologically and philosophically a little *simpliste.*

Enough has already been written about the absence of a sense of evil in the work of the Concord essayists. It is only one of the elements that resulted in the gradually progressive grayness of the last volumes of Thoreau's Journal. Far more important is the fact that Thoreau asked of nature a gift which nature cannot, without cooperation, accord. He asked a continual renewal of moments of youthful ecstasy. Unhappy indeed is the boy or girl who has not known those moments of inexplicable rapture in the open air. There is a corresponding experience accorded to those in later years—awe. In ecstasy the *self* is infused with happiness; in awe the self recedes before a realization of the vastness and mystery of the non-self. Many never cross the bridge from one to the other. Thoreau despised and dreaded Science; to inquire too narrowly into the laws of nature seemed to him to threaten those increasingly infrequent visitations of irrational joy. "If you would obtain insight, avoid anatomy," he wrote. With what a sad smile Goethe would have shaken his head over these words —for it was precisely from his studies of the skeleton of the vertebrates and the structure of plants that Goethe's life was flooded, even in the eighties, with an awe which retained much of the character of a juvenile ecstasy. Indeed, Goethe at eighty would not have written the words which Thoreau wrote at thirty-three:

> In youth, before I lost any of my senses, I can remember that I was all alive, and inhabited my body with inexpressible satisfaction . . . !

As the years passed, Thoreau increasingly mourned his lost youth and the intoxication which nature had afforded him then. For a time the humming of the telegraph wires aroused transports; it was his "redeemer"; then they too lost their peculiar powers. Finally, in his last years he turns from the almost passive notation of the phenomena about him and introduces into his observations an element of progression and exploration into the unknown. He counts the rings in stumps and makes notes on the succession of trees. Those who are conversant with these things tell us that he is discovering the science of ecology. He seems, however, to be deriving no warming satisfaction from this innovation; his notes lie buried in his Journal and the work is repeated independently by others.

I am eager to arrive at all the things that call forth our admiration for Thoreau, but I must delay a moment to point out that we have brushed against two traits in him which are not characteristic of the American: the fixed orientation toward childhood, and the view of nature as engaged in close personal conversation with man. These are characteristic, however, of the region from which he came.

A portion of Massachusetts and several states of our South are enclaves or residual areas of European feeling. They were cut off, or resolutely cut themselves off, from the advancing tide of the country's modes of consciousness. Place, environment, relations, repetitions are the breath of their being. One evidence of it is a constant preoccupation with how old one is and a striking obsession with early youth (how many of the brilliant novels which have lately come to us from the South turn upon childhood). In New York and Chicago and the West one's age is of relatively little importance; those who are *active* between twenty-five and sixty are contemporaries. They dine and dance and work and enjoy themselves together. This is bound up with the American sense of time, which I shall develop in later lectures. Time is something we create, we call into being, not something we submit to—an order outside us.

Similarly, there are aspects of Thoreau's relation to nature that are not those we feel to be prevalent elsewhere among us. The gods of glade and brook and pond are not the gods of plain, seacoast, forest, desert, and mountain. The former are almost in reach; one can imagine oneself in dialogue with them; they can enter into an almost personal relation with those who have turned from the company of men. But the gods of great space are enigmatic; we are never sure that we have read aright the message of their beauty and terror; we do not hastily put words into their mouths. Yet the more we feel an "otherness" in nature, the more we recognize that we ourselves are natural. "It appears to be a law," wrote Thoreau, in April 1852, "that you cannot have a deep sympathy with both man and nature." "I loved nature because she is not man, but a retreat from him." There is no such law, nor have any other American voices expressed any sentiment like it, unless we take note of a moment in Emily Dickinson's life when she wrote:

> I thought that nature was enough
> Till human nature came.

Nature failed Thoreau, as it will ultimately fail anyone who wishes to divide it up, to pick and choose only limited congenial aspects of it, for ecstasy or for retreat, or who wishes to employ one aspect of it to confound another.

And the question: "Life! who knows what it is, what it does?" It would seem that Thoreau had considerably compromised his inquiry by divesting himself of the testimony and the companionship of others and by repeating his question to a wooded vale.

Yet millions have testified and are testifying to the powerful clarifications that he brought back from Walden Pond. And all his triumphs came from his embattled individualism, from pushing it to the limits that border on absurdity, and from facing—"face to face"—the loneliness consequent upon it. He came back with the answer that life, thought, culture, religion, government—everything—arises from subjectivity, from inwardness. Our sole self is the first and last judge of values, including the values of communal life.

Here I traced briefly the long, gradual millenniary convergence of emphasis on the individual—religion's, government's, art's; and showed how through an historical accident the settling of America, by that "selection of a selection" of European individualists, constituted an acceleration, perhaps a "leap," in the forward movement of this centering of emphasis.

Thoreau does not urge us to live in shacks merely to save money and time; to eschew railroad trains, newspapers, and the postal service; to lay in two sets of washable clothing and a bar of soap; to refuse these jobs which deform our souls between nine and five. These are not ends in themselves. "Simplify, simplify, simplify!" All these are injunctions in order that we may refine our ear to the promptings of our subjective, inward self. The evil of community is that it renders us stupid—and cowardly. *Walden* is a manual of self-reliance so much more profound than Emerson's famous essay that the latter seems to be merely on the level of that advice to melancholics which directs them to take walks and drink a lot of milk.

Thoreau did not merely meditate about the problem of living: he costingly, searchingly exemplified it, and his work rings with the validity of that single-minded commitment. One of the rewards of independence, apparently, is that you are certain that you are the master of your choices, you are not left to doubt whether or not you are free.

Yet there is no air of triumph about the latter end of Thoreau's life. It is difficult to be an American. In some aspects of his life and thought Thoreau is one of our most conspicuous, most outrageous Americans. But the spiritual situation in which these citizens of the New World find themselves is so new, so demanding, and so uncharted, that only by keeping in contact with its total demands can one maintain one's head above the surface. A partial American will drown. Thoreau did not grasp the New-World sense of the innumerability of the human race—nor did Emerson, for all his employment of the word "universal." Thoreau had a parochial, a wood-lot view of nature and her mighty laws. Is there a Thoreau who

can tell us that once one has grasped and accepted a basic
solitude, all the other gifts come pouring back—love, friendship, and nature? One reads the life story of Thoreau with
anxious suspense.

And Abraham Lincoln?
And Melville—and Poe?

EMILY DICKINSON

I

Gerard Manley Hopkins wrote to Robert Bridges:

> To return to composition for a moment: what I want there to be more intelligible, smoother, and less singular, is an audience.

And again:

> There is a point with me in matters of any size when I must absolutely have encouragement as much as crops rain; afterwards I am independent.

Father Hopkins's verses first reached print twenty-six years after his death.

Emily Dickinson's closest friends included two men, each of whom, as editor, read hundreds, perhaps thousands, of poems a year with a view toward publication in periodicals; and a third, her mentor Colonel Higginson, was in a position strongly to urge their publication; yet none ventured to publish one of hers. Dr. Holland felt that her verses were "too ethereal," Colonel Higginson that they were too irregular. The Colonel could be very severe; she quotes back to him—

The third of the Charles Eliot Norton lectures as printed in *The Atlantic Monthly* for November 1952.

with an air of docile gratitude and contrition—some words he had written:

> Such being the majesty of the art you presume to practise, you can at least take time before you dishonor it.

Had she been accorded an audience, would her verses have been "more intelligible, smoother, and less singular"? Not only did she write some two thousand poems, the greater part of which were seen by no other eyes than her own, but she so arranged it that most of these poems—if they were someday to be read by others—would not appear to lay claim to literary evaluation. She left them ostentatiously "unfinished," unready for print. From time to time she seems to have started upon the task of preparing definitive copies, only to have flagged in the endeavor or to have shrunk from the presumption.

I find a relation between an aspect of Emily Dickinson's home life as a girl and her practice as a writer. This relation has its parallel in her attitude to literary fame, to the doctrine of personal immortality, and to the greater number of her friends. This recurrent pattern in her thought and behavior can be described as the movement of "five steps forward and two steps back."

So much for the lecture which I delivered in the series and which I shall not attempt to reproduce here. I am of such a nature—being neither scholar, biographer, nor critic—that I cannot listen for long to a discussion of a great poet without being filled with impatience to hear or read one or more of the subject's poems. Great poetry, like comparable painting and music, architecture and drama, cannot be described; in a certain sense it cannot be remembered. It comes into being only when we are confronting it—and confronting it in a state of concentration. In my lecture, then, I took good care to read a number of Emily Dickinson's poems, surrounding each one with moments of silence for self-collection.

It is unsuitable, however, that I present a selection from her po-

etry here. So, instead of the lecture, I submit a series of reflections which came to me as I prepared for that occasion. They have the character of a progression, for they are based upon a series of questions which I put to myself, and are the answers I assembled to them. I was later to find that many of my students—and not only my students—felt little sympathy for Emily Dickinson's poetry. Some whose opinion I valued dismissed it with faint praise, some with impatience, some with contempt. It is a pleasure to remember, however, that the antipathy of the students never sprang (as it so often did in the case of their elders) from a disapproval of the irregularities in her versification. Young people are seldom moved to dictate to a writer how a poem or book should be written; they regard it—for a few years, alas—as self-evident that every person would wish to do a thing in his own way and that original thought would wear an original dress.

The *tone* of Emily Dickinson's letters and of many of her poems—where have I heard that before? This effusive affection combined with ostentatious humility; this presentation of the self as a little being easily overlooked, asking only a crumb, yet somehow urging strong egotistical claims; above all, the practice of alluding to great matters, to love and loss and death and God, in elliptical jokes and mannered periphrases—where have we heard that before?

Within the space of one letter to the Hollands (of "Mid-May 1854") Emily Dickinson manages to say:

> . . . if you have not all forgotten us . . . darling friends, for whom I would not count my life too great a sacrifice . . . if you won't forget me . . .

That is to say, she *shall* have the honors of love; she shall love most and best; she shall enjoy stoically nourishing an unrequited passion. Mr. Bowles is going away on a trip; she writes to Mrs. Bowles:

I'll remember you, if you like me to, while Mr. Bowles is gone, and that will stop the lonesome, some, but I cannot agree to stop when he gets home from Washington.

Does that not practically dictate an answer on Mrs. Bowles's part, and an effusive one? In a letter of condolence—and to a clergyman!—on the death of a child, she writes:

I hope Heaven is warm, there are so many barefoot ones.

On such great subjects bathos is ever lying in wait for those who are not content to say a thing simply.

We have heard this tone before. It belongs to women who in childhood have received too heavy an impress from their relation to their fathers. It may be called the tone of a *misplaced coquetry.* Its general character is that of archness. It is perfectly in order (and arises from profound natural springs) when it is exhibited by a young woman as a response to a young man who is showing deep interest in her. It has certainly no place in mature friendship.

II

It is not difficult to trace the steps of this mental formation. The growing child wishes to get its way; it wishes to be succeeding and (note the word) winning. It tests out the relationships of the family toward this end. There are certain forms of appeal and persuasion that are successful with the father but have no effect whatever on the mother. The growing girl exercises her coquetry (as kittens scratch trees) on every man she meets, but particularly on those whose eyes rest attentively upon her. It is a game in which a girl concedes that she is somewhat attracted but, advancing provocatively and retreating provocatively, refuses to declare the extent. It is played with the most calculated dissimulation, and its enactment between daughter and father is mere harmless dress-rehearsal for later encounters—in most cases. From time to time, however, the game has been, as it were, surprised by inappropriate intensities.

Squire Dickinson was a very grim patriarch indeed. Study his photograph. His daughter was to say of him that "his soul was pure and terrible," that "he never learned to play," and to speak of his "lonely life and lonelier death." Yet he was a complex man. Startling is the story that he set the churchbells of Amherst ringing to call the attention of the town to a particularly fine sunset. At Jenny Lind's concert,

> Father sat all evening looking *mad,* and yet so much amused that you [his son] would have *died* a-laughing . . . it wasn't sarcasm exactly, nor it wasn't disdain, it was infinitely funnier than either of those virtues, as if old Abraham had come to see the show, and thought it was all very well, but a little excess of *monkey.*

The wife of this Abraham seems to have been a nonentity ("I never had a mother") who gradually lapsed into invalidism. Two facts should be sufficient (by the play of opposites) to reveal the extent to which the Squire was a strong and frustrated man with a compelling effect upon his children: one, it appears that he had never kissed his son or daughters; and, two, his son was later to dye his blond hair red and later still to wear a red wig—the color of his father's hair.

What was it that Emily Dickinson wished to win from this man? The same thing that he wished to win from her and which he could find nowhere else—love, attentive love, and the sense of one's identity rebounding from some intelligent and admired being. Oh, he watched her, and naturally in his case the watchfulness could chiefly express itself only in rebuke. Of her reading:

> Father was very severe to me . . . he gave me quite a trimming about "Uncle Tom" and "Charles Dickens" and those "modern literati" . . . we do not have much poetry, father having made up his mind that it's pretty much all real life. Father's real

life and mine sometimes come into collision but as yet escape unhurt.

Of her gardening:

I got down before father this morning, and spent a few minutes profitably with the South Sea rose. Father detecting me, advised wiser employments, and read at devotions the chapter of the gentleman with one talent. I think he thought my conscience would adjust the gender.

And she watched him.

Many a patriarchal father has misjudged his rôle in this game, particularly when he has long since quenched any spontaneous femininity in his wife. (Unquestionable authority is an offense against love, as it is against anything else, and it is ever seeking new territories to overwhelm.) This game can be played by the eyes alone, even in the grimmest face. New England was formerly filled with women whose imaginations had been thus overswayed. Their growth in the affective life had been arrested—some had even been frozen, as by shock or trauma—and they must continue to repeat the mechanisms of that phase forever.

Such I feel to have been Emily Dickinson's story, but Emily Dickinson was a genius—that is to say, was charged with extraordinary resources of the life-force which could break through dams and repair ravage. The die, however, had been cast. The forms of speech that are characteristic of a winning child will constantly reappear, the bright remarks that set the dinner table laughing and bring a slight smile even to the most dignified father's face. Above all, the expressions of affection will be drolly indirect: "I'm lonely since you went away, kind of shipwrecked like! Perhaps I miss you!" This infantile note may recur at any moment right up to her death, and it was against this that the reparative force of her genius had to struggle. She has left us a large amount of mature poetry, and it is with something like awe that we can see the operation of

genius fashioning great verse even in this tone which elsewhere can so often distress us.

One other aspect of her letters will show us how deeply her
affective life had been troubled. Emily Dickinson constantly
indulges in the fantasy that her loved ones are dead.

Much has been written about her preoccupation with mortality and graves, and with the promise of a beatific hereafter.
Certain authorities have directed us to pay no particular attention to this strain, saying that it did not exceed the measure
indulged in by many of her contemporaries. Emily Dickinson,
however, was individual in her treatment of other aspects of
thought and life—in love and friendship, in the description of
nature, in philosophical speculation—and I am prepared to
find that both in amount and in kind her allusions to these
matters were also unusual. At all events this recurring vision
of her friends as "repealed" is certainly an idiosyncrasy.

Among her first letters to Samuel Bowles—she hopes the
family is well:

> I hope your cups are full. I hope your vintage is untouched.
> In such a porcelain life one likes to be *sure* that all is well lest
> one stumble upon one's hopes in a pile of broken crockery.

And later, to Mrs. Bowles:

> We are all human, Mary, until we are divine, and to some of
> us that is far off, and to some as near as the lady ringing at the
> door; perhaps *that's* what alarms.

(There is the old inconsistency of the pietistic convention: it
is very alarming that one's friends may at any moment become
divine.) There are scores of these anticipated farewells; what
is strange and disquieting about them is that Emily Dickinson
almost never includes herself among the disappearing. To
Mrs. Holland:

> I'm so glad you are not a blossom, for those in my garden fade,
> and then a "reaper whose name is Death" has come to get a

few to help him make a bouquet for himself, so I'm glad you're
not a rose. . . .

And several years later:

Death! Ah! democratic Death! . . . Say, is he everywhere?
Where shall I hide my things? Who is alive? The woods are
dead. Is Mrs. H. alive? Annie and Katie—are they below, or
received to nowhere?

And to Mrs. Holland twenty-one years later:

God's little Blond Blessing—we have long deemed you, and
hope that his so-called "Will"—will not compel him to revoke
you.

She explained this idiosyncrasy to Colonel Higginson (who
had gone off to war and received the foreboding message in
his camp) saying:

Perhaps death gave me awe for friends, striking sharp and
early, for I held them since in brittle love, of more alarm than
peace. I trust you may pass the limit of war . . . ;

but the explanation is insufficient. No long experience of life
is necessary to alert us to the fact that there is an element of
latent cruelty in these manifestations. They confirm our sense
of how deep a wound she had received.

These are the characteristic expressions of the envious and
of those who feel themselves to have been "shut out" from
life's major prizes. (I once heard a woman say to another:
"What darling little boys you have! We all hope—don't we?
—that there'll be none of these dreadful wars fifteen years
from now.") One last example: What was Mrs. Holland to
make of the following effusion, received at a time when she
was occupied with three children and with furthering the career of her husband, who, after long struggles, was beginning
to be regarded as one of the most popular writers and lecturers
in the country? "How kind of some to die, adding *impatience*

to the rapture of our thought of Heaven!" Here she inserts a poem beginning "As by the dead we love to sit," and continues:

> I had rather you lived nearer—I would like to touch you. Pointed attentions from the Angels, to two or three I love, make me sadly jealous.

The inappropriateness here is so great that we may well ask ourselves whether this is love at all or rather a dangerous self-indulgence in purely subjective emotion, perhaps an effort to ignite a real affection within herself—a phenomenon we occasionally find in those whose love has suffered shipwreck or been frozen with fright early in life. That she could and did love maturely we have ample evidence in the poetry and we turn there to see how she made her escape from this perilous situation.

III

As a poet Emily Dickinson started out with two great disadvantages—an enormous facility for versifying and an infatuation with bad models. Later she was to read absorbedly Shakespeare, Milton, Herbert, and the great English poets of her century, and one is aware of the influence they had upon her language, but one is also aware of how little an effect they had upon the verse forms she employed. Her point of departure was the lyric of the keepsake and the Christmas Annual and the newspaper and the genteel periodical—the avocation of clergymen and of ladies of refinement and sensibility. Even the better poets of the hymnbooks do not seem to have greatly influenced her. Although she was to make some startling innovations within this form, it is no less startling that she made no attempts to depart from the half-dozen stanzaic patterns with which she began. I choose to see in this fact an additional illustration of that *arrest* in her development which we have discovered elsewhere. She was extraordinarily bold in what she did within these patterns (she soon *burst their seams*), but the form of the poem and to some extent the kind of poem she admired as a girl continued to be the poem she wrote to the end.

She wrote to Colonel Higginson in April 1862 (she was then thirty-one years old): "I made no verse, but one or two, until last winter, sir." So far, very few poems have been, with assurance, dated prior to that time; but it seems to me that she here intended the qualification: no verse of the highest conscious intention. There are numbers of poems of about this time, and certainly early (hence, naturally, the darlings of the anthologists), such as "If I Can Stop One Heart from Breaking" and "I Taste a Liquor Never Brewed" and "To Fight Aloud Is Very Brave," which show evidence of having been preceded by a long experience in versifying. The passage from one stanza to the next is very accomplished indeed, and presupposes an extended practice, in public or in private. It appears certain to me that when, toward 1861, Emily Dickinson collected herself to write verse of the most earnest intention, she had to struggle not only against the pitfalls of a native facility, but against those of a facility already long exercised in a superficial effectiveness—in the easy pathos and in the easy epigram.

Even before she sent the first examples of her work to Colonel Higginson she had won a critical battle over her facility. She had found the courage to write poetry which "insulted the intelligence" of her contemporaries. What shocked Colonel Higginson was not that she occasionally employed "bad" rhymes (such abounded in the poetry of Mrs. Browning); nor that she substituted assonance for rhyme; nor even that she occasionally failed to rhyme at all (that practice he had accepted in Walt Whitman, whose work he recommended to her reading); but that all these irregularities were combined and deeply embedded in the most conventional of all verse forms.

At this distance we can venture to reconstruct her struggles.

A new tide had entered her being; she now wished to say with passion what she had been hitherto saying playfully, saying with coquetry. New intensities—particularly in new countries —call for new forms. A childhood fixation, however, prevented her from abandoning the stanzaic patterns of her early reading. She revolted from the regular rhyme, the eternal "my—die" and "God—rod," not because she was too lazy to impose it, but because the regular rhyme seemed the outer expression of an inner conventionality. She called the regular rhyme "prose"—"they shut me up in prose"—and in the same poem she calls it "captivity."

One of her devices shows us how conscious she was of what she was doing. She artfully offers us rhymes of increasing regularity so that our ear will be waiting for another, and then in a concluding verse refuses any rhyme whatever. The poem "Of Tribulation These Are They" gives us "white—designate," "times—palms," "soil—mile," "road—*Saved!*" (The italics are hers.) The effect is as of a ceiling being removed from above our heads. The incommensurable invades the poem. In "I'll Tell Thee All—How Blank It Grew" she flings all the windows open in closing with the words "outvisions paradise," rhymeless after three stanzas of unusually regular rhymes.

Her "teacher" rebuked her for these audacities, but she persisted in them. She did not stoop to explain or defend them. The Colonel's unwillingness to publish the work showed her that he did not consider her a poet, however much he may have been struck by individual phrases. She continued to enclose an occasional poem in her letters to friends, but they seem not to have asked to see "lots of them." The hope of encouragement and the thought of a contemporary audience grew more and more remote. Yet the possibility of a literary fame, of an ultimate glory, never ceased to trouble her. In poem after poem she derided renown; she compared it to an auction and to the croaking of frogs; but at the same time she hailed it as this consecration of the poet's "vital light." What did she do about it? She took five steps forward and two steps back. It is no inconsiderable advance toward literary pretension to write two thousand poems; yet the condition in which she left them is a no less conspicuous retreat. She called on posterity to witness that she was indifferent to its approval, but she did not destroy her work. She did not even destroy the "sweepings of the studio," the tentative sketches at the margin of the table. Had she left fair copies, the movement would have been five steps forward and one step back; had she directed that the work be burned by others, it would have been three steps back.

I am convinced that she went even further in her wish to appear indifferent to our good opinion; she deliberately marred many a poem; she did not so much insult our intelligence as flout it. As we read the more authentic work we are astonished to find that poem after poem concludes with some lapse into banality, or begins flatly and mounts to splendor. No one would claim that she was free of lapses of judgment and of taste, but the last three words of "How Many Times These Low Feet Staggered":

> Indolent housewife, in Daisies lain!

or the last verse of "They Put Us Far Apart":

> Not Either—noticed Death—
> Of Paradise—aware—
> Each other's Face—was all the Disc
> Each other's setting—saw—

are, poetically speaking, of an almost insolent cynicism—the first for flatness, the second for cacophony.

That is to say, Emily Dickinson frequently wrote badly *on purpose.* She did not aspire to your praise and mine, if we were the kind of persons who cannot distinguish the incidental from the essential. She had withdrawn a long way from our human,

human, human discriminations and judgments. As we have
seen, she was singed, if not scorched, in early life by the
all-too-human in her family relationships. Thereafter she was
abandoned—"betrayed" she called it—by the person (or, as
I prefer to see it, by the succession of persons) whom most she
loved. She withdrew from us: into her house; and even in her
house she withdrew—the few old friends who came to call
were required to converse with her through a half-open door.
She became more and more abstract in her view of people. She
did not repudiate us entirely, but she increasingly cherished
the thought that we would all be more estimable when we
were dead. She was capable of envisaging the fact that there
may be no life hereafter: "Their Height in Heaven Comforts
Not" acknowledges that the whole matter is a "house of supposition . . . that skirts the acres of perhaps." But only such
a company, unencumbered with earthly things, would understand what she was saying, and she took ample pains to dis-
courage all others. The poem that begins "Some work for
Immortality, the chiefer part for *Time*" is not primarily about
books sold in bookstores.

IV

In other words, those who dwell in "immensity" are not
finicking literary critics.

It is very difficult to be certain what Emily Dickinson meant
by "God," though there are innumerable references to Him.
Her relation to Him is marked by alternating advance and
retreat. He is occasionally warned not to be presumptuous;
that all the gifts He may have to show hereafter (the single
work from which she quotes most often is the Book of Revelation) are not likely to exceed certain occasions of bliss she has
known on earth. God, a supreme intelligence, was not a stable
concept in her mind. On the other hand, she lived constantly
close to another world she called Infinity, Immensity, Eternity,

and the Absolute. For her these concepts were not merely greater in degree from the dimensions of earth: they were different in kind; they were altogether *other;* they were nonsense. *There* dwelt her audience. If you set yourself to write verses for people down here on earth, in time, you were bound to miss the *tone*—the tone that is current in immensity. Immensity does not niggle at off-rhymes and at untidy verse-endings. Immensity is capable of smiling and probably enjoys those things which insult the intelligence of men. Walt Whitman wrote: "I round and finish little, if anything; and could not, consistently with my scheme. . . ." It would be difficult to assemble five of the maturer poems of Emily Dickinson which one could place before an antagonistic reader and say that they were "finished poems." For those two poets that word "finish" would smack strongly of poems servilely submitted for the approval of judges, princes, and connoisseurs. Art—the work of art—was slow in presenting itself as the project of a continent-conscious American. Hawthorne strove for it, but Hawthorne was not caught up into the realization of the New World's boundlessness; he even averted his face from it, and consciously. Poe's mind knew both the boundlessness and the work of art, and the double knowledge was among the elements that destroyed him. The work of art is the recognition of order, of limits, of shared tacit assumptions and, above all, of agreed-upon conventions. Walt Whitman and Emily Dickinson seemed to be at every moment advancing into new territories in relation to writing; the time for them had not come to consolidate what they had acquired, to establish their limits and to construct their conventions.

I have said before that Americans can find no support for their identity in place, in time, or in community—that they are really in relation only to Everywhere, Always, and Everybody. Emily Dickinson is a signal illustration of this assertion. The imagination of this spinster withdrawn into a few rooms in

Amherst was constantly aware that the universe surrounded
every detail of life. "I take no less than skies," she wrote, "for
earths grow thick as berries, in my native town." Her tireless
observation of the animals and plants about her has none of
that appropriative feeling that we found in the Concord writers; she knows well that they are living their life engaging in
no tender or instructive dialogue with man, and that their life
is part of a millennial chain. She "gives them back" to the
universe. In this constant recognition of the immensity of
dimensions of time and place, she is the least parochial of
American poets and exceeds even Walt Whitman in imaginative sweep. She could have rejoined Poe in the preoccupations
that lay behind his *Eureka*.

And can we say of her that she wrote for Everybody? Yes;
for when one has overcome the "low" desire to write for
anybody in particular—the cultivated, the chosen souls, one's
closest friends; when one has graduated from all desire to
impress the judicious or to appeal to the like-minded—then
and only then is one released to write for Everybody—only
then released from the notion that literature is a specialized
activity, an elegant occupation, or a guild secret. For those
who live in "immensity" it is merely (and supremely) the
human voice at its purest, and it is accessible to Everybody, not
at the literary level, but at the human. It is Everybody's fault,
not hers, if Everybody is not ready to recognize it. Perhaps
only when Everybody is dead will Everybody be in a condition
to understand authentic human speech. "Some work for Immortality, the chiefer part for *Time.*" In Emily Dickinson we
have reached a very high point in American abstraction. (It is
characteristic of her that her thought turned often to the Alps
and the Andes.) She was, as we have seen in the letters, the
least confiding of women, the shut-up, the self-concealing; yet
if the audience was large enough, if she was certain that Everybody would attend, her lips could unlock to floods of impassioned confession and uninhibited assertion.

The problem of the American loneliness which we discussed in relation to Thoreau is the problem of "belonging." He was a lonely man because the elements to which he tried to belong were near and few; Emily Dickinson, in all appearance the loneliest of beings, solved the problem in a way which is of importance to every American: by loving the particular while living in the universal.

CULTURE IN

A DEMOCRACY

CULTURE IN A DEMOCRACY

Many are deeply concerned about the preservation and survival of cultural values in the years that lie ahead of us: the Age of the Common Man, the Age of Democracy. They say: the gains which have been made—and which will be made—in the living conditions of the majority must be paid for by a loss in the conditions that encourage and produce superior works of the mind and spirit.

The danger is real.

In the previous thousands of years most artists, poets, and thinkers were dependent on the protection, encouragement, subvention of rulers, aristocracies, ecclesiastical hierarchies, and elites. What these privileged groups had in common, for the benefit of artists, were three things:

1. The relatively free disposal of their time. Most of them were not all day in banks or offices or workshops, or in the fields. They had time to cultivate themselves, as we say. And from this experience of free time they had the insight: that

An address, written in English and then professionally translated, delivered by the author himself in German in the Pauluskirche, Frankfurt am Main, 6 October 1957, on the occasion of his receiving the Peace Prize of the Association of German Publishers and Booksellers. It was printed in German along with introductory speeches by Reinhard Jaspert and Carl J. Burckhardt as *Drei Ansprachen anlässlich der Verleihung des Friedenspreises des Deutschen Buchhandels* (Frankfurt am Main: Börsenverein des Deutschen Buchhandels, 1957) and, separately, with slight variations in text, as *Kultur in einer Demokratie.* Copyright © 1957 by Thornton Wilder. All rights reserved (Frankfurt am Main: S. Fischer Verlag, 1957). This English text is printed from a typescript among the Wilder papers (YCAL).

artists and thinkers needed, above all things, uninterrupted time.

2. They ruled; they commanded; they were authoritarian. And from this characteristic in themselves they had the insight to accord to artists a certain freedom in the choice of subjects and in the manner of their execution.

3. They felt themselves to be distinctly separated from the rest of mankind. Though relatively few in number, they felt under no obligation to consult the tastes or wishes of the majority.

In the society toward which we move there will be fewer and fewer persons enjoying these forms of privilege, wealth, authoritarian independence, and, above all, in possession of extended and uninterrupted time.

Already we see that the encouragement and subvention of cultural activities is in the hands of bureaucrats—of committees, of institutions, of foundations, and of governmental organizations—that is to say, of men and women who sit at desks from nine in the morning until late in the afternoon. The money they dispense comes very directly from the people and they must be very attentive to the tastes and wishes of the majority. The majority of the people are engaged in less cultural activities from morning until late afternoon.

This is the danger.

You have had experience in Germany of culture supervised by bureaucrats and Russia is having that experience now.

Another aspect of this problem is much discussed in the United States. We have more and more universities with twelve to fifteen thousand students. These institutions are supported by the taxes paid by their parents. These taxpayers feel they have the right to influence the content of higher education. The administrators must be attentive to these demands. Can they maintain standards of scholarship under such pressures?

The leadership of elites is giving place to the leadership of majority opinion. That is culture under a democracy. And our attitude to it depends upon our belief in the potentialities—the so-to-speak intuitive capabilities—of the average man existing in a democracy.

I am going to base my reply on some words of Walt Whitman—some very strange, bold words.

He is discussing this problem in relation to the United States. But we may apply them to the situation everywhere in our Western world.

I have long felt that many of the manifestations we call Americanism would have taken place all over the world even though the Western hemisphere had not existed or had not been discovered. Their source was in Europe—technological development, a classless society—the fugitives who came to the New World merely entered into conditions which produced an *acceleration* of such tendencies. The extent to which they received there a certain direction, a certain color, is the subject of another discussion.

Here are Walt Whitman's words:

> Of the great poems received from abroad and from the ages, and today enveloping and penetrating America, is there one that is consistent with these United States, or essentially applicable to them as they are and as they are to be? Is there one whose underlying basis is not a denial and insult to democracy?

He asks a question. What did he mean?

That the *Iliad* and the *Divina Commedia* and the plays of Shakespeare and *Paradise Lost* and *Faust* were an insult to Democracy?

My friends, we approach a danger—cultural life under a democracy.

But we are also emerging from a danger. A danger that has hung over mankind for more than five thousand years: a poison, subtle and often sweet, that has been present in every activity of the cultural life and which is still present in the very structure of our language.

I shall try to show you that it has found its way into religious thinking, into our daily life, and into our assumption about the life of the family. That danger is withdrawing like bright-colored clouds from a sky at dawn; but it is present in all these "great poems of the past" and it lingers under the surface of thought and feeling.

This was the insult: that God and destiny had given to a small number of persons an unearned superiority and that to the majority He had given an inferior lot; that *privilege* is not only in the order of society, but that it is in the order of nature; and in the order of divine governance. This was the feudal lie: that leadership is transmitted in the chromosomes; and that only communities enjoying these mystical privileges can pro-duce and encourage and maintain all that is excellent, true, and beautiful.

But—you say—this is ridiculous. All that is long a thing of the past. Who takes seriously those kings and aristocracies and counts? We read about their marriages in the paper—and they resemble some childish marionette play.

Of the past?

But Mr. [T. S.] Eliot and many others still believe that only elites can produce an excellent thing.

And certainly we are profoundly indebted to those feudal elites for most of the treasury of culture. To Athens: one freeman to ten slaves. To the courts of Augustus, of Mantua, of the Medici, the Papacy, Charles, Philip II, Elizabeth I—to Versailles—to Weimar . . .

This fiction thrived by the help of a confusion of images—of metaphors. The Feudal Fiction reinforced itself by association with Divinity, Paternity, and the laws of gravity. God was a King and a Father; so all kings and fathers participated—by metaphor—in an element of divinity. God was above; and kings and fathers were above—and everybody else was *low*.

Since God was a Father, all men are children.

But God is not a King, He is spirit.

God is not a Father, He is spirit.

He does not wish us to be children, but to be men and women.

And as there are no more kings, it is now our duty not to be subjects, but to be co-rulers.

God is not above. He is within and over and under and around.

From this inextricable metaphorical confusion of God—King—Father—Above, we have developed the other confusion:

We are low, base, subject, childish, common, ordinary, and vulgar.

For a century and a half the majority of letters written in Germany were addressed as a conventional salutation to the *"Hoch Wohlgeborenen."* (That is, to the "Eminently Well-born.") The rest of us were, by implication, the low-born.

One of the principal evils of this confusion was the image of the son. No man has a father after twenty-one. Lucky is the man who, after twenty-one, has in his father his best friend. A son until twenty-one is obedient; thereafter—not.

Notice the nations that have given to their country a feminine noun. They have even twisted a masculine word to make a feminine noun: *la patria; la patrie.* We speak of our mother country. A father one obeys; a mother one protects.

Notice how the feudal lie has embedded itself in the languages:

A view of a mountain is *"herrlich"* (*i.e.,* "lordly"), "noble," or *"soberano";* and in English an evil act is "ignoble." In English we speak of a "noble experiment" and a "sovereign remedy." We hope our sons will be "gentlemen"—from the Latin *"gens";* that they will show "gentility" and will be capable of "gentle" deeds. The word "common" (in German: *"gemein"*) ought to be a beautiful word. I would wish to associate myself with the "common," the "ordinary," and the "vulgar."

Can't we save these words?

The evil that I am bringing to your attention is not so much that there were coteries of persons in high places, but that their jealous protection of their undeserved and unjustified privileges robbed the rest of the world of spiritual dignity— not only social dignity, but spiritual dignity.

We have all admired the phrase *"Noblesse oblige."* But have you observed the reverse of that famous saying—*"Bassesse condamne"?*

And let us remember for a moment all the other thousand-year-old lies that are gradually disappearing:

That a woman is incapable of responsibility in civil life;

That a woman in marriage has no rights in property and no rights in regard to her children;

That a man—under God and the state—may own and buy and sell total ownership of another man;

That children, because of the accident of their birth in needy families, may be made to work from dawn to sunset;

That a man because of race or color or religion is an inferior creature—

Oh, the journey to truth and freedom and the maturity of man is not yet ended. The world is still full of sweet and comforting lies.

But the lie I have described is losing its strength.

Edmund Burke said that if you tell a man a thing a thousand times he will believe it.

Now, the mass of men have been told a thousand times a day that they were God's stepchildren; that He had His favorites and that those favorites were above them.

Democracy is not only an effort to establish a social equality among men; it is an effort to assure them that they are not sons, nor subjects, nor low—that they should be equal in God's grace.

It will take some time. Call men dogs for five thousand years and they will crawl.

Those bright-colored clouds are receding.

And how about culture?

Let us not be too easily frightened. We are confronted by some unknown factors: the characteristics of the Man with Head Raised. Extended over all society, that is indeed something new.

Culture in a democracy has its dangers, but it has also this hope and this promise. It has a vast new subject to write about, to think about, to express, to explore: the Man with Raised Head.

That position, newly adopted, is uncomfortable and troubling—as some literature in recent years has shown us. It can even lead to despair.

Democracy has a large task: to find new imagery, new metaphors, and new myths to describe the new dignity into which man has entered.

ON DRAMA
AND THE THEATER

SOPHOCLES'S
OEDIPUS REX

One of the remarkable aspects of the survival of literary masterpieces down through the centuries is the diversity of reasons which the successive ages have found for admiring them.
They are like great, slowly revolving lamps which turn a different face to each new generation that confronts them. Many
of them have outlasted the spoken life of the language in
which they were written and the social and religious ideas that
played a large part in their inspiration, but such is their depth
and variety that ever new aspects emerge to replace those
which have lost their immediacy. The *Aeneid* was intended to
be an inspiring appeal to patriotic emotion; then for centuries
it was held to be a prophetical allegory of the Christian dispen-
sation; for a time it was looked upon as a book of magic, and
fortunes were told through the blindfold singling out of a line
from its pages; now it is most often praised for its passages of
melancholy and pathos. For centuries *The Divine Comedy*
served as a poem of piety and instruction; now even the foremost Italian critic [Benedetto Croce] regards it as a conglom-
erate of poetry and non-poetry and advises the reader to cull
from its vast doctrinal scaffolding the intermittent moments of
poetic and dramatic force. We have much anecdotic evidence
that *Don Quixote* was originally received as boisterous comedy;

The introduction for the edition of the play, in an English translation by Francis Storr,
issued in New York by The Heritage Press in 1955, as *Oedipus the King.*

now it is the peculiar treasure of the reflective. Similarly, the *Oedipus Rex,* though it contains much that has commanded uniform admiration in every age, presents a number of aspects which were more impressive to the Greeks than they are to us, and others, indifferent or imperceptible to the contemporaries of Sophocles, which particularly engage the modern mind. It is the task of the attentive reader first of all to reconstruct, as far as he is able, the values which were most apparent to the original audience. In the *Oedipus Rex* there was one that exceeded even its technical ingenuity, its psychological truth, and its eloquence, and that was its religious force. Apollo does not appear upon the scene, but the terror of his presence and his will is the true subject of the play. There has been little religious drama in Europe since the Greeks, and the theater has lost one of its most powerful effects—the shudder and awe induced by the presence of the numinous, by the *tremendum* of religious experience; and in order to do justice to this play we, over twenty centuries later, must attempt to recover something of this emotion.

When at the first performance Oedipus appeared at the doors of his palace and spoke the opening lines of the play, the Greek audience gazed at him not only with full knowledge of his past involuntary crimes and of his future misfortunes, but with an additional apprehension which may be underestimated by the modern spectator. They saw in him a man under the shadow of the hereditary curse which pursued all the descendants of Labdacus, a shadow recently enhanced by a second curse laid on his father by Pelops—the same Pelops who was himself accursed and whose malediction is wrought out in the lives of his own descendants, Agamemnon, Orestes, Electra, and Iphigeneia. In the eyes of the original audience the actions and motives of such a man would be understood to express the constant pressure of a force for destruction beyond his own control. In the same way, in the play about his daughter Antigone, the modern reader may forget that for the Greeks the heroine's courageous action and lofty sentiments were enhanced by the fact that she was not only the daughter of a great house, but a child of incest and enmeshed in the doom that weighed upon her family from the curses that had been pronounced upon it.

It is not difficult to see how the idea of the hereditary curse could develop in primitive society. It satisfied the longing for a balance of justice whereby a powerful, wicked man could be rendered uneasy in the belief that because of his enemy's curse his descendants would suffer in his stead, and whereby a wronged man with no power of direct retaliation could be comforted through the assurance that his curse had struck terror into his enemy's mind. Yet it is difficult to see how the Greeks throughout that century of unparalleled swift growth in philosophic thought could cling so tenaciously to this vestige of rudimentary ethics. It is doubly interesting, therefore, to watch the way in which the tragic poets sought to elevate the hereditary curse—an unavoidable *datum* in the legendary material they were transferring to the stage—and to raise it from the realm of superstition to religious insight. In the *Oedipus Rex,* the *Antigone,* and the *Oedipus at Colonus,* Sophocles has muted the allusions to the curse and has placed the action of a pursuing vengeance in the hands of Apollo under his attribute of presiding deity over the purity of the home. The Athenian audience knew that the pestilence with which the play opens had been sent by him; within one hundred lines of the opening Creon arrives from the god's temple at Delphi, followed presently by his priest Teiresias. The theatrical excitement inherent in this opening scene can best be illustrated by reference to another Greek play, the *Choephoroi* or *Libation-bearers* of Aeschylus. There the tomb of the still unavenged Agamemnon is in view of the audience. The Furies are imagined to be hovering near it, clamoring for the death of the murderers, Clytemnestra and Aegisthus. Electra turns about it, brooding on her revenge. Orestes, in disguise, returns from his long exile and makes his vows before it. The Queen has been visited by terrifying dreams and brings her offerings to appease it. The air is charged; to borrow an expression from children's games, the stage is "warm" and it grows to a white heat during the progress of the play. Similarly, the *Oedipus Rex* opens at the moment that the "other world" has chosen to intervene in human affairs, to set in motion the train of events that will bring to light the enormities in Oedipus's past. The action of *Macbeth* and *Hamlet* is likewise instituted by supernatural agencies, but the witches and the ghost of Hamlet's father are easily understood as externalizations of the promptings within the protagonists' minds. In the Greek plays, however, the gods are objective forces and the audience received the anguish of Oedipus and the suicide of Iocasta as being required by a power greater and "other" than subjective fancy, and under a necessity more significant than the hereditary curse which Sophocles has elevated to a larger fatality, the cleansing will of Apollo.

It is this concentration of the punishment in the hands of Apollo which gives to the play its character of cruelty; for Apollo is punishing a patricide and an incest which had long since been predicted by his oracles and which depended for their fulfillment on slight and easily preventable coincidences. Oedipus's cry:

> Apollo, friends, Apollo was he that brought these my woes
> to pass, these my sore, sore woes . . .

seems to be as true of their having taken place originally as of their being punished now. When a modern dramatist [Jean Cocteau] undertook to retell the same story, he called his play *The Infernal Machine,* and the impression that both plays make upon us is that of an innocent man's being driven into a trap of vindictive ingenuity and of then being punished for it with equal malice. The *Oedipus Rex* seems to say: Destiny is engaged in the conscious preparations of man's humiliation.

During the play, all absorbed in the mounting tension, Sophocles does not stop to consider the problem of Oedipus's responsibility for his involuntary crimes; but this is not the poet's last word on the life-story of his hero. In the *Oedipus at Colonus,* which tradition tells us was written some forty years later, he shows us Apollo making amends and repentant of the part he had played. In the later tragedy word comes from the oracle at Delphi that inestimable benefits will accrue to whatever country affords hospitality and sepulture to the aged outcast, and at the close of the play Oedipus dies accompanied by many signs of divine favor. It is as though Sophocles, like his hero, had been troubled during the intervening years by all the philosophical questions that inevitably arise from the earlier play, and as though he too had seen that it was indeed those "pure and awful gods" whom Oedipus had invoked who were ultimately responsible for his misfortunes. Had the *Oedipus at Colonus* disappeared with the reported eighty or ninety other plays of Sophocles, the *Oedipus Rex* would have remained no less a masterpiece of tragic art, but it would have been one degree further removed from us by reason of this extreme picture it presents of the helplessness of man. The catastrophes in the plays of Euripides, as in those of Shakespeare, proceed from flaws in the protagonists' characters rather than from the implacable workings of circumstance. The sufferings that men endure as a result of their weaknesses are no less "tragic," but they do not imply a universe in which the human struggle for felicity is doomed in advance to frustration. When people in general conversation today refer to the "starkness of Greek tragedy" it is this play that has primarily established the idea; but it is well to remember that the two most notable contributions to the form, Aeschylus's trilogy dealing with Agamemnon and his children, and the two plays of Sophocles dealing with Oedipus, both conclude in a spirit of reconciliation and hope.

The consideration of Oedipus's guilt brings us to another

element in the play, an idea in regard to human behavior so deeply imbedded in the Greek mind that its understanding requires of us a particular exercise of the historical imagination. Any exceptional endowment, they believed, or any responsible position which a man might hold constituted a moral danger and rendered him liable to a state of pride, of excessive self-confidence, of *hubris*. Under *hubris* a man lost his spiritual discernment. All exceptional achievement was a provocation to arrogance, and the Greeks watched the kings and heroes of their epic poems and tragedies with a particular excitement for signs of this moral blindness. It was in the light of this law that they saw Achilles withdraw from the battle, Agamemnon sacrifice his daughter and later accept the treacherous flattery of his wife, Creon condemn Antigone, and Oedipus at the opening of this play insult Creon and the priest of Apollo, Teiresias. The Greek distrust of the exceptional did not apply only to the possession of notable advantages, however; it constituted a rule for behavior in the daily life of the average individual as well. Of the two inscriptions on the temple doors at Delphi, "Know thyself" has become the more famous, but the other, "Nothing too much," was more characteristically Greek. The idea recurs with particular frequency in the work of Sophocles. When he came to treat the subject of Electra, the whole play became a study in perilous excess and rings with such admonitions as "Weep not too much," "Rejoice not too much," and "Love not too much." In the *Oedipus Rex* the first sign that the King is in danger of succumbing to this excessive self-confidence arrives with his acceptance of the words spoken by the priest of Zeus:

> It is not as deeming thee ranked with the gods . . . but . . .

The sentence implies the possibility of such a comparison which no mere rhetorical negative could save, and the Greek audience knew that his failure to repudiate the implication was a sign that his downfall was imminent. Oedipus's responsibility for the crimes in the past does not present itself to Sophocles as a problem until he writes the *Oedipus at Colonus;* he is absorbed by the sins into which Oedipus falls during the action of the play—those he finds reprehensible enough, as the third choral ode shows.

The reason for Sophocles's indifference at this stage of his life to the ethical problems behind his story may lie in a trait of his character on which the few surviving fragments of his biography throw some light. We are told that his attitude to the religious ideas of his time was that of unquestioning piety. In one play, now lost, he had occasion to present the utterances of a blasphemer, and an Alexandrian critic tells us that the speeches were singularly ineffective. Whereas both Aeschylus and Euripides were engaged throughout their lives in purifying the mythical heritage and pouring into it a wealth of didactic innovations, Sophocles was generally content to retell the old stories without examination of their often savage principles. Even with the example before him of Aeschylus's treatment of the Orestes story as an argumentation against the tribal requirement of eye-for-an-eye revenge, Sophocles shows us an Orestes obediently accepting the duty of murdering his mother and closes the play with such satisfaction at the achievement that one critic has described it as "a mixture of matricide and high spirits." It may be that it is Sophocles's readiness to reproduce the traditional legend and his serene acceptance of Apollo's dictates that lend to the *Oedipus Rex* its character of cruelty, and it therefore becomes all the more interesting to know that later, in the *Oedipus at Colonus,* he changed his views upon its meaning.

If these religious elements in the play were nearer to the minds of the ancients, there remains another which has attracted attention in modern times: the psychological interest in the old myth which has rendered Oedipus's name a label for certain recurrent patterns in behavior. Modern psychology holds that myth-making is one of the means whereby the generalized truths of human knowledge find expression and particularly the disavowed impulses of the mind escape the "censor" of acquired social control and find their way into indirect confession. Myths constitute the dreaming sub-conscious soul of the race telling its story. Greek mythology is peculiarly rich in these formulations of generalized truth. Prometheus, the benefactor, is perpetually the rebel against authority. Cassandra stands forever as the wisdom that is un-able to warn the crowd. The heel of Achilles and the choice of Hercules have passed into proverbial expression. The newer psychologists claim to have discovered that in the infan-tile life every child feels himself to be the rival to the father for the mother's love and harbors and finally suppresses the death-wish against the father. In the majority of cases the phase is outgrown but remains in the subconscious in the form of a sense of guilt. Whatever truth this theory contains would help to explain the haunting power which this play has con-tinuously exercised and the strange fact that the critics from antiquity to the present day constantly refer to the "universal-ity" of the figure of Oedipus, who would seem on the contrary to be a man struggling in highly exceptional circumstances. This attribute of universality is further enhanced by the sec-ondary myth which represents him as the man who was able to answer the riddle of the Sphinx:

> What is it that goes first on four feet, then on two, and finally on three?

The answer itself is mankind, and the myth seems to say that Oedipus represents man setting out on the journey of self-knowledge and inquiry. If it is true that readers and audiences have followed this tragedy with a profound unconscious self-identification with the accurst and guilty hero, then the mes-sage of the *Oedipus at Colonus* declaring that the gods absolve mankind of the crimes in which it had no choice becomes an affirmation comparable to that contained in the Book of Job.

At the festival where it was first produced the *Oedipus Rex* obtained the second prize. The winning play has long since been forgotten, and the *Oedipus Rex* has probably been revived more frequently than any other play of antiquity. At the close of the last century, in the great performance of Mounet-Sully, it was one of the most popular productions of the Comédie Française. Max Reinhardt's productions of it attracted vast audiences throughout the German-speaking world and England. Sir John Martin-Harvey toured with it for many years in England and America. The plays by Voltaire and Dryden modeled closely upon it enjoyed great success in their day. The second prize remains in the record, however, for our instruction. It would seem that no play could make a more immediate effect. It is a triumph of construction, an intricate "detective story," wherein two avenues of inquiry after a long, mounting progress of increasing tension finally meet in a passage of compact force forty lines long. It is a demonstration of psychological skill. The figure of the Queen is drawn with great precision, shielding her husband from the knowledge she foresees approaching, alternately condemning and upholding the authority of the oracles as best suits the direction of the argument at the moment, and finally giving up the struggle.

The characterization of Oedipus displays the same combination of large-scale draftsmanship and specific detail: the mind caught in the whirlpool of dread, long unable to credit the evidence before him (Voltaire, the embodiment of French reasonableness, refused to see the psychological truth of this blindness, and exclaimed: "He who was able to read the riddle of the Sphinx was unable to see what would be apparent to a child of ten!") and betraying his inner turmoil by lapses of the tongue and by abrupt and all but incoherent transitions in his questionings.

Perhaps the second prize which the Athenian judges conferred upon the play should remind us primarily that masterpieces are difficult. Their survival and the diversity in their appeal are evidence that they come to us from a removed thought-world not easy to penetrate. Sometimes their difficulty proceeds from an inner necessity on their authors' part continually to innovate in form and subject matter. This was the case with Euripides, each of whose works was a new scandal to his contemporaries and who never received a first prize in the dramatic contests throughout his long career. Sometimes the difficulty proceeds, as in the case of the second part of Goethe's *Faust* and of the last quartets of Beethoven, from the extreme condensation and symbolic formulation that the artists' long meditations have converted into an almost "private language." During the years following the appearance of such works the public has the opportunity of adjusting itself to them; other works are composed under their influence by less original hands, and finally a body of critical commentary collects about them to facilitate their understanding. But the difficulty is eternally there, and as it is not essentially a difficulty of style or manner but of a relation to life, it is our duty to insist on rediscovering it and wrestling with it. The aids to masterpieces are often nothing but means to avoid their fundamental power and reduce to matters of "taste" and "interest" what should be a perpetually renewed conflict.

One may venture to suggest that the difficulty of the *Oedipus Rex* lies in two realms. In the first place, it is not easy to accord one's adherence, moment by moment, to a mind that treats so painful a subject with such composure. We are accustomed to seeing a greater conformity between style and matter: the imaginative tumult in Michelangelo's composition for the Judgment Day; the impassioned extensions of language and syntax in Aeschylus's treatment of the crimes of the *Oresteia*. Sophocles nowhere betrays this human participation in the overwrought emotions of his characters, and many distinguished scholars and critics have found something "chilling" in the measured beauty of the language and the impeccable intellectual ordering of the action. Sophocles's name is often linked with those of Raphael and Mozart, artists who chose to efface from their work all evidence of the emotional stress they underwent in contemplating the tragic background of life. It is not easy to follow such natures, but this deep equanimity before the spectacle of evil is one of the exacting values of the play. A still greater difficulty, however, resides in the fact that we rise to a prolonged act of concentration. There are no other examples in literature of so single-minded a discipline. The Elizabethan tragedies, by the use of sub-plots and the frequent change of scene, invited an intermittent relaxation; the *Antigone* even has moments of humor; the *Oresteia* has lyrical digressions and episodes in varying mood. Time after time in the *Oedipus Rex* our minds fall back, unwilling to carry the weight of realization and forever ready to follow the action on easier levels, as ingenious narrative or as absorbing characterization. Having chosen a subject in the realm of the incommensurable, the will of the gods, and having, through reasons in his own temperament, refused to endow it with the mitigating element of a sympathetically emotional treatment, Sophocles transferred it with an inflexible purity to the realm of the mind. This evocation of pity, terror, and religious awe under the control of an elevated objectivity estranged his contemporaries. In the intervening years the world has corrected the error, but it remains as drastic an experience as on the occasion of its first performance, and its rewards are in proportion to its difficulty.

GEORGE BERNARD SHAW

Somewhere Shaw writes:

> I am more responsible than anyone outside of Scandinavia for the improved position of women in the modern world, and women in the mines of South America and in the mills of Bombay are indebted to me, even though they do not know my name.

It is an impressive boast. One wonders why he does not add to the number of his beneficiaries some hundreds of thousands of wives who, having discovered that their amiable bridegrooms are brutes, are better able to protect themselves and their children. One might also expect to find him pointing with pride at the innumerable enemies he has made, including those property owners who have been made more publicly responsible for what takes place throughout those holdings which had seemed to lie at such a vast distance from them.

We are indeed aware that society owes a large debt to Shaw; but it is important that we attempt to estimate the extent of the debt and in what ways and through what channels he was effective. This brings us to a consideration of the rôle performed by the Man of Letters as Reformer, and thinking of

Written in 1968, when Thornton Wilder was in the hospital convalescing from minor surgery, but never published. (The paraphrases of passages from Shaw's writings are not identifiable as specific texts.) Printed from a typescript among the Wilder papers (YCAL).

Shaw we are to keep in mind the work of Voltaire and Diderot and Ibsen and Dickens, to say nothing of those even greater writers whom the hurried and impatient reformers never think of including among the builders of our social institutions.

During the last quarter of the last century Irishmen were reminding each other with increasing intensity that their country had endured seven centuries of oppression. Their brains were continually suffused with fantasies of the death-wish against the invader and they never ceased from intoning the names of the martyrs who fell in those ever renewed and ever repressed rebellions. What are the results of seven centuries of hatred and frustration? One of the manifestations among Irish men of letters was the withdrawal into esoteric mystical constructions infinitely remote from the agitations of the market-place; another was the cultivation of a histrionic bellicosity —histrionic, not because it was unreal but because so much of it required that the Irishman continually seek out or invent ever new objects for his aggression. We see the same thing frequently in men and women who have spent their childhood (or who retrospectively imagine that they have spent their childhood) under a senseless and immitigable tyranny.

The result for Bernard Shaw was that he did not know what he knew, he was not visited by any ideas, save in contradiction to some already established error. He was incapable of thinking in pure gratuity; he could only think by ricochet. Hence, his thought was always contentious; its energy was sustained by exaggeration and it glittered with those illuminations derived from striking a half-truth which are inseparable from wit. Further, he was unable to express a thought without being aware of its repercussion in Audience. He was Audience-ridden, Audience-fettered, and that is a very sorry thing to be.

I was once invited to lunch by the Shaws in their apartment in Whitehall Court. I observed immediately that Shaw had the handshake of a shy man, the rapid tender and withdrawal. He

seized the conversation one beat too soon—and not from
vanity but from dismay. He stood with his back to the hearth
and harangued the guests on the virtues of vegetarianism. "I
shall outlive you all," he cried, beating his chest. "In a few
minutes you will go into the next room and my dear wife will
offer you the decaying carcasses of animals. . . ." That is what
it is to be dependent on reaction. Even in the anecdotes of his
gaiety—and he was not gay on that day—the pressure upon
him was like an anguish. And no wonder he was shy, for to
live by one's effect on others—even if it includes insulting
those whom one feels to be worthy of contempt—is a dependence very close to servility.

The social effectiveness of Shaw's writings had by its very
nature to be indirect. It was not his books and plays in themselves which began to crack and melt the great icebergs of
British inertia. His particular kind of wit and exaggeration
were precisely the kind which hardens the sinner in his sin.
British society was so deeply imbedded in its institutions, so
self-evident seemed the continuation of its inequities (it has
never been difficult to ascribe the world's inequities to God's
will, "as the dear Bishop so reassuringly explained to us last
Sunday at St. Cuthbert's") that the sharpest attacks against it
rang in their ears as frivolity and flattery. At its worst we see
this operation in the librettos of W. S. Gilbert: they pretended
to be corrosive; in fact, they were little short of soothing.

Shaw's social effectiveness was rendered possible by vulgarization. He was digested and rephrased by bright young men
(and now that this twentieth century advances we can say for
the first time in history that such work is also being carried on
by bright young women, and we are partially indebted to
Shaw that we can say it). The thousands of wives who saw *A
Doll's House* within the first half-century of its appearance
themselves went home revolving long thoughts; Dickens's
debtors' prisons, his Dotheboys School and his Circumlocu-

tion Office aroused an immediate uneasiness in every self-respecting reader. Vulgarizers those writers had also, but the works themselves were masterpieces and masterpieces energize with or without mediation. Shaw was a bright young man who vulgarized Ibsen and Ellen Key [Swedish feminist and writer, 1849–1926] and Nietzsche, but he produced no masterpieces and the radiance of his brightness was obscured by his frenetic need of Audience's immediate praise and blame.

So now, partly as a result of Shaw's vigorous writing, millions of women in industry receive larger wages and work shorter hours and millions of wives know that if their husbands turn unamiable they are in a better position to take their children and walk out of the front door. These are great and merciful advances. It would be rash, nevertheless, to affirm that the totality of society is further advanced in its right to the pursuit of happiness than it was fifty years ago. Nor would one, on the other hand, compare these reformers to men who lift a yoke from one pair of shoulders only to discover that it has fallen on another, or to surgeon apprentices who are able to lance a patient's boil but who cannot purify a patient's blood. Misery and inhumanity never sleep, nor are they so easily abolished; they merely displace themselves. The trouble with the immediate and topical reformer is that he has an incomplete conception of the human need. Shaw attacked the institution of marriage without having any instinctive sympathetic understanding of the nature of woman; and he attacked the abuses of property without having any clear picture of the relation of property to the life in a home—especially the life of the workingman who would presumably benefit in a society under socialism. Like all Audience-fettered writers, he found it very difficult to be attentive to how freedom operates in other people. He has testified to his lifelong indebtedness to Charles Dickens. From Dickens he borrowed the outer contours of characterization; his cockney *raisonneurs,* for example, have some of the impudence and self-assurance of Dickens's originals; but he could not borrow Dickens's joy in the spontaneous separateness of everyone who has ever lived. It is to this that people refer when they say of certain writers: "All the characters talk like the author."

This trait furnishes another reason why Shaw's work depended on its vulgarization by bright young people and it throws light on a certain obtuseness whereby he could allocate so much credit to himself for a worldwide reformation. It is perhaps fortunate that such reformers enjoy so largely the sense of initiating a cause and of carrying it on singlehandedly, as Shaw did relative to the improved situation of women. At most we must see him as an accelerator. As far back as 1860 Queen Victoria had been trembling with indignation at the advancing tide. She hoped to curb "this mad, wicked folly of Women's Rights, with all its attendant horrors, on which her poor mad sex is bent."

Shaw affected to be in dialogue with Shakespeare all his life. He invented the fiction that everyone had always misunderstood Shakespeare and attributed to him many great qualities which he did not possess and remained blind to other qualities which he (Shaw) would now indicate. Shaw's quarrel with Shakespeare lay deeper, however. In one of the prefaces he draws a parallel between Shakespeare and John Bunyan. (I am writing these lines while convalescent in a hospital and furnish only a paraphrase of the text.)

> Five pages of Bunyan are worth a hundred by these myriad-minded opalescent-men who refrain from advancing to the ramparts of the struggle for human betterment and planting their banners there.

But it was Shakespeare who did so much toward preparing the improved situation of women. It is a poor writer who cannot arrest the attention of his readers with the presentation of an erratic young woman or with, at best, the picture of an admirable young woman, like Gretchen or Tess or Anna Karenina, caught up in situations that result in havoc and destruction. Shakespeare was one of the few writers in all literature who could present a young woman as both virtuous and interesting. He fashioned nine of them and they continue to affect the spiritual weather of the world. A number of them he places in situations of utter destitution (several are not even permitted to acknowledge that they are women), but they are unafraid, resourceful, observant, and thoughtful, and they are singularly exempt from the notion that they ceased to have any significance save in relation to some man. All of them are finally married, but we have the sense that they would have remained no less the objects of our admiration had we known them many years later as spinsters. There is food for thought in observing how few sisters they have (Nausicaä joins hands with Natasha Rostov) in world literature and how many notable writers attempted the task and failed. The vulgarization of Shakespeare was not carried on by bright young men writing editorials but by millions of persons in many lands gazing with emotion and delight at the way in which, to borrow a phrase of our grandfathers, Shakespeare "bore witness" for womankind.

The theater appears to be the most Audience-subservient of the arts. Like a magnet, it attracts all sorts of Audience-infatuate natures. It has another face, however; at its best it is the purest of the modes for presenting the human situation. Its masters have passed through all the solicitations of self-assertion and have come out on the farther side. To them the audience in the theater is neither student nor flatterer nor fool —Molière to the contrary—nor even judge. It is mere humanity, shoulder to shoulder—the dramatist in their midst—agaze at this mirror held up to nature. Shaw achieved no complete play at this elevation. Occasionally we are aware of it in a first act—those of *John Bull's Other Island* and *The Doctor's Dilemma*, for instance. He announced that he had written *Heartbreak House* "in the manner of Chekhov" and, again, for one act the example of the great Russian has lifted him above himself, the women particularly seeming to be alive in their separateness and their freedom; but soon thereafter the solicitations of self-assertion win the field. Millions have taken delight in these plays and will continue to do so for some time; it is only in juxtaposition to masterpieces that we are able to perceive that there is a difference.

FOREWORD TO
THE ANGEL THAT TROUBLED THE WATERS
AND OTHER PLAYS

It is a discouraging business to be an author at sixteen years
of age. Such an author is all aspiration and no fulfillment. He
is drunk on an imaginary kinship with the writers he most
admires, and yet his poor overblotted notebooks show nothing to prove to others, or to himself, that the claim is justified.
The shortest walk in the country is sufficient to start in his
mind the theme, the plan, and the title, especially the title, of
a long book; and the shortest hour when he has returned to
his desk is sufficient to deflate his ambition. Such fragments as
he is finally able to commit to paper are a mass of echoes,
awkward relative clauses, and conflicting styles. In life and in
literature mere sincerity is not sufficient, and in both realms
the greater the capacity the longer the awkward age. Yet
strange lights cross that confusion, authoritative moments that
all the practice of later maturity cannot explain and cannot
recapture. He is visited by great depressions and wild exhilara-
tions, but whether his depressions proceed from his limitations
in the art of living or his limitations in the art of writing he
cannot tell. An artist is one who knows how life should be
lived at its best and is always aware of how badly he is doing
it. An artist is one who knows he is failing in living and feeds
his remorse by making something fair, and a layman is one

The foreword for his *The Angel That Troubled the Waters and Other Plays,* published
in New York by Coward, McCann & Geoghegan, Inc. in 1928.

95

who suspects he is failing in living but is consoled by his successes in golf, or in love, or in business.

Authors of fifteen and sixteen years of age spend their time drawing up title pages and adjusting the tables of contents of works they have neither the perseverance nor the ability to execute. They compass easily all the parts of a book that are inessential. They compose dignified prefaces, discover happy quotations from the Latin and the French, and turn graceful dedications. This book is what is left of one of these projects.

The title was to have been *Three-Minute Plays for Three Persons.* I have lately found one of my early tables of contents for it, written in the flyleaves of a First-Year Algebra. Quadratics in those days could be supported only with the help of a rich marginal commentary. Usually these aids to education took the shape of a carefully planned repertory for two theaters, a large and a small. Here my longer plays were to alternate with *The Wild Duck* and *Measure for Measure* and were cast with such a roll of great names as neither money nor loyalty could assemble. The chapter on Combinations and Permutations ended short by several inches, and left me sufficient space to draw up a catalogue of all the compositions I had heard of that were the work of Charles Martin Loeffler. This list of *Three-Minute Plays* was drawn up in Berkeley, California, in the spring of 1915. It contains several that have since been rejected, two that are in the present volume, "Brother Fire" and "Proserpina and the Devil," and the names of many that were unwritten then and that still, through the charm of their titles, ask to be written.

Since then I have composed some forty of these plays, for I had discovered a literary form that satisfied my passion for compression. Since the time when I began to read I had become aware of the needless repetition, the complacency in most writing. Who does not know the empty opening paragraphs, the deft but uninstructive transitions, and the closing paragraphs that summarize a work and which are unnecessary to an alert reader? Moreover, their brevity flatters my inability to sustain a long flight, and the inertia that barely permits me to write at all. And finally, when I became a teacher, here was the length that could be compassed after the lights of the House were out and the sheaf of absurd French exercises corrected and indignantly marked with red crayon. In time the three minutes and the three persons became a habit, and no idea was too grandiose—as the reader will see—for me to try and invest it in this strange discipline.

There were other plans for this book. There was to have been a series of Footnotes to Biographies, suggested by Herbert Eulenberg's *Schattenbilder,* represented here by the Mozart, the Ibsen, and the St. Francis plays. There were hopes of a still more difficult series. Dürer's two sets of woodcuts illustrating the Passion were to serve as model for a series of plays that would be meditations on the last days of Our Lord. Two of them are in this book. There was to have been a series illustrating the history of the stage, and, again, two of them are in this book. How different the practice of writing would be if one did not permit oneself to be pretentious. Some hands have no choice: they would rather fail with an oratorio than succeed with a ballad.

During the years that these plays were being written I was reading widely, and these pages are full of allusions to it. The art of literature springs from two curiosities, a curiosity about human beings pushed to such an extreme that it resembles love, and a love of a few masterpieces of literature so absorbing that it has all the richest elements of curiosity. I use the word "curiosity" in the French sense of a tireless awareness of things. (It is too late to arrest the deterioration of our greatest English words. We live in an age where "pity" and "charity" have taken on the color of condescensions; where "humility" seems to mean an acknowledgment of failure; where "simplicity" is foolishness and "curiosity" is interference. Today "hope" and "faith" itself imply a deliberate self-deception.)

The training for literature must be acquired by the artist alone, through the passionate assimilation of a few masterpieces written from a spirit somewhat like his own, and a few masterpieces written from a spirit not at all like his own. I read all Newman, and then I read all Swift. The technical processes of literature should be acquired almost unconsciously on the tide of a great enthusiasm, even syntax, even sentence-structure; I should like to hope, even spelling. I am thinking of some words of Renan commenting in the *Souvenirs d'enfance et de jeunesse* upon his education:

> *Pour moi,* [je] *crois que la meilleure manière de former des jeunes gens de talent est de ne jamais leur parler de talent ni de style, mais de les instruire et d'exciter fortement leur esprit sur les questions philosophiques, religieuses, politiques, sociales, scientifiques, historiques; en un mot, de procéder par l'enseignement du fond des choses, et non par l'enseignement d'une creuse rhétorique.*

The last four plays here have been written within a year and a half. Almost all the plays in this book are religious, but religious in that dilute fashion that is a believer's concession to a contemporary standard of good manners. But these four plant their flag as boldly as they may. It is the kind of work that I would most like to do well, in spite of the fact that there has seldom been an age in literature when such a vein was less welcome and less understood. I hope, through many mistakes, to discover the spirit that is not unequal to the elevation of the great religious themes, yet which does not fall into a repellent didacticism. Didacticism is an attempt at the coercion of another's free mind, even though one knows that in these matters beyond logic, beauty is the only persuasion. Here the schoolmaster enters again. He sees all that is fairest in the Christian tradition made repugnant to the new generations by reason of the diction in which it is expressed. The intermittent sincerity of generations of clergymen and teachers has rendered embarrassing and even ridiculous all the terms of the spiritual life. Nothing succeeds in dampening the aspirations of the young today—who dares use the word "aspiration" without enclosing it, knowingly, in quotation marks?—like the names they hear given to them. The revival of religion is almost a matter of rhetoric. The work is difficult, perhaps impossible (perhaps all religions die out with the exhaustion of the language), but it at least reminds us that Our Lord asked us in His work to be not only as gentle as doves, but as wise as serpents.

A PREFACE FOR
OUR TOWN

For a while in Rome I lived among archeologists, and ever
since I find myself occasionally looking at the things about me
as an archeologist will look at them a thousand years hence.
Rockefeller Center will be reconstructed in imagination from
the ruins of its foundations. How high was it? A thesis will be
written on the bronze plates found in New York's detritus
heaps—"Tradesmen's Entrance," "Night Bell."

In Rome I was led through a study of the plumbing on the
Palatine Hill. A friend of mine could ascribe a date, "within
ten years," to every fragment of cement made in the Roman
Republic and early Empire.

An archeologist's eyes combine the view of the telescope
with the view of the microscope. He reconstructs the very
distant with the help of the very small.

It was something of this method that I brought to a New
Hampshire village. I spent parts of six summers tutoring at
Lake Sunapee and six at the MacDowell Colony at Peter-
borough. I took long walks through scores of upland villages.

And the archeologist's and the social historian's points of
view began to mingle with another unremitting preoccupation
which is the central theme of the play: What is the relation
between the countless "unimportant" details of our daily life,

Written in the winter of 1938 but not published. Printed from a typescript in the
Wilder papers (YCAL).

on the one hand, and the great perspectives of time, social history, and current religious ideas, on the other?

What is trivial and what is significant about any one person's making a breakfast, engaging in a domestic quarrel, in a "love scene," in dying? To record one's feelings about this question is necessarily to exhibit the realistic detail of life, and one is at once up against the problem of realism in literature.

William James used to warn his students against being impressed by the "abject truth." Most works in realism tell a succession of such abject truths; they are deeply in earnest, every detail is true, and yet the whole finally tumbles to the ground—true but without significance.

How did Jane Austen save her novels from that danger? They appear to be compact of abject truth. Their events are excruciatingly unimportant; and yet, with *Robinson Crusoe,* they will probably outlast all Fielding, Scott, George Eliot, Thackeray, and Dickens. The art is so consummate that the secret is hidden; peer at them as hard as one may; shake them; take them apart; one cannot see how it is done.

I wished to record a village's life on the stage, with realism and with generality.

The stage has a deceptive advantage over the novel—in that lighted room at the end of the darkened auditorium things seem to be half caught up into generality already. The stage cries aloud its mission to represent the Act in Eternity. So powerful is the focus that it brings to bear on any presented occasion that every lapse of the author from his collaborative intensity is doubly conspicuous: the truth tumbles down into a heap of abject truths and the result is doubly trivial.

So I tried to restore significance to the small details of life by removing scenery. The spectator through lending his imagination to the action restages it inside his own head.

In its healthiest ages the theater has always exhibited the least scenery. Aristophanes's *The Clouds*—423 B.C. Two houses are represented on the stage, *inside* of one of them we see two beds. Strepsiades is talking in his sleep about his racehorses. A few minutes later he crosses the stage to Socrates's house, the Idea Factory, the "Thinkery." In the Spanish theater Lope de Vega put a rug in the middle of the scene—it was a raft in mid-ocean bearing a castaway. The Elizabethans, the Chinese used similar devices.

The theater longs to represent the symbols of things, not the things themselves. All the lies it tells—the lie that that young lady is Caesar's wife; the lie that people can go through life talking in blank verse; the lie that that man just *killed* that man —all those lies enhance the one truth that is there—the truth that dictated the story, the myth. The theater asks for as many conventions as possible. A convention is an agreed-upon falsehood, an accepted untruth. When the theater pretends to give the real thing in canvas and wood and metal it loses something of the realer thing which is its true business. Ibsen and Chekhov carried realism as far as it could go, and it took all their genius to do it. Now the camera is carrying it on and is in great "theoretical peril" of falling short of literature. (In a world of actual peril that "theoretical peril" looks very farfetched, but ex-college professors must be indulged.)

But the writing of the play was not accompanied by any such conscious argumentation as this. It sprang from a deep admiration for those little white towns in the hills and from a deep devotion to the theater. These are but the belated gropings to reconstruct what may have taken place when the play first presented itself—the life of a village against the life of the stars.

In an earlier draft of the play there were some other lines that led up to those which now serve as its motto. The Stage Manager has been talking about the material that is being placed in the cornerstone of the new bank at Grover's Corners, material that has been chemically treated so that it will last a thousand or two thousand years. He suggests that this play has been placed there so that future ages will know more about the life of the average person;

more than just the Treaty of Versailles and the Lindbergh Flight—see what I mean?

Well, people a thousand years from now, in the provinces North of New York at the beginning of the Twentieth Century, people et three times a day—soon after dawn, at noon, and at sunset.

Every seventh day, by law and by religion, there was a day of rest and all work came to a stop.

The religion at that time was Christianity; but I guess you have other records about Christianity.

The domestic set-up was marriage, a binding relation between a male and one female that lasted for life.

. . . Anything else? Oh, yes, when people died they were buried in the ground just as they were.

Well, people a thousand years from now, this is the way we were—in our growing-up, in our marrying, in our doctoring, in our living, and in our dying.

Now let's get back to our day in Grover's Corners. . . .

PREFACE TO *THREE PLAYS:*
OUR TOWN, THE SKIN OF OUR TEETH,
THE MATCHMAKER

Toward the end of the 'twenties I began to lose pleasure in going to the theater. I ceased to believe in the stories I saw presented there. When I did go it was to admire some secondary aspect of the play, the work of a great actor or director or designer. Yet at the same time the conviction was growing in me that the theater was the greatest of all the arts. I felt that something had gone wrong with it in my time and that it was fulfilling only a small part of its potentialities. I was filled with admiration for presentations of classical works by Max Reinhardt and Louis Jouvet and the Old Vic, as I was by the best plays of my own time, like *Desire Under the Elms* and *The Front Page;* but at heart I didn't believe a word of them. I was like a schoolmaster grading a paper; to each of these offerings I gave an A plus, but the condition of mind of one grading a paper is not that of one being overwhelmed by an artistic creation. The response we make when we "believe" a work of the imagination is that of saying: "This is the way things are. I have always known it without being fully aware that I knew it. Now in the presence of this play or novel or poem (or picture or piece of music) I know that I know it." It is this form

The preface to *Three Plays: Our Town, The Skin of Our Teeth, The Matchmaker,* published in New York by Harper and Brothers in 1957. A slightly abridged version appeared in *Harper's* magazine for October 1957 under the title "A Platform and a Passion or Two."

of knowledge which Plato called "recollection." We have all murdered, in thought; and been murdered. We have all seen the ridiculous in estimable persons and in ourselves. We have all known terror as well as enchantment. Imaginative literature has nothing to say to those who do not recognize—who cannot be *reminded*—of such conditions. Of all the arts the theater is best endowed to awaken this recollection within us —to believe is to say "yes"; but in the theaters of my time I did not feel myself prompted to any such grateful and self-forgetting acquiescence.

This dissatisfaction worried me. I was not ready to condemn myself as blasé and overfastidious, for I knew that I was still capable of belief. I believed every word of *Ulysses* and of Proust and of *The Magic Mountain,* as I did of hundreds of plays when I read them. It was on the stage that imaginative narration became false. Finally, my dissatisfaction passed into resentment. I began to feel that the theater was not only inadequate, it was evasive; it did not wish to draw upon its deeper potentialities. I found the word for it: it aimed to be *soothing.* The tragic had no heat; the comic had no bite; the social criticism failed to indict us with responsibility. I began to search for the point where the theater had run off the track, where it had chosen—and been permitted—to become a minor art and an inconsequential diversion.

The trouble began in the nineteenth century and was connected with the rise of the middle classes—they wanted their theater soothing. There's nothing wrong with the middle classes in themselves. We know that now. The United States and Scandinavia and Germany are middle-class countries, so completely so that they have lost the very memory of their once despised and ludicrous inferiority (they had been inferior not only to the aristocracy but, in human dignity, to the peasantry). When a middle class is new, however, there is much that is wrong with it. When it is emerging from under the shadow of an aristocracy, from the myth and prestige of

those well-born Higher-ups, it is alternately insecure and ag-
gressively complacent. It must find its justification and reassurance in making money and displaying it. To this day, members
of the middle classes in England, France, and Italy feel themselves to be a little ridiculous and humiliated. The prestige of
aristocracies is based upon a dreary untruth, that moral superiority and the qualifications for leadership are transmittable
through the chromosomes, and the secondary lie, that the
environment afforded by privilege and leisure tends to nur-
ture the flowers of the spirit. An aristocracy, defending and
fostering its lie, extracts from the arts only such elements as
can further its interests, the aroma and not the sap, the grace
and not the trenchancy. Equally harmful to culture is the
newly arrived middle class. In the English-speaking world the
middle classes came into power early in the nineteenth century
and gained control over the theater. They were pious, law-
abiding, and industrious. They were assured of eternal life in
the next world and, in this, they were squarely seated on
Property and the privileges that accompany it. They were
attended by devoted servants who knew their place. They
were benevolent within certain limits, but chose to ignore
wide tracts of injustice and stupidity in the world about them;
and they shrank from contemplating those elements within
themselves that were ridiculous, shallow, and harmful. They
distrusted the passions and tried to deny them. Their questions
about the nature of life seemed to be sufficiently answered by
the demonstration of financial status and by conformity to
some clearly established rules of decorum. These were precar-
ious positions; abysses yawned on either side. The air was loud
with questions that must not be asked. These audiences fashioned a theater which could not disturb them. They thronged
to melodrama (which deals with tragic possibilities in such a
way that you know from the beginning that all will end happily) and to sentimental drama (which accords a total license
to the supposition that the wish is father to the thought) and

to comedies in which the characters were so represented that they always resembled someone else and not oneself. Between the plays that Sheridan wrote in his twenties and the first works of Wilde and Shaw there was no play of even moderate interest written in the English language. (Unless you happen to admire and except Shelley's *The Cenci.*) These audiences, however, also thronged to Shakespeare. How did they shield themselves against his probing? How did they smother the theater—and with such effect that it smothers us still? The box set was already there, the curtain, the proscenium, but not taken "seriously"—it was a convenience in view of the weather in northern countries. They took it seriously and emphasized and enhanced everything that thus removed, cut off, and boxed the action; they increasingly shut the play up into a museum showcase.

Let us examine why the box-set stage stifles the life in drama and why and how it militates against belief.

Every action which has ever taken place—every thought, every emotion—has taken place only once, at one moment in time and place. "I love you," "I rejoice," "I suffer," have been said and felt many billions of times, and never twice the same. Every person who has ever lived has lived an unbroken succession of unique occasions. Yet the more one is aware of this individuality in experience (innumerable! innumerable!) the more one becomes attentive to what these disparate moments have in common, to repetitive patterns. As an artist (or listener or beholder) which "truth" do you prefer—that of the isolated occasion, or that which includes and resumes the innumerable? Which truth is more worth telling? Every age differs in this. Is the Venus de Milo "one woman"? Is the play *Macbeth* the story of "one destiny"? The theater is admirably fitted to tell both truths. It has one foot planted firmly in the particular, since each actor before us (even when he wears a mask!) is indubitably a living, breathing "one"; yet it tends and strains to exhibit a general truth since its relation to a specific "realistic" truth is confused and undermined by the fact that it is an accumulation of untruths, pretenses, and fiction. The novel is pre-eminently the vehicle of the unique occasion, the theater of the generalized one. It is through the theater's power to raise the exhibited individual action into the realm of idea and type and universal that it is able to evoke our belief. But power is precisely what those nineteenth-century audiences did not—dared not—confront. They tamed it and drew its teeth; squeezed it into that removed showcase. They loaded the stage with specific objects, because every concrete object on the stage fixes and narrows the action to one moment in time and place. (Have you ever noticed that in the plays of Shakespeare no one—except occasionally a ruler—ever sits down? There were not even chairs on the English or Spanish stages in the time of Elizabeth I.) So it was by a jugglery with time that the middle classes devitalized the theater. When you emphasize *place* in the theater, you drag down and limit and harness time to it. You thrust the action back into past time, whereas it is precisely the glory of the stage that it is always "now" there. Under such production methods the characters are all dead before the action starts. You don't have to pay deeply from your heart's participation. No great age in the theater ever attempted to capture the audience's belief through this kind of specification and localization. I became dissatisfied with the theater because I was unable to lend credence to such childish attempts to be "real."

I began writing one-act plays that tried to capture not verisimilitude but reality. In *The Happy Journey to Trenton and Camden* four kitchen chairs represent an automobile and a family travels seventy miles in twenty minutes. Ninety years go by in *The Long Christmas Dinner.* In *Pullman Car Hiawatha* some more plain chairs serve as berths and we hear the very vital statistics of the towns and fields that passengers are traversing; we hear their thoughts; we even hear the planets over their heads. In Chinese drama a character, by straddling a stick, conveys to us that he is on horseback. In almost every No play of the Japanese an actor makes a tour of the stage and we know that he is making a long journey. Think of the ubiquity that Shakespeare's stage afforded for the battle scenes at the close of *Julius Caesar* and *Antony and Cleopatra*. As we see them today what a cutting and hacking of the text takes place—what condescension, what contempt for his dramaturgy.

Our Town is not offered as a picture of life in a New Hampshire village; or as a speculation about the conditions of life after death (that element I merely took from Dante's *Purgatory*). It is an attempt to find a value above all price for the smallest events in our daily life. I have made the claim as preposterous as possible, for I have set the village against the largest dimensions of time and place. The recurrent words in this play (few have noticed it) are "hundreds," "thousands," and "millions." Emily's joys and griefs, her algebra lessons and her birthday presents—what are they when we consider all the billions of girls who have lived, who are living, and who will live? Each individual's assertion to an absolute reality can only be inner, very inner. And here the method of staging finds its justification—in the first two acts there are at least a few chairs and tables; but when Emily revisits the earth and the kitchen to which she descended on her twelfth birthday, the very chairs and table are gone. Our claim, our hope, our despair are in the mind—not in things, not in "scenery." Molière said that for the theater all he needed was a platform and a passion or two. The climax of this play needs only five square feet of boarding and the passion to know what life means to us.

The Matchmaker is an only slightly modified version of *The Merchant of Yonkers,* which I wrote in the year after I had written *Our Town.* One way to shake off the nonsense of the nineteenth-century staging is to make fun of it. This play parodies the stock-company plays that I used to see at Ye Liberty

(margin note: Bold 1st part of 1st sentence)

Theatre, Oakland, California, when I was a boy. I have already read small theses in German comparing it with the great Austrian original on which it is based. The scholars are very bewildered. There is most of the plot (except that our friend Dolly Levi is not in Nestroy's play); there are some of the tags; but it's all "about" quite different matters. My play is about the aspirations of the young (and not only of the young) for a fuller, freer participation in life. Imagine an Austrian pharmacist going to the shelf to draw from a bottle which he knows to contain a stinging corrosive liquid, guaranteed to remove warts and wens; and imagine his surprise when he discovers that it has been filled overnight with very American birch-bark beer.

The Skin of Our Teeth begins, also, by making fun of old-fashioned playwriting; but the audience soon perceives that it is seeing "two times at once." The Antrobus family is living both in prehistoric times and in a New Jersey commuters' suburb today. Again, the events of our homely daily life—this time the family life—are depicted against the vast dimensions of time and place. It was written on the eve of our entrance into the war and under strong emotion and I think it mostly comes alive under conditions of crisis. It has been often charged with being a bookish fantasia about history, full of rather bloodless schoolmasterish jokes. But to have seen it in Germany soon after the war, in the shattered churches and beerhalls that were serving as theaters, with audiences whose price of admission meant the loss of a meal and for whom it was of absorbing interest that there was a "recipe for grass soup that did not cause the diarrhea," was an experience that was not so cool. I am very proud that this year it has received a first and overwhelming reception in Warsaw. The play is deeply indebted to James Joyce's *Finnegans Wake*. I should be very happy if, in the future, some author should feel similarly indebted to any work of mine. Literature has always more resembled a torch race than a furious dispute among heirs.

The theater has lagged behind the other arts in finding the "new ways" to express how men and women think and feel in our time. I am not one of the new dramatists we are looking for. I wish I were. I hope I have played a part in preparing the way for them. I am not an innovator but a rediscoverer of forgotten goods and I hope a remover of obtrusive bric-a-brac. And as I view the work of my contemporaries I seem to feel that I am exceptional in one thing—I give (don't I?) the impression of having enormously enjoyed it.

NOTING THE NATURE
OF FARCE

Surely highly civilized societies can never enjoy farce, farce which depends on extreme improbability and on the laughter aroused by the spectacle of someone's mental and physical anguish.

These long-lost twins that arrive in the same town; these girls dressed as boys that are not recognized by their closest friends; these deceived husbands under torment; these guardians beaten by mistake; these respectable and distraught ladies with men hidden all over their rooms.

Farce would seem to be intended for childlike minds still touched with grossness; but the history of the theater shows us that the opposite is true. Farce has always flourished in ages of refinement and great cultural activity.

And the reason lies where one would least expect it: farce is based on logic and objectivity.

The author of a farce may ask his audience to concede him two or three wild improbabilities, but thereafter he must proceed with an all the more rigorous consequence. The laughter is an explosion of almost grudging concession: "Yes, granted that premise, these things would inevitably follow."

The School for Scandal simmers along among a thousand mild improbabilities; it is a comedy; but *The Importance of Being*

Reprinted from *The New York Times* for January 8, 1939.

Earnest shows us what would be bound to happen if a man invented an invalid brother who needed his attendance whenever he wished to shirk a tedious engagement, and what would happen if his friend decided to impersonate this brother.

The pleasures of farce, like those of the detective story, are those of development, pattern, and logic.

A "pure" farce would be all pattern and would admit no mixture. Comedy, which is the clarification of unsocial human traits through exaggeration, may benefit by a dash of farce, especially toward the close of the evening; but farce dare not lean too far toward the exposition of character.

She Stoops to Conquer is not primarily about a man who mistakes a private house for an inn, which would be farce; but about a man so shy that he cannot converse at ease with a "lady of quality," which is comedy. *Twelfth Night* is not about a girl who dresses as a man in order to make her way out of destitution; but about a girl who is clear-eyed in a world of misguided "humorous" beings.

Since farce is an intellectual exercise, the only ornament it welcomes is the additional intellectual pleasure of lines of social comment and generalization. It is significant that "the fires of the French Revolution were lighted" during a soliloquy in Beaumarchais's *The Marriage of Figaro;* and the early farces of Molière cast a host of proverbial expressions into the French language.

And the cruelty of farce?

Theorists since Aristotle—whose lecture-notes on this matter were unfortunately lost—have tried to analyze the springs of laughter. In this century two distinguished hands have written books on the subject, Bergson and Freud.

Bergson says that we laugh when we see man—man who prides himself on living by choice, reason, and free will—reduced to being a victim of the same forces that govern things. Pretentious man reduced to an automaton is funny; a scrubwoman who slips on a banana peel is less funny than a bank president in a silk hat.

Freud says our laughter is a release of a grudge against a universe which has since infancy crossed our ambitions and defeated our egocentric wishes. Civilization, however, has educated us; we do not wish, even in our own eyes, to be transparent in the revelation of our wounded pride. We cannot give vent to our animus until incongruity or the verbal ingenuity of wit gives us the pretext and the permission.

A lady who had forgotten that Whistler hated Turner said to him: "Oh, Mr. Whistler, my husband has discovered in a secondhand shop what he thinks are two real Turners. Will you come and tell us whether they are real Turners or imitation Turners?" "Well, ma'am," replied Whistler, adjusting his monocle, "that is a fine distinction."

Wit is the permitted suspension of decorum and the retaliation of the underdog.

There has never been a "pure" farce. Terence's *Andria* is crossed with melancholy; Goldoni's *The Liar* is perfect in ingenuity and design, but is forever straying off into psychological finesse; Nestroy's *The Talisman* delays in Dutch genre-painting of three social strata. Perhaps—as with the "pure" detective story—it would not be so desirable after all. Perhaps a wavering among other elements makes it bearable: toward humor, its natural enemy, for humor is the acknowledgment of one's kinship with frailty; toward character-drawing; toward picturesqueness, a static quality; even toward pathos—perhaps all these are necessary to keep it from the ultimately empty triumph of its two fundamental drives: logic and objectivity.

SOME THOUGHTS ON
PLAYWRIGHTING

Four fundamental conditions of the drama separate it from the other arts. Each of these conditions has its advantages and disadvantages, each requires a particular aptitude from the dramatist, and from each there are a number of instructive consequences to be derived. These conditions are:

I. The theater is an art which reposes upon the work of many collaborators;

II. It is addressed to the group-mind;

III. It is based upon a pretense and its very nature calls out a multiplication of pretenses;

IV. Its action takes place in a perpetual present time.

I

THE THEATER IS AN ART WHICH REPOSES
UPON THE WORK OF MANY COLLABORATORS.

We have been accustomed to think that a work of art is by definition the product of one governing selecting will. A landscape by Cézanne consists of thousands of brushstrokes each commanded by one mind. *Paradise Lost* and *Pride and Prejudice*, even in cheap frayed copies, bear the immediate and exclusive

A contribution to *The Intent of the Artist,* edited by Augusto Centeno, published in Princeton by the Princeton University Press in 1941.

message of one intelligence. It is true that in musical performance we meet with intervening executants, but the element of intervention is slight compared to that which takes place in drama. Illustrations:

1. One of the finest productions of *The Merchant of Venice* in our time showed Sir Henry Irving as Shylock, a noble, wronged, and indignant being, of such stature that the merchants of Venice dwindled before him into irresponsible schoolboys. He was confronted in court by a gracious, even queenly Portia, Miss Ellen Terry. At the Odéon in Paris, however, Gémier played Shylock as a vengeful and hysterical buffoon, confronted in court by a Portia who was a *gamine* from the Paris streets with a lawyer's quill three feet long over her ear; at the close of the trial scene Shylock was driven screaming about the auditorium, behind the spectators' backs and onto the stage again, in a wild Elizabethan revel. Yet for all their divergences both were admirable productions of the play.

2. If there was ever a play in which fidelity to the author's requirements was essential in the representation of the principal rôle, it would seem to be Ibsen's *Hedda Gabler,* for the play is primarily an exposition of her character. Ibsen's directions read:

> Enter from the left Hedda Gabler. She is a woman of twenty-nine. Her face and figure show great refinement and distinction. Her complexion is pale and opaque. Her steel-gray eyes express an unruffled calm. Her hair is of an attractive medium brown, but is not particularly abundant; and she is dressed in a flowing loose-fitting morning gown.

I once saw Eleonora Duse in this rôle. She was a woman of sixty and made no effort to conceal it. Her complexion was pale and transparent. Her hair was white, and she was dressed in a gown that suggested some medieval empress in mourning. And the performance was very fine.

One may well ask: Why write for the theater at all? Why not work in the novel, where such deviations from one's intentions cannot take place?

There are two answers:

1. The theater presents certain vitalities of its own so inviting and stimulating that the writer is willing to receive them in compensation for this inevitable variation from an exact image.

2. The dramatist through working in the theater gradually learns not merely to take account of the presence of the collaborators, but to derive advantage from them; and he learns, above all, to organize the play in such a way that its strength lies not in appearances beyond his control, but in the succession of events and in the unfolding of an idea, in narration.

The gathered audience sits in a darkened room, one end of which is lighted. The nature of the transaction at which it is gazing is a succession of events illustrating a general idea—the stirring of the idea; the gradual feeding out of information; the shock and counter-shock of circumstances; the flow of action; the interruption of action; the moments of allusion to earlier events; the preparation of surprise, dread, or delight—all that is the author's and his alone.

For reasons to be discussed later—the expectancy of the group-mind, the problem of time on the stage, the absence of the narrator, the element of pretense—the theater carries the art of narration to a higher power than the novel or the epic poem. The theater is unfolding action and in the disposition of events the authors may exercise a governance so complete that the distortions effected by the physical appearance of actors, by the fancies of scene-painters, and the misunderstandings of directors, fall into relative insignificance. It is just because the theater is an art of many collaborators, with the constant danger of grave misinterpretation, that the dramatist learns to turn his attention to the laws of narration, its logic, and its deep necessity of presenting a unifying idea stronger than its mere collection of happenings. The dramatist must be by instinct a storyteller.

There is something mysterious about the endowment of the storyteller. Some very great writers possessed very little of it, and some others, lightly esteemed, possessed it in so large a measure that their books survive down the ages, to the confusion of severer critics. Alexandre Dumas had it to an extraordinary degree; while Melville, for all his splendid quality, had it barely sufficiently to raise his work from the realm of nonfiction. It springs, not, as some have said, from an aversion to general ideas, but from an instinctive coupling of idea and illustration; the idea, for a born storyteller, can only be expressed imbedded in its circumstantial illustration. The myth, the parable, the fable are the fountainhead of all fiction and in them is seen most clearly the didactic, moralizing employment of a story. Modern taste shrinks from emphasizing the central idea that hides behind the fiction, but it exists there nevertheless, supplying the unity to fantasizing, and offering a justification to what otherwise we would repudiate as mere arbitrary contrivance, pretentious lying, or individualistic emotional association-spinning. For all their magnificent intellectual endowment, George Meredith and George Eliot were not born storytellers; they chose fiction as the vehicle for their reflections, and the passing of time is revealing their error in that choice. Jane Austen was pure storyteller and her works are outlasting those of apparently more formidable rivals. The theater is more exacting than the novel in regard to this faculty and its presence constitutes a force which compensates the dramatist for the deviations which are introduced into his work by the presence of his collaborators.

The chief of these collaborators are the actors.

The actor's gift is a combination of three separate faculties or endowments. Their presence to a high degree in any one person is extremely rare, although the ambition to possess them is common. Those who rise to the height of the profession represent a selection and a struggle for survival in one of the most difficult and cruel of the artistic activities. The three endowments that compose the gift are observation, imagination, and physical coordination.

1. An observant and analyzing eye for all modes of behavior about us, for dress and manner, and for the signs of thought and emotion in oneself and in others.

2. The strength of imagination and memory whereby the actor may, at the indication in the author's text, explore his store of observations and represent the details of appearance and the intensity of the emotions—joy, fear, surprise, grief, love, and hatred—and through imagination extend them to intenser degrees and to differing characterizations.

3. A physical coordination whereby the force of these inner realizations may be communicated to voice, face, and body.

An actor must *know* the appearances and the mental states; he must *apply* his knowledge to the rôle; and he must physically *express* his knowledge. Moreover, his concentration must be so great that he can effect this representation under conditions of peculiar difficulty—in abrupt transition from the non-imaginative conditions behind the stage; and in the presence of fellow actors who may be momentarily destroying the reality of the action.

A dramatist prepares the characterization of his personages in such a way that it will take advantage of the actor's gift.

Characterization in a novel is presented by the author's dogmatic assertion that the personage was such, and by an analysis of the personage with generally an account of his or her past. Since in the drama this is replaced by the actual presence of the personage before us and since there is no occasion for the intervening all-knowing author to instruct us as to his or her inner nature, a far greater share is given in a play to (1) highly characteristic utterances and (2) concrete occasions in which the character defines itself under action and (3) a conscious preparation of the text whereby the actor may build upon the suggestions in the rôle according to his own abilities.

Characterization in a play is like a blank check which the dramatist accords to the actor for him to fill in—not entirely blank, for a number of indications of individuality are already there, but to a far less definite and absolute degree than in the novel.

The dramatist's principal interest being the movement of the story, he is willing to resign the more detailed aspects of characterization to the actor and is often rewarded beyond his expectation.

The sleepwalking scene from *Macbeth* is a highly compressed selection of words whereby despair and remorse rise to the surface of indirect confession. It is to be assumed that had Shakespeare lived to see what the genius of Sarah Siddons could pour into the scene from that combination of observation, self-knowledge, imagination, and representational skill, even he might have exclaimed, "I never knew I wrote so well!"

II
THE THEATER IS AN ART ADDRESSED
TO A GROUP-MIND.

Painting, sculpture, and the literature of the book are certainly solitary experiences; and it is likely that most people would agree that the audience seated shoulder to shoulder in a concert hall is not an essential element in musical enjoyment.

But a play presupposes a crowd. The reasons for this go deeper than (1) the economic necessity for the support of the play and (2) the fact that the temperament of actors is proverbially dependent on group attention.

It rests on the fact that (1) the pretense, the fiction, on the stage would fall to pieces and absurdity without the support accorded to it by the crowd, and (2) the excitement induced by pretending a fragment of life is such that it partakes of ritual and festival, and requires a throng.

Similarly, the fiction that royal personages are of a mysteriously different nature from other people requires audiences, levées, and processions for its maintenance. Since the beginnings of society, satirists have occupied themselves with the descriptions of kings and queens in their intimacy and delighted in showing how the prerogatives of royalty become absurd when the crowd is not present to extend to them the enhancement of an imaginative awe.

The theater partakes of the nature of festival. Life imitated is life raised to a higher power. In the case of comedy, the vitality of these pretended surprises, deceptions, and *contretemps* becomes so lively that before a spectator, solitary or regarding himself as solitary, the structure of so much event would inevitably expose the artificiality of the attempt and ring hollow and unjustified; and in the case of tragedy, the accumulation of woe and apprehension would soon fall short of conviction. All actors know the disturbing sensation of playing before a handful of spectators at a dress rehearsal or performance where only their interest in pure craftsmanship can barely sustain them. During the last rehearsals the phrase is often heard: "This play is hungry for an audience."

Since the theater is directed to a group-mind, a number of consequences follow:

1. A group-mind presupposes, if not a lowering of standards, a broadening of the fields of interest. The other arts may presuppose an audience of connoisseurs trained in leisure and capable of being interested in certain rarefied aspects of life. The dramatist may be prevented from exhibiting, for example, detailed representations of certain moments in history that require specialized knowledge in the audience, or psychological states in the personages which are of insufficient general interest to evoke self-identification in the majority. In the Second Part of Goethe's *Faust* there are long passages

dealing with the theory of paper money. The exposition of the nature of misanthropy (so much more drastic than Molière's) in Shakespeare's *Timon of Athens* has never been a success. The dramatist accepts this limitation in subject matter and realizes that the group-mind imposes upon him the necessity of treating material understandable by the larger number.

2. It is the presence of the group-mind that brings another requirement to the theater—forward movement.

Maeterlinck said that there was more drama in the spectacle of an old man seated by a table than in the majority of plays offered to the public. He was juggling with the various meanings in the word "drama." In the sense whereby drama means the intensified concentration of life's diversity and significance he may well have been right; if he meant drama as a theatrical representation before an audience, he was wrong. Drama on the stage is inseparable from forward movement, from action.

Many attempts have been made to present Plato's dialogues, Gobineau's fine series of dialogues, *La Renaissance,* and the *Imaginary Conversations* of Landor, but without success. Through some ingredient in the group-mind, and through the sheer weight of anticipation involved in the dressing-up and the assumption of fictional rôles, an action is required, and an action that is more than a mere progress in argumentation and debate.

III
THE THEATER IS A WORLD OF PRETENSE.

It lives by conventions: a convention is an agreed-upon falsehood, a permitted lie.

Illustrations: Consider at the first performance of the *Medea,* the passage where Medea meditates the murder of her children. An anecdote from antiquity tells us that the audience was so moved by this passage that considerable disturbance took place.

The following conventions were involved:
1. Medea was played by a man.
2. He wore a large mask on his face. In the lip of the mask was an acoustical device for projecting the voice. On his feet he wore shoes with soles and heels half a foot high.
3. His costume was so designed that it conveyed to the audience, by convention: woman of royal birth and Oriental origin.
4. The passage was in metric speech. All poetry is an "agreed-upon falsehood" in regard to speech.
5. The lines were sung in a kind of recitative. All opera involves this "permitted lie" in regard to speech.

Modern taste would say that the passage would convey much greater pathos if a woman "like Medea" had delivered it—with an uncovered face that exhibited all the emotions she was undergoing. For the Greeks, however, there was no pretense that Medea was on the stage. The mask, the costume, the mode of declamation were a series of signs which the spectator interpreted and reassembled in his own mind. Medea was being re-created within the imagination of each of the spectators.

The history of the theater shows us that in its greatest ages the stage employed the greatest number of conventions. The stage is fundamental pretense and it thrives on the acceptance of that fact and in the multiplication of additional pretenses. When it tries to assert that the personages in the action "really are," really inhabit such-and-such rooms, really suffer such-and-such emotions, it loses rather than gains credibility. The modern world is inclined to laugh condescendingly at the fact that in the plays of Racine and Corneille the gods and heroes of antiquity were dressed like the courtiers under Louis XIV; that in the Elizabethan Age scenery was replaced by placards notifying the audience of the location; and that a whip in the hand and a jogging motion of the body indicated that a man was on horseback in the Chinese theater; these devices did not spring from naïveté, however, but from the vitality of the public imagination in those days and from an instinctive feeling as to where the essential and where the inessential lay in drama.

The convention has two functions:

1. It provokes the collaborative activity of the spectator's imagination; and

2. It raises the action from the specific to the general.

This second aspect is of even greater importance than the first.

If Juliet is represented as a girl "very like Juliet"—it was not merely a deference to contemporary prejudices that assigned this rôle to a boy in the Elizabethan Age—moving about in a "real" house with marble staircases, rugs, lamps, and furniture, the impression is irresistibly conveyed that these events happened to this one girl, in one place, at one moment in time. When the play is staged as Shakespeare intended it, the bareness of the stage releases the events from the particular and the experience of Juliet partakes of that of all girls in love, in every time, place, and language.

The stage continually strains to tell this generalized truth and it is the element of pretense that reinforces it. Out of the lie, the pretense, of the theater proceeds a truth more compelling than the novel can attain, for the novel by its own laws is constrained to tell of an action that "once happened"— "once upon a time."

IV

THE ACTION ON THE STAGE TAKES PLACE
IN A PERPETUAL PRESENT TIME.

Novels are written in the past tense. The characters in them, it is true, are represented as living moment by moment their present time, but the constant running commentary of the novelist ("Tess slowly descended into the valley"; "Anna

Karenina laughed") inevitably conveys to the reader the fact that these events are long since past and over.

The novel is a past reported in the present. On the stage it is always now. This confers upon the action an increased vitality which the novelist longs in vain to incorporate into his work.

This condition in the theater brings with it another important element:

In the theater we are not aware of the intervening storyteller. The speeches arise from the characters in an apparently pure spontaneity.

A play is what takes place.

A novel is what one person tells us took place.

A play visibly represents pure existing. A novel is what one mind, claiming to omniscience, asserts to have existed.

Many dramatists have regretted this absence of the narrator from the stage, with his point of view, his powers of analyzing the behavior of the characters, his ability to interfere and supply further facts about the past, about simultaneous actions not visible on the stage, and, above *all,* his function of pointing the moral and emphasizing the significance of the action. In some periods of the theater he has been present as chorus, or prologue and epilogue, or as *raisonneur.* But surely this absence constitutes an additional force to the form, as well as an additional tax upon the writer's skill. It is the task of the dramatist so to coordinate his play, through the selection of episodes and speeches, that, though he is himself not visible, his point of view and his governing intention will impose themselves on the spectator's attention, not as dogmatic assertion or motto, but as self-evident truth and inevitable deduction.

Imaginative narration—the invention of souls and destinies —is to a philosopher an all but indefensible activity.

Its justification lies in the fact that the communication of ideas from one mind to another inevitably reaches the point where exposition passes into illustration, into parable, meta-phor, allegory, and myth.

It is no accident that when Plato arrived at the height of his argument and attempted to convey a theory of knowledge and a theory of the structure of man's nature, he passed over into storytelling, into the myths of the Cave and the Charioteer; and that the great religious teachers have constantly had re-course to the parable as a means of imparting their deepest intuitions.

The theater offers to imaginative narration its highest pos-sibilities. It has many pitfalls and its very vitality betrays it into service as mere diversion and the enhancement of insignificant matter; but it is well to remember that it was the theater that rose to the highest place during those epochs that aftertime has chosen to call "great ages" and that the Athens of Pericles and the reigns of Elizabeth I, Philip II, and Louis XIV were also the ages that gave to the world the greatest dramas it has known.

RICHARD BEER-HOFMANN'S
JAAKOBS TRAUM

Richard Beer-Hofmann in *Jaakobs Traum* retells the story of the deception which Rebecca and Jacob played upon Isaac and interprets the vision which came to Jacob at Bethel. In the unfinished trilogy to which this play serves as prologue he recounts the life of King David.

The retelling of the great myths forms a large part of the literature of all countries; the last fifty years have shown a surprising increase in this form of literature. In the light of Beer-Hofmann's distinguished achievement it is of interest to consider the problems which accompany the treatment of such themes and, in particular, his solution of them.

A number of origins may be ascribed to the myth, and any definition of the myth should reflect the variety of such origins and the possibility of any given myth being at one or other of the phases through which all myths pass.

A myth at the moment when it is employed as the basis of a work of literature, however, may be defined as a story:

1. Whose historical authenticity is so far irrelevant as to permit to the narrator an assumption of omniscience in regard to what took place;

The introduction for an English translation, by Ida Bension Wynn, of the play by Richard Beer-Hofmann, published in New York by Johannespresse in 1946, as *Jacob's Dream*.

2. Whose antiquity and popular diffusion confer upon it an authority which limits the degree of variation that may be employed in its retelling; and

3. Whose subject matter is felt to have a significance which renders each retelling a contribution to the received ideas of the entire community to which, in a very real sense, it belongs.

Such a definition, however, still includes the animal fables of worldly wisdom and the fairy tales of childhood.

A fourth clause in the definition must be sought further.

The most persistent myths are stumbling blocks; they are not reassuring but disturbing. The writer who sets out to retell them discovers that a mere filling-in of the story with visual and psychological details is not sufficient. The survival of these stories seems to be due to their being questions and not answers in regard to the human situation.

Their tenacity is endlessly surprising. They are among the few things of which it may be said with assurance that they have a long future. Speculations as to their origin do not sufficiently explain this persistence. Anthropologists assure us that they may have come to us from any of three sources or from any combination of the three. They may have been put forward to explain natural phenomena. Helen and Siegfried, the golden-haired, were each originally the sun, hidden by the clouds, captured by the Trojans and by the Nibelungen. Myths may be the reports of historical events and persons, exaggerated in the course of innumerable retellings, assimilated to natural phenomena and reinforced by emotional fantasies, religious, patriotic, or instinctual. They may testify to the relations of tribes and races and the syncretism which took place among their religions. Under this interpretation Europa and the Bull-God should be understood to read Europa the Cow-Goddess and Zeus the Man-God; Leda, and not her lover, was the swan. Psychologists are saying that many myths have their origin in the unavowed fantasies of the subconscious and that an Oedipus is slain in every family and that a Moses is sanctified by his murderers in many a religion.

These elements may play a large part in the formation and persistence of many myths. In those, however, which are most frequently retold another element is more constantly recognizable and is more frequently seized upon by the poets who in successive ages have chosen to retell them.

They are questions and not answers in regard to the human situation. In the majority of cases the questions seem to have to do with the mind disengaging itself from the passions or finding its true position in the presence of the established authorities, human or divine. They are concretizations of man's besetting preoccupation with the mind and the mind's struggle to know itself; and each retelling requires that some answer be furnished to the question that infuses every part of the story.

These stories, then, are not reassuring, but disturbing. Soothing stories have been plentiful in all ages—and to the philosophical sense few stories are as soothing as adventure stories—but each of these circulates for a time and is forgotten. To survive, a story must arouse wonder, wonder in both the senses in which we now employ the word: astonishment at the extent of man's capability for good and evil, and speculation as to the sources of that capability. Not least troubling have been those which seem to have been raised by dogma to the realm of the unquestionable. Nor have all the resources of the greatest writers engaged upon their acknowledged masterpieces been able to bring to definite solution the problems set by these old stories. Certain of them seem to grow even more urgent with the passing of time. Those, for instance, concerning Prometheus, Satan, Adam, Faust, Phaëthon, and Icarus converge upon a number of related questions: Can intellectual advance be made without disobedience? Must intellectual inquiry and mastery over nature be paid for by self-destruction? At each retelling, such stories as those of Job, Oedipus, Orestes (Orestes-Hamlet), Cassandra, and Tristram break through the established interpretations and re-insist upon questions which appeared to have been settled. Sometimes a figure of myth seems—like Ulysses of the *Odyssey*—to have achieved a state of rest, to be merely exemplary; but the great writers of the successive ages do not permit a characterization of such vitality to remain unquestioned. Sophocles and Euripides dealt harshly with him; Dante showed him under eternal torture in Hell; Shakespeare mocked him as the mouthpiece of a glib worldly wisdom; through him Tennyson voiced the all-but-despairing aspiration of his time; James Joyce in a vast parody made him an image of modern man, abashed and rootless, but "long-enduring" and "of many devices."

The story of the command which Abraham received to sacrifice Isaac is so appalling that only a mind which is cruel to itself can gaze at it fixedly. In the last century, however, Søren Kierkegaard wrung from it a reading of such power that, like a strong wind, it is blowing through the thought of the foremost religious philosophers of the Greek Orthodox, the Roman Catholic, and the Protestant faiths.

Jaakobs Traum retells two disturbing myths. Behind the story of Rebecca's fraudulent substitution of Jacob as leader of his people one hears Kierkegaard's urgent question: "Is there a teleological suspension of the ethical?" Beer-Hofmann does not hesitate in his answer, either in this play or in *Der Junge David:* there is a line of succession in the leadership of men that is indicated by spiritual insight and which is justified in overriding the customs and received opinions of any localized community.

The second myth retold is that of God's message to Jacob at Bethel, the famous promise to the Jewish people:

. . . and in thee and in thy seed shall all the families of the earth be blessed. And behold I am with thee and will keep thee whithersoever thou goest, and will bring thee back into this land; for I will not leave thee, until I have done that which I have spoken to thee of.

Beer-Hofmann's interpretation of these words avoids none of the difficulty of understanding them in the light of the thousands of years of persecution; with prophetic power he describes the new trials which were to be visited on the Jewish people during the years following the writing of the play. There are few more impressive passages in modern literature than those in this work wherein it is developed that suffering can be experienced as a "distinction." It is a doctrine which is not easy to express in words; those in comfort do not wish to hear it and those under trial are wary of receiving facile consolations. Beer-Hofmann's statement irresistibly recalls three other passages on the subject: Milton's two sonnets on his blindness and the invocation to Light in *Paradise Lost;* Pascal's prayer on his illness; and the Baron von Hügel's letters on "the uses of pain," written to a friend dying of an incurable disease.

There are three pitfalls in the way of writers who undertake to retell a myth: they may seek to transpose it into rationalistic and realistic terms; they may seek to make it the vehicle of autobiographic identification; and they may rely solely upon its antiquity and accumulated authority for force, without convincing us that they have wrestled with the basic ideas inherent in the story and found their authority within their own creative vision. It is instructive to see the way in which Beer-Hofmann has avoided each of these dangers.

A myth, passing from oral tradition into literature, moves most congenially into poetry and particularly into the poetic drama. Even the most rationalistic reader consents to receive as *given* the elements of the supernatural and the incredible that are involved in these ancient stories. Their validity rests on the general ideas they contain. The novel carries with it the inevitable requirement of presenting the realistic atmosphere of the daily life, which in the case of such ancient stories means the accompaniment of varying amounts of archeological and anthropological learning. The characters whom we have endowed with the life of significant ideas must be endowed with a different kind of life—that of the recognizable quotidian. The noble narratives which Thomas Mann has based upon the story of Joseph occasionally exhibit the constraint imposed by this transposition. So great, however, is the gulf between the two kinds of reality that it can be said that it has seldom been bridged in either direction, save by parody, a method peculiarly suitable to this literary problem. By this method Cervantes achieved the force of myth against the background of the Spanish roads and taverns of his time. A result in the opposite direction, from sublimity to the naturalistic, frequently skirts the ludicrous, a danger that even the suave tact of Renan did not escape in his *Vie de Jésus.*

Among the most interesting aspects of *Jaakobs Traum* is the art with which Beer-Hofmann gradually moves from the relatively realistic presentation of Isaac's ranch at the opening and by gradual infusion of other-worldly elements prepares us for the vast perspectives of the close.

Der Junge David is not based on mythical material. The chapters of the Books of Samuel which it retells are historical narrative. But the great prologue which is *Jaakobs Traum* has established the framework and tenor of the world of myth, which is universal application and basic issues, and it may be assumed that the conclusion of the trilogy would have carried the retelling of David's life back into the thought-world presented to us at the close of the prologue.

Myths do not easily lend themselves to being retold as the vehicle of an individual author's self-identification. They come to us molded by the pressure of innumerable storytellers and listeners; their heroes and heroines are legion. The writers who announce themselves as Cassandra, as Cain, as Dedalus arouse in us a feeling of embarrassment. The gulf between the mythical type and the isolated individual is too great for any writer to cross; assertion passes into rant and pathos into bathos. The myth is everyman's and no man's. It is not impossible that the lack of organic directness in Shelley's *Prometheus Unbound* is a result of the poet's inability to decide as to the extent to which he will project himself as the great revolutionary of Greek tradition.

Beer-Hofmann has a profoundly urgent message to convey. Nothing indicates the elevation of his thought more clearly than the way by which this message comes to us divested of personal assertion yet of undiminished intensity. It is unnecessary to enlarge upon the third of the three pitfalls I have indicated above: he does not rely on the solemn authority of the Biblical story to project his work; all has been thought through and made his own. He has accomplished the ultimate requirement of this type of literature: to preserve the universality of a story which is the property of the whole world without robbing it of its immediacy to each individual who addresses himself to it.

Those already familiar with the original text will discover with pleasure that the present translation is both faithful and musical. The fact that Beer-Hofmann worked closely with the translator, weighing over the exact shade of his intention, has furnished us a number of readings which are particularly precious, constituting as they do a sort of gloss or amplification of the original.

It is to be hoped that *Der Junge David* will also soon be presented to English readers.

The loss which the world of letters sustained with the death of Beer-Hofmann will be felt for a long time. It is a consolation, however, to know that an ever widening circle of readers will come to know the beauty and power of his work.

GOETHE AND

WORLD LITERATURE

GOETHE AND
WORLD LITERATURE

We come upon certain recurrent ideas distributed throughout Goethe's works and conversations to which he was continually adding new shades of meaning until they appear to
us as being each a galaxy of associated meanings rather than
a single definable doctrine. They never come to a rest, neither in his mind nor in their power to bewilder us, to escape
us, to stimulate us, and to provoke us into a breathless effort
to join in the hunt that will capture them. The greatest
among these are, of course, those that deal with the nature
of nature, with the rôle of the demonic, and with the "Shaping Force" in the universe.

And among these is that of "World Literature."

When Goethe spoke of a world literature he did not mean,
as we are likely to, the treasury of masterpieces of all tongues
and all ages. He seems—on a number of occasions, at least—
to have meant literature of all times and languages, the merely
good as well as the great, in so far as it can be felt to illustrate
the concept so dear to him of the unity of all mankind.

An essay delivered as a lecture at the Goethe Convocation in Aspen, Colorado, in
1949. First published, with some introductory paragraphs relating to the Convocation, under the title "World Literature and the Modern Mind," in *Goethe and the
Modern Age: The International Convocation at Aspen, Colorado, 1949.* Edited by Arnold
Bergstraesser (Chicago: Henry Regnery Company [1950]), it subsequently appeared
with the present title and without the introductory paragraphs in *Perspectives USA* for
Fall 1952, the text used for this printing.

Here, in the *Conversations,* is a *locus classicus.* It is Wednesday, the 31st of January 1827. Goethe is talking to Eckermann, that excellent young man. Of him Goethe wrote to Marianne Willemer—she who is in eternity Suleika:

> To understand him one has merely to realize that he is a man of simple soul who wishes at all times to stand in a pure relation toward himself and toward the world about him.

It was that purity—that absence of vanity and self-assertion, that unspotted attentiveness—that brought him a great triumph. It brought him that admirable aural memory and that self-effacing trust which enabled him to present us with one of the very great books of the world. Scholars are increasingly warning us—as they are in the cases of those other reporters of conversation, Boswell and the Evangelists—that Eckermann is not always to be trusted and that he was not above "cooking up" his material; let us not distrust, however, the evidence of our senses that from these pages, almost seven hundred of them, there emerges a figure of overwhelming characterizing force, as uniform as it is grand. Eckermann wrote down many a saying of his friend which he did not understand and Goethe knew that he did not understand them. These sayings are like darts that Goethe cast over Eckermann's head and which have fallen at our feet. There are many which we do not understand and which are flying over our heads to fall at the feet of generations still unborn. It is sufficient to say that we may trust the trust which Goethe reposed in Eckermann.

On this Wednesday Goethe was talking about a Chinese novel he had been reading. And then he talked about the poetry of Béranger. And always, what talk! what charm! what sense!

> I see every day more clearly [continued Goethe] that poetry is a property common to all mankind and that it makes its appearance everywhere and in all ages, by the hundreds and hundreds and ever more hundreds. One man makes it a little

better than another and swims along on the surface a little longer than another—that's all. Friedrich von Matthisson, therefore, mustn't think that he's *the one,* and I mustn't think that I'm *the one;* but each of us must merely tell himself that the poetic gift is not such a very uncommon thing. No one has any particular reason to impute to himself a peculiar merit when he has made a good poem.

(So much for the friends and strangers who have been writing in to inform us that this Goethe about whom we are occupying ourselves was pompous, stuffy, and egocentric.)

> Indeed, [he continues] if we Germans don't start looking about outside the narrow circle of our immediate surroundings, we are apt to fall all too easily into this pedantic arrogance. I take great pleasure in looking into the works of other nations and I advise everyone to do it also. National literature no longer means very much. The epoch of world literature is at hand and everyone must now get to work to hasten the advent of that epoch. However, while extending this high appreciation to foreign works we should not bind ourselves to any particular one and regard it as the final model—whether it be the Chinese or the Serbian or Calderón or the *Nibelungenlied.* When we feel the need of model and exemplar we should always return to the ancient Greeks in whose works the beautiful human being is constantly presented. All the others we should regard merely historically; to the full extent we should extract the good that is in them and make it our own.

This epoch of world literature which in 1827 Goethe felt to be at hand—how does it appear to us now, one hundred and twenty-two years later? The years succeeding his prophecy were to produce Leopardi, Balzac, Flaubert, Ibsen, Baudelaire, Melville, and so on. Were they closer to his conception of a world literature than his admired Voltaire, Diderot, Rousseau, Byron, Sir Walter Scott, Manzoni, Schiller, and Lessing?

"National literature no longer means very much." As Don

José Ortega y Gasset was telling us the other day:*"Man is the animal with the long memory," and one of the contributions of the scientific activity of the last century and a half has been to reinforce this memory and to extend it in ways that confuse the very operation of memory itself. Every college student is under the impression that he remembers the days of Greece and Rome and that he was present at our Civil War. This leads to many false judgments, but at least one result of it is that modern man is aware that billions—not merely millions— have lived and died and that no description of mankind is adequate which does not find its proportionate place within a realization of all the diversity of life on the entire planet over a vast extent of time.

The aid which science has rendered to history and the in-creased facilities for communication in our time have pro-voked an ever more voracious appetite for information con-cerning other ways of life and an ever deeper dismay at the multitude of souls who live and have lived—and also will live. This appetite grows by what it feeds on and, growing, induces an unrest, a strained self-examination, and a dread. The mind of modern man has become a hold-all of flying leaves torn from some vast encyclopedia; but these leaves are not merely items of information. Each one is variously vibrant with emo-tion; each one may mean for us a panacea or consolation, or dire warning, or a stick to beat a dog with, or a subject for our moralizing. World literature will arrive when all this vast body of information is felt as a unity and literature is not only *not* national—it is planetary.

Goethe spoke too soon. Among the writers in any list one could furnish of those working since 1827, there are few who were shaken by these enlarged dimensions. They may, indeed,

*EDITOR'S NOTE: Ortega y Gasset's lecture at the Goethe Convocation in Aspen, "Concerning a Bicentennial Goethe," had preceded Thornton Wilder's. (It was delivered in Spanish, but accompanied by an English version prepared and spoken by Mr. Wilder.)

have had a vision of the cosmos, of the magnitude and diversity of created life, but such illuminations seemed external to that segment which they had selected to explore in depth; it is not absent from Manzoni's Lombardy or Hölderlin's Hellas, but it is separate.

It is now during the second quarter of the twentieth century that we are aware of the appearance of a literature which assumes that the world is an indivisible unit. Its subject has become planetary life. Without attempting to make a comparison of these writers with their predecessors in respect to degrees of genius, it is possible to make a comparison in respect to fields of reference. It is not as an expression of Alexandrian wit that T. S. Eliot juxtaposes a verse from Gérard de Nerval and a Sanskrit invocation, that he furnishes a sort of *cento* of quotations from a dozen literatures; the differences between languages and cultures begin to grow less marked to one who is accustomed to contemplating the unity of the human spirit. *Finnegans Wake* of James Joyce not only uses twenty languages as a sort of keyboard, but the characters themselves coalesce with a multitude of persons of myth and history. The *Cantos* of Ezra Pound require our familiarity with the civilizations which Frobenius claims to have distinguished in African prehistory, as well as a close knowledge of Chinese history, the Italian Renaissance, and the economic problems of the American Revolution. Such material is not imbedded in these works as allusion, illustration, or as ornament; it is there as *ambiance,* as the "nation" has been in what Goethe was calling national literature.

For better or worse, world literature is at hand. Our consciousness is beginning to be planetary. A new tension has been set up between the individual and the universe. It is not new because poets and entire literatures have been lacking in the sense of the vastness of creation, but new in the response provoked in the writer in relation to his own language and his own environment.

Where in literature do we find signs of one or other aspect
of this planetary consciousness? For all its xenophobia, the Old
Testament abounds in the consciousness of the human as multitude and of time as incommensurable. The *Iliad* precisely
states its rosters in the thousands but conveys them in the
millions. I do not find this sense in the *Aeneid.* As one reads
The Divine Comedy his head reels and his heart shrinks before
it. Over and over one has felt it before Dante himself exclaims:
"I had not known that death had undone so many." (A phrase
which T. S. Eliot calls upon in *The Waste Land;* an emotion
scarcely to be found elsewhere in all European literature, for
all its Dances of Death, its *Oraisons Funèbres,* and its *Urn-
Burials.*) I find it in *Don Quixote,* on that road which seems to
have no beginning and no end. I do not find it in Shakespeare
—diversity of souls is not the same thing as multiplicity of
souls. I do not find it in English literature. (Can an island-
dweller expand his imagination beyond a million?) The mark
of national literature is that the foreigner is either exotic (that
is, an object of aesthetic curiosity) or symbolic (like the "noble
savage" or the "noble Roman"). I do not find it in French
literature, not even in Pascal. Occasionally Victor Hugo seems
to be blowing himself up to achieve it (it is one of the advantages of exile; it may be noted that the three examples I have
chosen from our time are all *déracinés*), but the efforts end in
rhetoric. All Oriental literature is filled with it; it is the pre-
dominant note in the Sanskrit. It is in Tolstoi and in Gogol,
though clearer in Dostoevski. It might well be expected in
countries that are continent-wide. It is a characteristic of classical American literature: it informs the "catalogues" of Walt
Whitman, it blanches the face of Melville, and it even vibrates
in the poems of Emily Dickinson, who for so many years never
passed beyond her garden gate.

Though the consciousness of the multiplicity of souls is not
the only ingredient in world literature, it is an essential one.
It is often present without being accompanied by its temporal

component: the realization of the deep abyss of time. Nor does the presence of these realizations in itself constitute a superiority. For the present all we can say is that once a mind is aware of it, it is not possible to *un-know* it.

And it is the character of the modern mind that it knows this thing. The literature that it writes must express it: that every man and woman born is felt to be in a new relation to the whole. Now every child in the street is acquiring it. It has brought more urgent questions to the "revealed" religions. Søren Kierkegaard was obsessed with it; it had a part in his proud claim that faith was even more "absurd" than we had acknowledged it to be. Is it not likely (is it not already seeming?) to bear a pressure on ethics and morals? In the light of it we can read Shakespeare and he can sustain it. Molière can sustain it. Can Ibsen? Can Balzac?

Generally speaking, could national literature ever know this thing? Could the imagination in those walled countries imagine (and with a *frisson*) the existence of more than a hundred thousand souls? Over one's wall and beyond one's channel dwelt those others—the ridiculous foreigners, the barbarians, despised, or dreaded, or fantastically admired. As we read European literature the very names for other nationals have a derisive sound: *"i Tedeschi," "los Franceses," "die Engländer,"* "the Americans." Derision is remote from awe.

It is characteristic of Goethe that he opened our eyes to this coming world literature. In his nature, the scientist and the poet had long stood in close relation. Examining under his microscope the structures of vertebrates and plants, he had long been accustomed to the millions of years required for an alteration in the species; delighting in the literatures of other countries, he had found ever new confirmation of his deepest belief in the unity of human minds.

He did not shrink from anachronism. He married Faust to Helena; he superimposed Weimar upon Shiraz, the city of the Persian poets. But for him world literature did not mean the elimination of local, of national and racial characteristics, a watering-down of specific detail. Goethe—like all eye-natures —rejoiced in the specific and the individual. Our diversity remains, as it remains in nature where no tree, no valley, and no eye is ever identical with another. Only the relation between one thing and another (as that relation exists in our minds) is changed and it is in the light of that change that he says: National literature no longer means very much.

It is not a new thing that man is frightened as he views himself in the immensity of the universe. Science has merely made that immensity more palpable. The distance between the stars was always thought to be immense, but it is only recently that a measure has been named to record it: they talk of light-years. As the realization of these dimensions began to dawn in Europe in the last century, expressions of this fright made their appearance in literature.

Kierkegaard did not hesitate to cry out his fright, and from his fright he made his magnificent "leap" into confidence. That leap, however, is inimitable; it is not available to everyone, though he claims that the leap is precisely the continuation, the logical product, of the dread. At all events, his remorselessly honest description of his fright is one of the greatest contributions of the nineteenth century.

Nietzsche was frightened. Fright struck from him a veritable aurora borealis of brilliant defenses and fertile suggestions; but his principal bulwark against these alarms appears to us more and more meretricious.

Carlyle and Emerson and Browning return again and again to the threat to identity under the glacial tracts of time and space, but it is precisely because they do not seem to be sufficiently frightened that their works do not seem to "prepare the coming of a world literature."

Goethe was not frightened. It can almost be said that Goethe derived his confidence from gazing deep into the very matters that awoke alarm in others.

At first glance the theory which he erected as a bulwark seems to be not unlike the vague pantheisms that flourished at the margins of American Unitarianism. Goethe took much from Spinoza but invested his God-in-Nature with so specific a function that Spinoza's share is scarcely recognizable. His attitude to the Christian tradition is alternately respectful and hostile. He has told us that he viewed many aspects of God as represented in the Old Testament with revulsion and certain representations of divine operation in the New Testament as "blasphemies against God and His revelation of Himself in Nature."

From the heart of the universe, he declared, there pours out a stream of energy ceaselessly operative. This energy presses on all things; its action is to mold chaos into significant form. This is the doctrine of *Gestaltung.*

> No one will realize that the highest and unique operation of Nature and Art is *Gestaltung* and that the *Gestalt* is the require-ment that, under the laws of order, each thing may become, may be, and may remain an individual and significant entity.

This law he had seen in the microscope; he had seen it in history, in art, and most of all in his own life—this urging on of the random and the incoherent toward meaningful shape.

The shapes toward which all things tend are not determined in advance. (Goethe held many reservations against Plato.) This *Wirkende* achieving force—is *ewig*—it will never come to an end. Our becoming, our striving, Faust's striving, is pulled as it were through the iron gates of necessity, chance, hope, and love, and the puzzling contrary obstacles set by the demonic, but the pattern toward which we move is not deter-mined in advance. The world and each one of us in it are the collaborators on our ultimate form ("ultimate" itself only ap-plicable to a stage, since the operation is eternal).

This *ewig Wirkende* views all this activity with a sort of remote and genial benignancy. In some passages of Goethe

our Nature-God glows with love, but the love which exists in
Goethe's concept of nature is of another thought-world than
that which is radical in Christian doctrine.

The *ewig Wirkende* has no tears. It does not hear our sup-
plications. It does not grieve over our mistakes. The whole
erring planet may go up in smoke, but the *ewig Wirkende* will
continue gloriously, joyously, pressing chaos into new significant forms. It has enough material in hand; it has enough time
at its disposal; it is the All and it is eternal.

There is, however, another factor. This God-in-Nature
wishes us well—you and me and all artists and all species of
animals and plants; it wishes us to develop into ever more
excellent states, but—

But— We cannot be sure that it will—as it were—connect
with us, as we could wish. It is capricious. It does not necessarily reward our merits of hard work or our longing.

All we can do is to work, to wait, and to hope—and perhaps
be passed over.

Because nature is also playing. There are these demonic
forces lurking about its action. Play is a by-product of joyous
creativity. It interrupts and impedes the equalized beneficent
operation of this force.

Yet Goethe was not afraid. He did not feel himself outside
of nature. He was not at war with what is. But Goethe was,
above all, a poet. And for this idea let us listen to him speaking
as a poet. It is a passage from *"Die Natürliche Tochter"*:

> *Jawohl! das ewig Wirkende bewegt,*
> *Uns unbegreiflich, dieses oder jenes,*
> *Als wie von ungefähr, zu unserm Wohl,*
> *Zum Rate, zur Entscheidung, zum Vollbringen,*
> *Und wie getragen werden wir ans Ziel.*
> *Dies zu empfinden ist das höchste Glück,*
> *Es nicht zu fordern, ist bescheidne Pflicht,*
> *Es zu erwarten, schöner Trost im Leiden.*

(Yes, yes, the Eternally Fashioning Principle, in ways
Incomprehensible to us, moves this or that,
As though at random, to our benefit,
To taking counsel, to arriving at decision, to achievement;
And we are, as it were, borne, carried on to our goal.
To feel this is the highest happiness there is;
Not to demand it is our humble duty;
And to await it expectantly is sweet consolation in sorrow.)

"And to await it expectantly is sweet consolation in sorrow."
What do we do while we await it? We work. We are nature
—and productivity and fertility are the first law of nature.

What do we work at? There the life of Goethe helps us as
much as the writings—through *Faust* rings wide the conviction that *Wirken*—effective action—alone reconciles us to life
and leads us into the sense of the oneness of all existing.

So many people think Goethe moved only among great
abstractions. No—what respect he had for miners and shoe-
makers, for mothers bringing up their children, for the beautiful girl in the first *Wilhelm Meister,* who knew all about agricul-
ture and arboriculture. All in Goethe is energy and activity.
He wrote to Schiller:

> Anything that merely adds to my information without aug-
> menting my productivity or communicating an immediate
> vital impulse I find odious.

It was from such sources as these that it came about that
Goethe was not frightened. There are many ways of not being
frightened by death, but Goethe's way was very characteristic
of him.

Again he is talking—and now you are to imagine him as
very, very old:

> If I remain ceaselessly active to the end of my days nature is
> under an obligation to allot me another form of existence,
> when the present one is no longer capable of containing my
> spirit. . . . I do not doubt the continuance of our existence. May

it then be that He who is eternally Living will not refuse us
new forms of activity, analogous to those in which we have
been tested.

One of these things we're to work for, he tells us, is the
advent of world literature. Well, in one sense it's here—it's
here with a vengeance. But the other qualifications of a world
literature are struggling to be born.

To anyone but Goethe the prevision of a world, a planetary
literature would have frightening implications. I think it did
not even occur to him to be frightened. He had long since
made his peace with nature. He had found his place among
two hundred thousand billion and had accepted his moment
in uncountable light-years.

And if it meant that he had shrunk, shrunk, shrunk, it also
meant that he had not shrunk into anything foreign to him, or
hostile to him—he had merely taken his place in the thing he
had imitated all his life—the *ewig Wirkende.*

ON READING

THE GREAT LETTER

WRITERS

ON READING THE
GREAT LETTER WRITERS

The very nature of letter writing is such that when we get together to discuss it there should never be more than a dozen persons. The great letter sequences are full of passages that you and I were never meant to see. I grant that some of the letters that I shall discuss were written with one eye on a larger audience; but many a letter by even the most conscious artists in this literature was not intended for the Complete Edition. There are letters even of Horace Walpole, the virtuoso, that he did not label *"Confidential: Please burn"* because he assumed as a matter of course that they would not be wrapped in ribbons and returned to him with the rest. Moreover, until the last fifty years, letters had always been edited, and the letter writers who might have had a lurking suspicion that their pages might be published someday never doubted that the local passages or the humdrum passages or the intimate passages would be cut out. They did not foresee the type of attention that the twentieth century would bring to such work; "morbid" they would have called it.

Moreover, there is an extraordinary aspect about the letter writers' work whereby one understands that even the consciousness of other readers does not impair or undermine the

The Daniel S. Lamont Memorial Lecture delivered at Yale University on May 4, 1928, as "English Letters and Letter Writers." Brief quotations appeared in *The Yale Daily News* for May 5th, but the complete text was never published. Printed from an autograph manuscript among the Wilder papers (YCAL). Present title supplied by the editor.

sincerity and the singlemindedness of the letters they address
to the friends they really love. In the old sense, there is a
"mystery" here. It is related to the mystery behind all creative
literature above a certain level. Art is confession; art is the
secret told. Art itself is a letter written to an ideal mind, to a
dreamed-of audience. The great letter-sequences are written
to close friends. But even the closest friends cannot meet the
requirements of the artist, and the work passes over their
shoulder to that half-divine audience that artists presuppose.
All of Mme. de Sévigné's life was built about those wonderful
letters. On one plane they were written to regain her daughter's affection, to attract her daughter's admiration and love.
But Mme. de Sévigné knew that her daughter merely brought
an amused, an indulgent, a faintly contemptuous appreciation.
And time after time the letter rises beyond the understanding
of the daughter and becomes an *aria* where the overloaded
heart sings to itself for the sheer comfort of its felicity, sings
perhaps to the daughter as she might have been. In such
passages Mme. de Sévigné even defeated the purpose of the
rest of the letter, even risked drawing upon herself her daughter's vexation and ill-humor. But sing she must. The audience
of a work of art is never clear in a true artist's mind, but is
made of souls that he has guessed at—old hero worships reper-
sonified and loves transferred: as though the audiences at
concerts and art galleries and the company of book-buyers
were made up of Michelangelos and Platos and Violas and
Imogens and Cardinal Newmans. Your letters and mine are
messages to friends and we do them as well as we can to please
the friends; but the great letters are letters to friends plus the
most exacting spirits the mind can imagine.

But art is not only the desire to tell one's secret; it is the
desire to tell it and to hide it at the same time. And the secret
is nothing more than the whole drama of the inner life, the
alternations between one's hope of self-improvement and
one's self-reproach at one's failures. "Out of our quarrels with

other people we make rhetoric," said William Butler Yeats; "out of our quarrels with ourselves we make literature." Self-reproach is the first and the continuing state of the soul. And it is the way we go about assuaging that reproach that makes us do anything valuable.

I have had to say all this in order to make clear what I am looking for in great letters. My friends: in literature, I am fond of grace and charm and suavity; but I am not *very* fond of it. But isn't that the quality that most of the great letter writers are praised for? Yes. But I confess that if Horace Walpole offered me nothing more than the brilliant picture of his times (and a very limited picture it is, as one discovers in reading that great and almost exactly contemporaneous document, [John] Wesley's *Journal*); if he offered me nothing but his parliamentary news, and dowager tattle, I should not return to him as I do. And if William Cowper brought merely his charming news of eight persons, three Belgian hares, one dog, one cat, and one garden, I doubt whether he would be so surely surviving into a world of railroads, aviation, and steel construction. And yet that is all that many critics and readers seem to mention. Every great letter writer in the world, save one, presents behind all the verbal felicity an infinitely more satisfying pleasure. They have all left signposts, footprints, clues of the life of their more-than-usual, their extraordinary hearts. All but one, and I wash my hands of Voltaire. His armor is complete. He was perfectly contented with his brains. In all those volumes he left no sign that he had ever found his superb mind unequal to face the impressiveness of nature, the complexity of human relationships, or the pain and loneliness in man's situation. Sometimes I think that in one novel, or rather novelette, *L'Ingénu,* he allowed instinctive emotion to claim itself to be richer than intelligence. But at least in all that immense correspondence, that dazzling correspondence, he preserves his *sang-froid.* But all the great letter writers except

Voltaire offer much richer treasure than their literary skill, and
the only reason that so many people approach them so lightly
is this:

This great branch of literature has been betrayed into the
hands of the anthologists. The whole aim of reading the great
letter-sequences has been reduced to skipping toward the
much-advertised *tours-de-force.* Even in St. Paul thousands of
people regard I Corinthians 13 as a sort of wall motto, never
caring to restore it to its place in that great curve of anxious
exhortation that is presently to mount still more impressively
(yet never losing the character of a letter) to climax after
climax in the passages on the resurrection. Regarding the
Epistle merely as literature, as technique, I have to find myself
merely happily laughing with admiration at such a display.

The first rule in reading the great letter writers is this: *Read
them in extent.*

What we get then through reading these letters in great
length is this:

Gradually a face hovers between the words.

Gradually a personality (unmistakable for any other, just as
you and I are unmistakable for any other) defines itself. When
one has passed the hundredth letter not only the profile of the
personality is becoming clear to us but that wonderful phenomenon takes place: we hear the voice of the writer in the
very word order. There is a William Cowper sentence cadence; there is an Edward FitzGerald sentence cadence (and
very beautiful it is too); and this particular music is of course
linking itself up with the portrait, with the traits, with the
smile, I can almost say: with the glance from the author's eyes.

This particular joy you scarcely ever derive from novels. For
the most part they are engaged on other business. But of
course one receives it from Jane Austen. One receives it ap-
pallingly from Richardson, where it is identified with the heroine. I am told one receives it from Turgenev, though naturally
it is untranslatable and has its home in the vowel-and-conso-

nant accidents of the language. And there are times when it becomes so penetrating in Shakespeare that one swears that one has seen him.

But this isn't all. These letter writers have survived from hundreds and thousands of others who likewise had literary gifts just because they not only reported the world about them persuasively, but because they had this great talent for designing their own portrait in and between the lines. And if they are so gifted at talking about themselves, isn't it possible that every now and then they will let the cat out of the bag—that is, tell the secret of which I was speaking a few moments ago; bring us news from the furthest corners of their spirits, mark for us some of the road? After all, nothing is interesting for long save this, and there is a possibility that these writers with their special gift for writing themselves over will admit us to their happiness or suffering.

I am supposed to be speaking about English writers, but I want to say a few more words about the greatest of all letter writers, Mme. de Sévigné. Indeed, she has almost a place in English letters, since two of our greatest loved her with a special love. Horace Walpole read and reread the volumes of her correspondence that kept making their first appearance in his time; he called her "Notre Dame des Rochers," and when he finally received the manuscript of one of her letters he treasured it above everything else he possessed. And Edward FitzGerald went so far as to prepare a little atlas and biographical dictionary and practically a concordance of her letters for his own use. The anthologists have made havoc with her reception in France. All students in that country, especially the girls, are obliged to study and imitate and comment upon a volume of her *Selected Letters.* And all the showpieces, all the stunt letters are there. But the way to enter the fair country that is her mind is to begin by not looking for the anecdotes of the court, or the flowerets of language, or the inimitable little jokes through which she sees life (for later "all these things shall be added unto you"), but to enter it as Marcel Proust said his grandmother did, by the door of the heart. For me the key to Mme. de Sévigné is an acquaintance with her grandmother. Her grandmother was Mère Marie de Chantal, the co-worker of St. François de Sales. Mère Chantal was canonized as a Saint of the Church almost during Mme. de Sévigné's lifetime. She was one of those saints like St. Teresa who found no difficulty in living two full lifetimes in one, a Mary and a Martha. Her writings are among the minor classics of the Church. They are full of an overwhelming fixed adoration of God, and one has only to read them for a few pages to realize that it is the same blinding intensity that has been inherited by the granddaughter and fixed by some tragic accident upon a human being. And Mme. de Sévigné knew it, and the anthologies do not include those bitter and heartbroken passages in which the cards are really laid on the table:

> This is my destiny [she writes to her daughter]; and the sufferings which follow upon my love for you, being offered to God constitute my penitence for an attachment which should be only for him.

Do I exaggerate?
She writes her friend Guitant:

> I still am in the dark as to whether my dear daughter is coming back to Paris or not. However, I am preparing her rooms in our Carnavalet and we shall see what Providence has decreed. I ceaselessly keep this idea of Providence, Providence in my mind. All my thoughts are resigned to this sovereign will. There is my devotion. There is my scapulary. There is my rosary. There are my vigils. And if I were worthy of believing that I had a spiritual rôle to play I should say that it lay in that. But I am not worthy: for what is one to do with a mind that sees clearly, but with a heart of ice?

One has to read thirty or forty letters to come upon such passages, but, having found them, all the rest glows with an even greater beauty. For example, I have never seen quoted in any book or article on Mme. de Sévigné a short phrase that explains the miracle of the style, and perhaps of all style:

> Farewell, my blessed child; now I can go on telling you that I love you without fear of boring you, since you are willing to endure it in favor of my style: you excuse the importunity of my heart through your approval of my intelligence, isn't it just that?

Nor this terrible word:

> All that is hateful in me, my daughter, proceeds from my lifetime of devotion to you.

In one of my books [*The Bridge of San Luis Rey*] I made literary use of this situation with distinct allusion to Mme. de Sévigné: and I keep receiving indignant letters from lovers of the Frenchwoman saying that I imagined it; that she, being the incarnation of grace and charm and the salon, was too sane to allow of such an interpretation.

Let us proceed now to some English letter writers and read them from this point of view: what I call *reading on three levels:* the surface level, that is the *literary exercise;* the second level, which I call the *profile of a personality;* and the third level, which is *news of the soul.*

Horace Walpole is continually being dismissed as a gossip. But the word "gossip" has many definitions good and bad and Horace Walpole succeeded in illustrating most of them. At times he certainly illustrated the lowest: gossip, I think, is the art of retelling someone else's tragedy as though it reflected credit on oneself. He certainly illustrated the middle ground of gossip: a preoccupation with other people's affairs in that effort we all make to persuade ourselves that our lives are eventful. We bring from childhood the passionate expectation that life will be colorful, but life is seldom ever as exciting as it was when we were five and six and seven years old. Some few people create a glamorous world by overpraising their neighbors and their friends, but most people by detracting from them. Horace Walpole did both. I no longer believe that this kind of thing is malice and the desire to undermine other people's practice of the pleasures our consciences forbid us. I think it is just disappointed hero worship. We discover that even the nicest girls in the world are not so nice as Shakespeare's girls and the noblest men when we meet them fall short of Plutarch's. Well, Horace Walpole was always making even the vivid eighteenth century more vivid than it had any right to be. Harry Seymour Conway was not so wonderful as Harry thought; nor was the Duchess of Bedford so detestable; the eternal witticisms of George Selwyn were not so bright as he claims they were and I think Dr. Johnson was not so uninteresting. The funerals and coronations of the Georges were not so fascinating as he makes them. The gossip colors up life, to escape from the boredom of its monotony and expectedness. Walpole tells lies, like someone whistling in the dark to keep up his courage. But there is a third definition of gossip on this rising scale and that is an unquenchable curiosity about human traits and the springs of conduct; we have no English word for it and we borrow and debase the French word *"curiosité."* This is an interest in human beings so intense and so unremitting that it approaches and resembles love. It is impossible to people who despise human nature or believe it incapable of any very happy surprises. To the eyes of this curiosity nothing one discovers is really repugnant. It is this attitude we define when we say that the angels are never shocked by what they see among us. Psychoanalysis and the new half-truths from Vienna are widely decried because they are said to discover the disgusting in half the conduct of life. On the contrary, they supply this *curiosité* with new resources of charity and pity. They do not remove the responsibility for failure, but they distribute the blame over a wider number of elements.

Horace Walpole did not have, to please me, enough of this highest use of gossip; but it is there. Yet in his letters there is much material about himself where we may employ our *curiosité*. And none more striking than in the story of his failure to understand the aged Mme. du Deffand's frantic infatuation for him until, after her death, he himself found himself possessed by a frantic infatuation for one or both of the Miss Berrys. Two faintly embittered people, both intelligent as the serpent and the devil, had scoffed amusingly at love all their lives, to discover almost at the age of eighty that their lives were being laid waste because they wanted someone to say to them: You are the person I love most in the world. It is in that story that we reach my third level of approach. And the soul in the last struggle of pride and suffering stares up at one from the page. The quality one derives from Walpole then is the range and the possibilities in curiosity.

From the letters of Cowper we receive the unremitting gift of his gentle and shadowed spirit. These pages gain all their richness from the fact that they are written against a background of despair. William Cowper lived an even more uneventful life than Edward FitzGerald. He seemed to be forever holding the wool yarn for elderly ladies. If a bee enters by the window it is quite an exciting event in the poet's life. A balloon ascension in the neighborhood takes up about as much space in Cowper's letters as all the wars and revolutions of Europe. A snake was caught under the kitchen door; an electioneering delegation intruded one evening into the parlor. These are the excitements of Olney. Most of the encyclopedists feel that the gentle, tolerant humor with which these are communicated to us is the reason for Cowper's fame.

But there are layers and layers beneath that surface which [Sir Walter] Scott has immortalized in the phrase "Cowper's divine chit-chat." If you take up the complete letters (and there is still no really complete *Letters*) and if you are patient and watchful you will see another plane that William Cowper did not intend you to see: some very subtle and gradual shifting of likes and dislikes and cautions and hesitations among the modest *dramatis personae.* The world in which these people live is so quiet that psychological shades become dramatic. We are in the wonderful world that Jane Austen ruled: Relativity is at work, and all the coloring of Carlyle's *French Revolution* is extracted from the exchanged visits of a few neighbors. When Dr. John Newton was a wandering preacher the gentle and high-strung poet came under his influence. Dr. John Newton applied the methods of an almost hysteric revivalism to the young man. He was converted. But at the age of forty he was informed from Heaven in a dream that he had committed the unpardonable sin and would never be saved. Now what is the attitude one takes to the revivalist who converts one to Eternal Life, even though one discovers soon after that the conversion was useful only to form the conviction that one is eternally damned? Love and respect, of course; love and respect, tempered, ladies and gentlemen, by the most implacable dislike. One writes faithful and affectionate letters, but one's horror is betrayed every fifteen months by some shade. Another illustration: One lives side by side for years with a devoted, intelligent elderly lady. Business of reading aloud for years Captain Cook's voyages to the South Seas and the news sheets about the court of Poland and the perhaps justified restlessness of the American colonies. But other ladies all over fifty come to look at the flowers, come to have their skeins of worsted held and to listen to the first readings of "John Gilpin" and the new translation of Homer. All three, all four are united in politeness, congeniality, and affection. But the balance of affection in a group can never remain poised at an equation, and even those gentle hearts are capable of laying claims on one another. Suddenly one member of the group drops out of the letters as though she had never been. Years later there are allusions so deft, wrapped in their formal latinity, that you almost tell yourself that you imagine it. The editor informs us in a footnote what happened, but going back we see that we could have gathered it from the tiny overstatements, and from the not-so-tiny reticences.

But there is a layer even below this, and here lies the deep interest in Cowper. Cowper was convinced that he had committed The Unpardonable Sin. No one is quite sure what that sin is in the scripture and no one is quite sure what Cowper did that he called The Unpardonable Sin. He says that once in his boyhood he had had to improve upon some occasion from God. At all events he was quite convinced that there was heavenly grace for every repentant sinner in the world, except himself. And the smell of sulphur is never absent for long from the parlor and garden at Olney. His dearest friends (several of them are clergymen), knowing his impeccable life, his deeply religious mind, and even his sense of humor, try to argue with him, sometimes with some harshness. But he mildly holds his ground; he knows the Biblical texts about forgiveness and the limitless possibilities of divine love. All that is perfectly true—except for William Cowper.

Now are you prepared to be both impatient and even angry at the poet and yet to believe that he believes it? Or are you among those horsey people who in the presence of mental suffering stride about crying: "Just think of other things, my dear. Get some good exercise, drink a lot of milk, and read P. G. Wodehouse"?

Again we are in a relative world. The reality of a person's sufferings to himself is what must concern us. The child that has been hurled across the room by a father temporarily drunk does not understand and make allowance for the effect of alcohol. The child's world goes dark. The despair of the heart is not any the less because of a lack in reasoning power or education.

Loving William Cowper then is a spiritual exercise. One must learn not to be exasperated by him. One must think of Mary Unwin, who had several times a day to flatter this spiritual vanity in him—this delusion in him that he was unique, the horrible exception to God's mercy—she had to protest even at breakfast that he must be mistaken, and yet not protest too hard. For I am sorry to have to tell you that William Cowper liked to mention his eternal damnation quite frequently. Mary Unwin had also to comfort him before and after his visits of insanity. And one day after years of faithful friendship she had to enter a room and discover him trying to hang himself from the ceiling. Again, because we know this profoundly moving background the divine chit-chat speaks to us with a quality beyond mere grace and humor.

But there remains one letter writer with whom this method does not carry us far. Edward FitzGerald's letters move in an atmosphere of high tragic implication, but he has buried the Key. Watch as carefully as you choose, and with all the practice you have acquired from the letters of Mme. de Sévigné, Cowper, Swift, Charles Lamb, St. François de Sales, Lady Mary [Wortley Montagu], Jane Welsh Carlyle—for all these are full illustration of the three levels of interest. Even as St. Paul is, even as Cicero is.

With FitzGerald the surface is beautiful. I may say that it seems to me that Edward FitzGerald taught me how to read —his way of reading so closely and of finding importance in passages of Shakespeare and Milton and Cervantes that I had always thought were the mere business, or even padding, of masterpieces. He is the most beautiful illustration in all English literature of how to be bookish in the best sense, loving great books as though they were people. "Well, well," he says every year, "I hope to read *Don Quixote* once more before I die." The second plane he conducts as well, in my opinion, as anyone else in English—even better than Charles Lamb, whose verbal fooling repels me a little, wonderful though he is. The profile of the personality of Edward FitzGerald is one of the great gifts of the time. I can't help but believe that it comes over even better in the letters than it did in life, a not uncommon phenomenon in people with the literary gifts. (Goldsmith is another illustration.) Carlyle and Tennyson and Thackeray loved him very dearly and left unshakable testimony, but always with a touch of Victorian didactic superiority in regard to his absence from the battlefields. As I say, we have no facts on the third level, but we have that atmosphere that has led to his being called the Hamlet of letter writers, the enigmatic FitzGerald. What was the matter? What was his soul suffering from? Wasn't it just the inadequacy of the view on life that he borrowed and modified from Omar Khayyám? Wasn't it just a refusal to cope with the dismaying look of experience and the longing for death? He had made a number of dear friends ("My friendships are more like loves," he would say) and they died or moved away and became wrapped up in their wives and children and wrote him perfunctory letters. And his own death delayed and delayed and delayed.

Novels I suppose are pure literature and diaries are pure life. Autobiographies are life, but life that has been adroitly rearranged for the show window. The great books of confession, the Rousseau and the Augustine, are all too few. So that we come back to the great letter writers for the happiest mixture of both. When even fiction is not real enough, when even Dostoevski and Stendhal, for all their inner truth, remind us that actually on the planet the brothers Karamazov never lived—a childish test, but an eternally human objection against novels. And when on the side of real life we tire of biographies, because they happened all too palpably on the planet and repel us with that awful thought, What would Keats or Walt Whitman or Queen Victoria say if they read their biography? Wouldn't they cry out: But this is only one tenth of the truth; all that is really myself escaped?

Between these two discontents: between the fictional character of fiction and the all-too-graphic character of biographic work, there are letters. These people not only really lived as you and I are living, but they are reporting themselves faithfully. You may read them for their style, or for the acquaintance of their personality, or you may read them for the dark patterns in their life and for the courage they bring to it.

JAMES JOYCE

JAMES JOYCE
1882–1941

During thirty-five years of self-imposed exile James Joyce never ceased from the contemplation of Dublin. From Trieste, from Rome, from Zürich, earning his living in the appalling treadmill of the Berlitz schools, night after night he relived the Dublin of 1900, its sights and sounds and smells and inhabitants—bound to Dublin in love and hate, parallel, irreconcilable, each emotion whipping on its contrary; a love that could only briefly make peace with the hatred through the operation of the comic spirit; a hatred that could only intermittently make peace with the love through the intensity of artistic creation. This unresolved love and hate recurred in every aspect of his life: it went out toward his youth, toward the religion in which he was brought up, toward the rôle of artist, toward the very phenomenon of language itself. It compelled him to destroy and to extol; to annihilate through analysis and to make live through passionate comprehension.

The price that must be paid for a love that cannot integrate its hate is sentimentality; the price that must be paid for a hate that cannot integrate its love is, variously, empty rhetoric, insecurity of taste, and the sterile refinements of an intellect bent on destruction.

Between these perils Joyce won some great triumphs.

An article contributed originally to *Poetry*, Chicago, for March 1941. The essay was reprinted separately with the same title in Aurora, New York, by the Wells College Press in 1944.

Like Cervantes, he groped confusedly for his subject and his form. The history of a writer is his search for his own subject, his myth-theme, hidden from him, but prepared for him in every hour of his life, his *Gulliver's Travels,* his *Robinson Crusoe.* Like Cervantes, unsuccessfully, Joyce tried poetry and drama. Knowing the incomparable resources of his prose rhythms, one is astonished at these verses—a watery musicality, a pinched ventriloqual voice. Knowing the vital dialogues in *Dubliners* and that electrifying scene, the quarrel at the Christmas dinnertable, in *A Portrait of the Artist as a Young Man,* one is astonished at the woodenness of his play *Exiles.*

Like Cervantes, he turned with greater success to short narratives, and, like him, found in the dimensions of the long book his form and his theme.

Ulysses brought a new method into literature, the interior monologue. The century-long advance of realism now confronted this task: the realistic description of consciousness. To realism, mind is a babbler, a stream of fleeting odds and ends of image and association. Joyce achieved this method with a mastery and fullness of illustration that effaces any question of precursors. He alone has been able to suggest the apparent incoherence and triviality of this incessant woolgathering, and yet to impose upon it a coordination beyond itself, in art. With what consternation the Masters would have beheld this sight. Shakespeare reserved divagation for Juliet's nurse, Jane Austen for Miss Bates. Hamlet's interior monologue is based upon the assumption that for a short time the human mind may pursue its idea in purity. Yet all art is convention, even the inner monologue. Joyce's discovery has the character of necessity, a twentieth-century necessity, and again it was wrung from him by the operation of his love and hate. There is destruction in that it saps the dignity of the mind; there is profound sympathy in the uses to which he put it for characterization. With it he explores three souls, Stephen Dedalus and the Blooms; one failure and two great triumphs.

Dedalus is confessedly autobiographical; how can unreconciled love and hate make a self-portrait? Here the price is paid, sentimentality. Dedalus extends his bleeding heart, not without complacency; he mocks himself for it, but even in the mockery we surprise the sob of an Italian tenor. The miracle of the book is Leopold Bloom, Joyce's anti-self, *l'homme moyen sensuel,* and his wife, Marion—transcendent confirmations of the method itself. If we could surprise the interior monologue of any person—it seems to affirm—we would be obliged to enlarge the famous aphorism: to understand that much is not only to forgive that much; it is to extend to another person that suspension of objective judgment which we accord to ourselves; a homage to the life-force itself in the play of consciousness relegating all questions of approval or disapproval.

Ulysses exemplifies, as a technical problem, the mastery of the long book—where Proust and so many others have failed. This has been achieved, perilously, by a resort to curious architectural devices and by the play of the comic spirit—these Chinese boxes of complicated schematization: each chapter marked by one color; each chapter representing an organ in the human body; each under the sign of a theological virtue and its allied vice; each bearing a relation—partly as parody, partly for emotion—to a corresponding book of the *Odyssey.* At first glance how unlike the abounding creativity of the great books—of Rabelais, Cervantes, and Dante—are these devious ingenuities and buried cross-references; and yet *Ulysses* has the climate of the great books. It circulates in the resources of the style, equal to every mood and to every game; in the lofty requirement that the reader give his whole attention to every word; in the omnipresence of a surpassingly concrete Dublin; in the humanity of the characters; and in the earnestness of an element that one can only call "confessional."

After *Ulysses,* Joyce went through a period of disorganization: the search for the new subject; the increasing threat to his eyesight.

One day a friend sent him a postcard picturing the Bay of Dublin and Howth Head—that promontory in which Celt and Dane and Saxon have always seen the outline of a sleeper's head. Joyce resolved to write the thoughts of that sleeping man. For seventeen years he worked on *Finnegans Wake,* peering over the page with fading vision, elaborating its complexities, like some ancient illuminator fashioning the traceries of the *Book of Kells.* A book in sleep-language—the inner monologue unlocked to still greater possibilities of apparent incoherence and hence requiring a still more elaborate schematic scaffolding. Those who have deciphered even a small part of the work have glimpsed the grandeur of the plan: the sleeper reliving the history of mankind and identifying himself with the heroes and sinners of the world's myth literature; his thoughts influenced by the stars that pass over his head and couched in a language which reproduces the talking-on-two-levels characteristic of sleep; a language in which all the tongues of the world have coalesced into a *pâté,* the barriers between them having become imperceptible at that level; the sleeper wrestling all night with the problem of original sin, with the sense of guilt acquired from offenses which his waking self knows nothing of. Toward dawn, his enemies mastered, identifying himself with Finn, the ancient Irish hero, he awakes to a new day in the eternal cyclic revolutions of lives and civilizations. Finn! Again wake!

We cannot know yet whether hate has buried this conception under the debris of language analyzed to dust or whether love through identification with human history, through the laughter of the comic genius, and through the incomparable musicality of its style, has won its greatest triumph of all.

Joyce recommended this work to the world as his greatest, and it may be that when we come to know it, our gratitude for so many excellences in the earlier books will be exceeded by all that we owe him for this one.

JOYCE AND
THE MODERN NOVEL

The subject I am going to treat tonight is the question we are so often asked: Why did Joyce have to write in so difficult a way? Why didn't he recount "simply" that Leopold Bloom identified Stephen Dedalus with a son he had lost? And why this impenetrable thicket of polyglot puns in *Finnegans Wake?* Why all these complicated things going on all the time? Readers turn to the various manuals on *Ulysses* and they find out each episode is controlled by an organ of the human body; each episode has a predominating color. Episode VII has reference to the lungs: its color is red-brown, and its art is rhetoric. In episode VI you attend a funeral; you must remember your *Odyssey* and the descent to Hell; the color of it is black and white, and its organ is the heart. Why must Joyce erect so many formal patterns?

There are a number of answers. In the first place, James Joyce was hunting for a style that would reveal the extent to which every individual—you and I, the millions of the people who walk this earth—is both sole and unique and also archetypical. To establish that each human being is archetypical, he had to draw on the human being whom he knew best: himself. So the book likewise is confession, and it is confession

---

Adapted by the author from a tape recording of a talk before the James Joyce Society in New York on 2 February 1954 and published in *A James Joyce Miscellany*. Edited by Marvin Magalaner for the James Joyce Society, 1947–1957 (New York: James Joyce Society, 1957).

at a very deep and agonizing level. It is a wonderful experience to unburden the heart in confession, but it is a very difficult thing to do. The subject longs to tell his charged secret and longs not to tell it. So the complications are partly one step forward and two steps back and two steps forward and four steps back. *Finnegans Wake* is, in spite of all we know of its comic force and its lyric beauty, an agonized journey into the private life of James Joyce.

Another thing that complicates the book is the comic spirit, a constant flow of bitter or tender wit.

In addition, there is an obsessive compulsion toward the all-inclusive—what you might call the kitchen-stove complex. Joyce will get everything in there including the kitchen stove if he possibly can. It is a sort of need to make the catalogue absolutely complete. Not a dozen, but every one of the Sutras of the Koran, every one of Tom Moore's *Melodies,* and, I suspect, every one of the Saints in the calendar. These, and many other series, he stuck into the book like plums into a vast plumcake.

How, as a literary method, does he render an individual archetypically? Joyce was fundamentally a great realistic writer. One of the greatest realistic writers that ever lived was Flaubert, and Joyce worshiped Flaubert. And *Madame Bovary* and *Un Coeur simple* are the greatest achievements of what we call the realistic method. People who open *Finnegans Wake* for the first time would say that certainly this was the least realistic book ever written. But the concrete world is there with a tremendous precision. For in order to pass to the general, one must retain a firm grasp on the particular. In order to see what Joyce accomplished, let us draw an illustration from the theater, making clear the limitations of the realistic theater and novel.

Let us pretend that we are attending a performance of *Romeo and Juliet* in 1910 or 1890. The curtain rises on the banquet scene in *Romeo and Juliet* where Romeo meets Juliet for the first time. What we see are real chandeliers, real rugs, tables laden with supposedly real food and drink, and it is all boxed in within a picture frame. So it was staged, not as Shakespeare intended, but as the nineteenth century staged it. The nineteenth century was a very bad century for the theater and a glorious century for the novel.

And what did it convey? It said that these events took place to one set of persons, at one moment in time, in one place. That is the theater of the Unique Occasion.

Now, you and I and everybody live a complete life under unique occasions. Every single moment of our life is unique in that sense. Every human being lives only unique occasions, just as we all die one death—our death and no one else's. Likewise, of the millions of times that "I love" has been said, each time it is really said just once. The participation in essential love or essential death is, as they now are saying, "existential"—totally individual.

The realistic novel is the art of these unique occasions. *Tess* and *Anna Karenina* and the novels of Jane Austen securely place their characters in one time and one place.

But I can hear you objecting that from all those books a true "generalization" arises, to which Emma Bovary herself has given her name—the type of an outlook on life—*Bovaryisme*. And we all know the other Emma, too, Jane Austen's Emma, is the kind of woman who goes around bossing, ineptly bossing, the affairs of others. Yes, they participate in "type," but they are lodged in specific circumstances and their generalization follows from the weight laid on particularization.

The realistic method is the glory of the novel; few novels have transcended it, and it was Joyce's point of departure. He wanted not to tell how Mr. So-and-so met Miss So-and-so and how they got married in such-and-such a place. It was this kind of realization that led to a search for a new way of making it arresting to us. Let us approach the problem from another angle:

After I'd graduated from college I was sent to Europe to study archeology. One day our class in Rome was taken out into the country to dig up a bit of the Etruscan world, a street.

Once thousands of persons had walked it. The rut was very deep. Those who have uncovered such a spot are never the same again.

Now in the twentieth century we all have something of the mind of an archeologist. The other centuries knew that many people had lived and died a long while ago, and they knew there were many people living on the earth. But the invention of the printing press (its consequences are still unfolding) had made these realizations far more actual. Now everybody knows them, not as something you learn in school and recite to one another, but "in their bones"—that millions and billions have lived and died, and that probably billions and billions (let us not despair of the human race) will live and die. The extent of this enlarged realization alters the whole view of life.

You have lost some husband, brother, or parent in the war. Your grief is very real to you. Yet now we know as never before that a great many died in this war and in the wars of Carthage and Troy and Ur, and in the Thirty Years War— what end is there to any human thing in which you are not also companion to billions? It does not diminish your grief, but it orients it to a larger field of reference.

This shift in outlook brings two results. We are less interested in the anecdote, in the "plot," Mr. So-and-so met the attractive Miss So-and-so. We wish them well; but the mere account of their progress no longer arrests us in the same way. As Gertrude Stein said,

> If you read any of the four greatest novels of the Twentieth Century for *what happens next,* you might as well throw the book away at the beginning: Proust, Joyce, *The Magic Mountain, The Making of Americans.*

Plot must be stated differently in order to arrest the attention. The railway stations will continue to sell all sorts of things, but we are talking about adequate reading for adults. The "anecdote" has lost its importance.

The second result is an urgent search for the validity of individual experience. Though I realize that my joy or my grief is but "one" in the ocean of human life, nevertheless it *has* its reality. I know that the existential thing pouring up in me, my joy or my fear, is a real thing and yet that the intensity with which I feel it can be called absurd. It is absurd to claim that "I," in the vast reaches of time and place and repetition, is worth an assertion. This problem drove man back into a journey of self-examination. What is my "I"? What is the reality of my "I"? That's where the New Psychology came in.

Now, Joyce is the great novelist of these two things. He is the novelist who has most succeeded in placing man in an immense field of reference, among all the people who have lived and died, in all the periods of time, all the geography of the world, all the races, all the catastrophes of history. And he is also the one who has most dramatically engaged in a search for the validity of the individual as an absolute.

To express his insights he was driven to fashion a new technique. It is interesting now to see that the search began early. He felt the need of burying beneath the narratives an almost compulsive network of cross-relations, categories, and systems. For a generation *Dubliners* appeared to be a collection of remarkable but loosely related stories. We now know that they fall into a series of interlocking, illustrative patterns.

Now, how would we "present" any individual, or ourselves —ourselves in this room—existing and somehow related to totality? How do we do it in such a way that we would be freed a little from the terror of shrinking to nullity?

First we would seek for our place in myths. Myths are the dreaming soul of the race, telling its story. Now, the dreaming soul of the race has told its story for centuries and centuries and centuries, and there have been billions of stories. They're still telling them. Every novel for sale in a railway station is the dreaming soul of the human race telling its story. But the myths are the survival of the fittest of the billions of stories most of which have been forgotten. No chance survival there. The retelling of them on every hand occurs because they whisper a validation—they isolate and confer a significance—Prometheus, Cassandra, Oedipus, Don Quixote, Faust.

Joyce not only drew on myth; he used history as though it were myth. He made a hero who was Everyman, and to describe him to us he played on the vast repertory of myth and history as upon a clavier. Then he added to his technique another procedure: the dream.

Every great writer has been interested in dreams. Think of how interested in dreams Shakespeare was. Joyce had read the classics of psychoanalysis—though he seems to make fun of them—and there he found what he wanted. There he found the use which our subconscious makes of the symbol—the symbol as clarification and aid, and the symbol substituted for the thing disavowed; there he found the pun and slip of the tongue as betrayal; there also he found the thing which Jung extended much further than Freud: the fact that all of us are motivated by an unconscious reliance on these myths and symbols which help us over difficulties. *Finnegans Wake* is overwhelmingly committed to a belief in the unconscious.

In *Ulysses* Joyce had explored the pressures of the unconscious on the conscious mind. He had gone further than anybody else in unmasking its apparent incoherences. There are no incoherences in the human mind, not even under insanity. Having done a book of the mind awake, he decided to show the mind asleep—to write a Night Book. For this he was driven to invent a technique—a night language. He was greatly helped by the discoveries of Freud.

Freud once said to me,

> Oh, I don't think that writers will be able to use the tenets of psychoanalysis for two or three hundred years. Numbers of my friends—Arnold Zweig and Stefan Zweig and Franz Werfel—have been using psychoanalysis in their novels; but it still

comes out as clinical document, as schemata. Only in two or three hundred years will the *Dichter* have assimilated it at so deep a level that they'll know it without knowing they know it. And it will come out as pure novel.

But already the greatest novelist of the twentieth century had digested it so deeply that he could play with it, turn it around, illustrate it; it was there as a deep visceral "knowing," a sort of sovereign and joyous possession.

The hero of *Finnegans Wake* is the most "generalized" character in all literature, but he is also completely a unique and individualized person. We overhear and oversee him in bed above his tavern at the edge of Dublin. His conscience is trying him for some obscure misdemeanors committed—or perhaps only partially envisaged—during the day. He is in disgrace. He identifies himself with Lucifer fallen from Heaven, Adam ejected from Paradise, Napoleon defeated at Waterloo, Finnegan of the old ballad laid out for his wake. It is the Book of Falls, and as the night advances he plunges deeper and relives all the crimes of which man is capable; he stands trial (the very constellations of the night sky are sitting in judgment). He submits his defense and extenuation. Finally dawn arrives; the sun climbs through the transom of the Earwickers' bedroom. The last chapter is a wonderful sunburst of Handelian rhetoric; all the resurrection myths of the world are recalled along with Pears' soap advertisements and the passing trains and the milkman. The phoenix is reborn; Everyman re-awakes.

The technique, then, had to ensure a constant oscillation between the homeliest particularizations and the vastest generalization. Joyce, with what I call his compulsion toward all-inclusiveness, had to make sure of including the red man, and the yellow man, and the black man, and the brown man, to include allusions to Australia and Africa and the other continents.

I am told that "twelve-tone series" composers have to touch every one of the notes of the scale before they are allowed to repeat any one of them. Joyce requires of himself a similar obligation. And not only man and his cultures: the physical universe is represented: the constellations of both hemispheres. Light and dark are there in the colors of the spectrum. The universe of sound is there in Guido d'Arezzo's scale—all half-hidden polyglot puns. Also the elements of matter: gold, silver, copper, lead, carbon.

All these devices were necessary to "orient" the individual within the universe. To them one ingredient more has been added: Joyce was a great comic genius. The comic spirit is constantly relieving us of the burden of life's logical implications. Confront life logically and you might as well resign at once. Human beings cannot bear much wrong and cannot bear much logic and they cannot bear too much self-examination; and the comic spirit was given to us as reconciliation and as an alibi from drawing the last deductions. Push *Don Quixote* and *Le Misanthrope* just a little further and you find agonizing material; the comic spirit has saved them from the precipices over which they hang: defeat and despair. It is necessary to remember this book was written over just such a precipice. There's a limit to which the human heart can endure or sustain itself, even with the aid of the comic spirit. Joyce seems to have sustained himself with his humor, his exercise of confession, and his all but unimaginable industry. He submitted to eleven operations upon his eyes. Finally, he spent hours a day, with diminishing eyesight, fashioning these complicated verbal constructions, always guarding their relation to the heart of the book and bearing in mind their resemblance to the ornamentation of the *Book of Kells.*

Since man in the twentieth century is increasingly aware of the futility of the anecdote alone, and seeks an orientation to a larger universe, do all books henceforward have to be written like this?

I think we are going through a phase when books must reflect these preoccupations. Notice *The Magic Mountain*—Hans Castorp's education. It is about a man learning how to live and think in the twentieth century. Its "Anecdote" is negligible. It is as though for the time being we resigned from that excessive interest in that thing which has fascinated the world for so long: individual personality; the pendulum is now swinging and we are interested in the great types.

Many will say: "Do I have to read this? I'm a busy housewife. I have three children. I belong to the PTA. Do I have to read books like this?"

Did you ever read Rousseau's *Émile* or *La Nouvelle Héloïse?* I never did—but I can pretty well believe that all of us, whether we know it or not, have been in large part formed by them. Every century has its underground books which have permeated thought. Often they have been transmitted through relatively few readers. I believe those two great books of Rousseau are shaping us still—though many of us will probably never read them. *Finnegans Wake* is going to be passed on through its ardent enthusiasts to generations still unborn. It will take its part in the emergence from parochialism and nationalism and the complacencies of "our system" and "our technological superiority."

The terrible thing is to live in our twentieth century with nineteenth-century mentality. To be "out of phase"—that's what is blighting. That's what starves and frightens and shipwrecks so many souls. The realizations of new dimensions and new obligations pour in on us from the world of science, but we would rather retreat into the accustomed and the soothing. Joyce and Pound and Eliot have advanced into the new territory; they have shown us how understanding can reduce fear. The difficulties they present to readers are the exact counterparts of the difficulties we experience in living at this time, and their triumphs are notification and guide to us as to where we may find clarification and strength.

GERTRUDE STEIN

GERTRUDE STEIN'S
NARRATION

In November of 1934 Miss Gertrude Stein delivered before an audience of five hundred students at the University of Chicago the lecture on "Poetry and Grammar" which is now printed in the volume *Lectures in America.* At the invitation of the university she returned in March 1935 to read before approximately the same audience the four lectures contained in this volume. In addition ten conferences were arranged during which Miss Stein amplified the ideas contained in these lectures by means of general discussion with some thirty selected students.

There are a number of ways in which these lectures may be approached. In the first place they are in themselves models of artistic form. The highly individual idiom in which they are written reposes upon an unerring ear for musical cadence and upon a conviction that repetition is a form of insistence and emphasis that is characteristic of all life, of history, and of nature itself.

> If a thing is really existing there can be no repetition. . . . Then we have insistence insistence that in its emphasis can never be repeating, because insistence is always alive and if it is alive it is never saying anything in the same way because emphasis can

The introduction to *Narration: Four Lectures by Gertrude Stein,* published in Chicago by the University of Chicago Press in 1935.

never be the same not even when it is most the same that is
when it has been taught.

In the printed version of the lectures the individuality of the
idiom has been enhanced by the economy of the punctuation,
which has been explained by Miss Stein as being a form of
challenge to a livelier collaboration on the part of the reader.

> A comma by helping you along holding your coat for you and
> putting on your shoes keeps you from living your life as ac-
> tively as you should lead it. . . . The longer, the more compli-
> cated the sentence the greater the number of the same kinds
> of words I had following one another, the more the very many
> more I had of them I felt the passionate need of their taking
> care of themselves by themselves and not helping them, and
> thereby enfeebling them by putting in a comma. . . . A long
> complicated sentence should force itself upon you, make your-
> self know yourself knowing it.

Another approach to these lectures lies in seeing them as
object lessons of the teaching method. Nothing is learned save
in answer to a deeply lodged and distinctly stated question.
Beginning with a calculated simplicity, these lectures first prepare and provoke the correct questions in the listeners' minds.
One is irresistibly reminded of the request that Dante put to
his guide, and which might serve as a motto for all education:

> . . . io 'l pregai che mi largisse il pasto
> Di cui largito m'avea il disio. *
>
> (. . . I prayed him to bestow on me the food, for
> which he had already bestowed on me the appetite.)

These are real rewards, but the great reward of these lectures lies in the richness and vitality of the ideas contained in
them. We soon discover that we are not to hear about narration from the point of view from which the rhetorics usually
discuss the subject. We hear nothing of the proportion of

*Inferno, XIV, 92–93.

exposition to narrative, of where to place a climax, of how to heighten vividness through the use of illustrative detail. Here we return to first principles, indeed:

> Narration is what anybody has to say in any way about anything that can happen, that has happened or will happen in any way.

There is an almost terrifying exactness in Miss Stein's use of the very words that the rest of the world employs so loosely: "everybody," "everything," and "every way." Consequently the discussion leads at once into the realms of psychology, philosophy, and metaphysics, to a theory of knowledge and a theory of time. These matters are treated, however, not in the Latinizing jargon of the manuals, but in the homely language of colloquial usage. The great and exhilarating passage in the third lecture, describing the difference between "existing" and "happening," that begins:

> The inside and the outside, the outside which is outside and the inside which is inside are not when they are inside and outside are not inside in short they are not existing, that is inside. . . .

—such a passage might have been rendered in terms of "subjective and objective phenomena"; it might have been more academically impressive; it could not have been clearer; and it would have lost that quality of rising from the "daily life" and from our "common knowledge" which is the vitalizing character of Miss Stein's ideas.

These ideas are presented to us in a highly abstract form. Miss Stein pays her listeners the high compliment of dispensing for the most part with that apparatus of illustrative simile and anecdote that is so often employed to recommend ideas. She assumes that the attentive listener will bring, from a store of observation and reflection, the concrete illustration of her generalization. This is what renders doubly stimulating, for example, the treatment of the differences between English and American literature, and the distinction between prose and poetry—a critical principle which from the earlier lecture has already made so marked an impression and which in the present lectures receives a further development. In the present series, however, the outstanding passages will undoubtedly be those dealing with the psychology of the creative act as the moment of "recognition" and the discussion of the relations between the artist and the audience—a subject now the center of critical speculation in many quarters and which here receives distinguished and profound treatment.

Miss Stein has said that the artist is the most sensitive exponent of his contemporaneousness, expressing it while it still lies in the unconscious of society at large. In the first lecture in this book and in the lectures she has previously given she has described the character of the new points of view of this age, the twentieth century which was made by America, as the nineteenth was made by England, and with the result that "the United States is now the oldest country in the world." These lectures in their method and in their content are brilliant examples of the breadth and movement and energy that the perspective of time will reveal to have been our characteristic.

GERTRUDE STEIN'S
THE GEOGRAPHICAL HISTORY
OF AMERICA

This book grew out of Miss Stein's meditations on literary masterpieces. Why are there so few of them? For what reasons have they survived? What qualities separate the masterpieces from the works that are almost masterpieces? The answers usually given to these questions did not satisfy her. It was not enough to say that these books were distinguished by their "universality," or their "style," or their "psychology," or their "profound knowledge of the human heart." She thought a great deal about the *Iliad* and the Old Testament and Shakespeare, about *Robinson Crusoe* and the novels of Jane Austen— to quote the works that appeared most frequently in her conversation during the months that this book was approaching completion—and the answer she found in regard to them lay in their possession of a certain relation to the problems of identity and time.

In order to approach their treatment of identity and time Miss Stein made her own distinction between Human Nature and the Human Mind. Human Nature clings to identity, its insistence on itself as personality, and to do this it must employ memory and the sense of an audience. By memory it is reassured of its existence through consciousness of itself in time-

The introduction to Gertrude Stein's *The Geographical History of America or The Relation of Human Nature to the Human Mind,* published in New York by Random House, Inc., in 1936.

succession. By an audience it is reassured of itself through its effect on another—" 'I am I,' said the little old lady, 'because my dog knows me.' " From Human Nature, therefore, come all the assertions of the self and all the rhetorical attitudes that require the audience—wars, politics, propaganda, jealousy, and so on. The Human Mind, however, has no identity; every moment "it knows what it knows when it knows it." It gazes at pure existing. It is deflected by no consideration of an audience, for when it is aware of an audience it has ceased to "know." In its highest expression it is not even an audience to itself. It knows and it writes, for its principal expression is in writing and its highest achievement has been in literary masterpieces. These masterpieces, though they may be about human nature, are not of it. Time and identity and memory may be in them as subject matter—as that existing at which the Human Mind gazes—but the absence from the creative mind of those qualities has been acknowledged by the vast multitudes of the world who, striving to escape from the identity-bound and time-immersed state, recognize that such a liberation has been achieved in these works.

If then Miss Stein is writing metaphysics, why does she not state her ideas in the manner that metaphysicians generally employ?

There are three answers to this question.

In the first place, a creative metaphysician must always invent his own terms. Even though his concepts may have something in common with those of his predecessors—with such concepts as "subjective," "objective," "soul," "imagination," and "consciousness"—he cannot in certain places employ those terms, because they come bringing associations of (for him) varying validity and bringing with them the whole systems of which they were a part. The contemporaries of Kant complained (as the contemporaries of Professor Whitehead are now complaining) that the philosopher's terminology was arbitrary and obscure.

In the second place, Miss Stein is not only a metaphysician; she is an artist. In varying degrees artists, likewise, have always sought to invent their own terms. The highest intuitions toward a theory of time, of knowledge, or of the creative act have always passed beyond the realm of "textbook" exposition. When the metaphysician is combined with the poet we get such unusual modes of expression as the myths in Plato, the prophetic books of Blake, and the difficult, highly figured phrases in Keats's letters. Miss Stein's style in this book might be described as a succession of "metaphysical metaphors." On the first page, for example, we read:

> If nobody had to die how would there be room enough for any of us who now live to have lived. We never could have been if all the others had not died. There would have been no room.
> Now the relation of human nature to the human mind is this.
> Human nature does not know this. . . .
> But the human mind can. . . .

(Human Nature, hugging identity-survival, cannot realize a non-self situation. The Human Mind, knowing no time and identity in itself, can realize this as an objective fact of experience.)

Similarly, further down we come upon the question:

> What is the use of being a little boy if you are going to grow to be a man?

(Since the Human Mind, existing, does not feel its past as relevant, why does succession in identity have any importance? What is the purpose of living in time? One cannot realize what one was like four seconds ago, four months ago, twenty years ago. "Only when I look in the mirror," said Picasso's mother, "do I realize that I am the mother of a grown-up man.")

This book is a series of such condensations, some of them, like the plays and the "detective stories" about pi-

geons, of considerable difficulty. These latter, it is only fair
to add, have, with a number of other passages, so far exceeded the delighted but inadequate powers of this commentator. The book presupposes that the reader has long
speculated on such matters and is willing and able to assimilate another person's "private language"—and in this
realm what can one give or receive, at best, but glimpses
of an inevitably private language?

The third reason that renders this style difficult for many
readers proceeds from the author's humor. Metaphysics is
difficult enough; metaphysics by an artist is still more difficult;
but metaphysics by an artist in a mood of gaiety is the most
difficult of all. The subject matter of this book is grave indeed;
and there is evidence throughout of the pain it cost to express
and think these things. (It is not without "tears" that Human
Nature is found to be uninteresting and through a gradual
revelation is discovered to be sharing most of its dignities with
dogs.) But Miss Stein has always placed much emphasis on the
spirit of play in an artist's work. The reward of difficult thinking is an inner exhilaration. Here is delight in words and in
the virtuosity of using them exactly; here is wit; here is mockery at the predecessors who approached these matters with so
cumbrous a solemnity. One of the aspects of play that most
upsets some readers is what might be called "the irruption of
the daily life" into the texture of the work. Miss Stein chooses
her illustrations from the life about her. She introduces
her friends, her dogs, her neighbors. Lolo, about whom
gather the speculations as to the nature of romance, lived
and died in a house that could be seen from Miss Stein's terrace in the south of France. She weaves into the book the
very remarks let fall in her vicinity during the act of writing. Similarly, at one period Picasso pasted subway tick-
ets upon his oil paintings; one aspect of the "real" by juxtaposition gives vitality to another aspect of the real, the
created.

But why doesn't Miss Stein at least aid the reader by punctuating her sentences as we are accustomed to find them? And why does she repeat herself so often?

A great many authors have lately become impatient with the inadequacy of punctuation. Many think that new signs should be invented; signs to imitate the variation in human speech; signs for emphasis; signs for word-groupings. Miss Stein, however, feels that such indications harm rather than help the practice of reading. They impair the collaborative participation of the reader.

> A comma by helping you along holding your coat for you and putting on your shoes keeps you from living your life as actively as you should live it. . . . A long complicated sentence should force itself upon you, make yourself know yourself knowing it.

The answer to the charge of repetition is on many levels. On one level Miss Stein points out that repetition is in all nature. It is in human life:

> . . . if you listen to anyone, behind what anyone is saying whether it's about the weather or anything, you will hear that person repeating and repeating himself.

Repeating is emphasis. Every time a thing is repeated it is slightly different.

> The only time that repeating is really repeating, that is when it is dead, is when something is being taught.

Then it does not come from the creating mind, but from unliving forms. Sometimes Miss Stein's repeating is for emphasis in a progression of ideas; sometimes it is as a musical refrain; sometimes it is for a reassembling of the motifs of the book and their re-emergence into a later stage of the discussion; sometimes it is in the spirit of play.

But if this book is about the psychology of the creative act, why is it also called *The Geographical History of America?*

Miss Stein, believing the intermittent emergence of the Human Mind and its record in literary masterpieces to be the most important manifestation of human culture, observed that these emergences were dependent upon the geographical situations in which the authors lived. The valley-born and the hill-bounded tended to exhibit a localization in their thinking, an insistence on identity with all the resultant traits that dwell in Human Nature; flat lands or countries surrounded by the long, straight lines of the sea were conducive toward developing the power of abstraction. Flat lands are an invitation to wander, as well as a release from local assertion. Consequently, a country like the United States, bounded by two oceans and with vast portions so flat that the state boundaries must be drawn by "imaginary lines," without dependence on geographical features, promises to produce a civilization in which the Human Mind may not only appear in the occasional masterpiece, but may in many of its aspects be distributed throughout the people.

Miss Stein's theory of the audience insists upon the fact that the richest rewards for the reader have come from those works in which the authors admitted no consideration of an audience into their creating mind. There have been too many books that attempted to flatter or woo or persuade or coerce the reader. Here is a book that says what it knows: a work of philosophy, a work of art, and a work of gaiety.

GERTRUDE STEIN'S
FOUR IN AMERICA

Miss Gertrude Stein, answering a question about her line

> Rose is a rose is a rose is a rose,

once said with characteristic vehemence:

> Now listen! I'm no fool. I know that in daily life we don't go around saying "is a . . . is a . . . is a . . ."

She knew that she was a difficult and an idiosyncratic author. She pursued her aims, however, with such conviction and intensity that occasionally she forgot that the results could be difficult to others. At such times the achievements she had made in writing, in "telling what she knew" (her most frequent formulization of the aim of writing), had to her the character of self-evident beauty and clarity. A friend, to whom she showed recently completed examples of her poetry, was frequently driven to reply sadly: "But you forget that I don't understand examples of your extremer styles." To this she would reply with a mixture of bewilderment, distress, and exasperation:

> But what's the difficulty? Just read the words on the paper. They're in English. Just read them. Be simple and you'll understand these things.

The introduction to Gertrude Stein's *Four in America,* published in New Haven by the Yale University Press in 1947.

Now let me quote the whole speech from which the opening remark in this introduction has been extracted. A student in her seminar at the University of Chicago had asked her for an "explanation" of the famous line. She leaned forward, giving all of herself to the questioner in that unforgettable way which has endeared her to hundreds of students and to hundreds of soldiers in two wars, trenchant, humorous, but above all urgently concerned over the enlightenment of even the most obtuse questioner:

> Now listen! Can't you see that when the language was new
> —as it was with Chaucer and Homer—the poet could use the
> name of a thing and the thing was really there? He could say
> "O moon," "O sea," "O love" and the moon and the sea and
> love were really there. And can't you see that after hundreds
> of years had gone by and thousands of poems had been writ-
> ten, he could call on those words and find that they were just
> worn-out literary words? The excitingness of pure being had
> withdrawn from them; they were just rather stale literary
> words. Now the poet has to work in the excitingness of pure
> being; he has to get back that intensity into the language. We
> all know that it's hard to write poetry in a late age; and we
> know that you have to put some strangeness, something unex-
> pected, into the structure of the sentence in order to bring
> back vitality to the noun. Now it's not enough to be bizarre;
> the strangeness in the sentence structure has to come from the
> poetic gift, too. That's why it's doubly hard to be a poet in a
> late age. Now you all have seen hundreds of poems about
> roses and you know in your bones that the rose is not there.
> All those songs that sopranos sing as encores about "I have a
> garden; oh, what a garden!" Now I don't want to put too
> much emphasis on that line, because it's just one line in a
> longer poem. But I notice that you all know it; you make fun
> of it, but you know it. Now listen! I'm no fool. I know that
> in daily life we don't go around saying "is a . . . is a . . . is a
> . . ." Yes, I'm no fool; but I think that in that line the rose is
> red for the first time in English poetry for a hundred years.

Four in America is full of that "strangeness which must come
from the poetic gift" in order to restore intensity to images
dusted over with accustomedness and routine. It is not required in poetry alone; for Miss Stein all intellectual activities
—philosophical speculation, literary criticism, narration—had
to be refreshed at the source.

There are certain of her idiosyncrasies which by this time
should not require discussion—for example, her punctuation and her recourse to repetition. Readers who still balk
at these should not attempt to read this volume, for it contains idiosyncrasies far more taxing to conventional taste.
The majority of readers ask of literature the kind of pleasure they have always received; they want "more of the
same"; they accept idiosyncrasy in author and period only
when it has been consecrated by a long-accumulated prestige, as in the cases of the earliest and the latest of Shakespeare's styles, and in the poetry of Donne, Gerard Manley
Hopkins, or Emily Dickinson. They arrogate to themselves
a superiority in condemning the novels of Kafka or of the
later Joyce or the later Henry James, forgetting that they
allow a no less astonishing individuality to Laurence Sterne
and to Rabelais.

This work is for those who not only largely accord to others
"another's way," but who rejoice in the diversity of minds and
the tension of difference.

Miss Stein once said:

> Every masterpiece came into the world with a measure of
> ugliness in it. That ugliness is the sign of the creator's struggle
> to say a new thing in a new way, for an artist can never repeat
> yesterday's success. And after every great creator there fol-
> lows a second man who shows how it can be done easily.
> Picasso struggled and made his new thing and then Braque
> came along and showed how it could be done without pain.
> The Sistine Madonna of Raphael is all over the world, on
> grocers' calendars and on Christmas cards; everybody thinks

it's an easy picture. It's our business as critics to stand in front
of it and recover its ugliness.

This book is full of that kind of ugliness. It is perhaps
enough to say: "Be simple and you will understand these
things"; but it is necessary to say: "Relax your predilection for
the accustomed, the received, and be ready to accept an extreme example of idiosyncratic writing."

Distributed throughout Miss Stein's books and in the *Lectures in America* can be found an account of her successive
discoveries and aims as a writer. She did not admit that the
word "experiments" be applied to them.

> Artists do not experiment. Experiment is what scientists do;
> they initiate an operation of unknown factors in order to be
> instructed by its results. An artist puts down what he knows
> and at every moment it is what he knows at that moment. If
> he is trying things out to see how they go he is a bad artist.

A brief recapitulation of the history of her aims will help us
to understand her work.

Gertrude Stein left Radcliffe College with William James's
warm endorsement, to study psychology at Johns Hopkins
University. There,* as a research problem, her professor gave
her a study of automatic writing. For this work she called upon
her fellow students—the number ran into the hundreds—to
serve as experimental subjects. Her interest, however, took an
unexpected turn; she became more absorbed in the subjects'
varying approach to the experiments than in the experiments
themselves. They entered the room with alarm, with docility,
with bravado, with gravity, with scorn, or with indifference.
This striking variation re-awoke within her an interest which

*EDITOR'S NOTE: Thornton Wilder was incorrect in locating Gertrude Stein's work
with motor automatism at Johns Hopkins. Her research was done under William
James while she was still at Radcliffe and its results were published in the *Psychological
Review* for September 1896 and May 1898.

had obsessed her even in very early childhood—the conviction that a description could be made of all the types of human
character and that these types could be related to two basic
types (she called them independent-dependents and depend-
ent-independents). She left the university and, settling in
Paris, applied herself to the problem. The result was the novel
of one thousand pages, *The Making of Americans,* which is at
once an account of a large family from the time of the grand-
parents' coming to this country from Europe and a description
of "everyone who is, or has been, or will be." She then went
on to give in *A Long Gay Book* an account of all possible
relations of two persons. This book, however, broke down
soon after it began. Miss Stein had been invaded by another
compelling problem: How, in our time, do you describe anything? In the previous centuries writers had managed pretty
well by assembling a number of adjectives and adjectival
clauses side by side; the reader "obeyed" by furnishing images
and concepts in his mind and the resultant "thing" in the
reader's mind corresponded fairly well with that in the
writer's. Miss Stein felt that that process did not work any
more. Her painter friends were showing clearly that the corresponding method of "description" had broken down in painting and she was sure that it had broken down in writing.

In the first place, words were no longer precise; they were
full of extraneous matter. They were full of "remembering"
—and describing a thing in front of us, an "objective thing,"
is no time for remembering. Even vision (a particularly over-
charged word), even sight had been dulled by remembering.
The painters of the preceding generation, the Impressionists,
had shown that. Hitherto people had known that, close to, a
whitewashed wall had no purple in it; at a distance it might
have a great deal of purple, but many painters had not allowed
themselves to see purple in a distant whitewashed wall because
they remembered that close to it was uniformly white. The
Impressionists had shown us the red in green trees; the Post-

Impressionists showed us that our entire sense of form, our very view of things, was all distorted and distorting and "educated" and adjusted by memory. Miss Stein felt that writing must accomplish a revolution whereby it could report things as they were in themselves before our minds had appropriated them and robbed them of their objectivity "in pure existing." To this end she went about her house describing the objects she found there in the series of short "poems" which make up the volume called *Tender Buttons*.

Here is one of these:

Red Roses

A cool red rose and a pink cut pink, a collapse and a sold hole, a little less hot.

Miss Stein had now entered upon a period of excited discovery, intense concentration, and enormous productivity. She went on to writing portraits of her friends and of places. She revived an old interest in drama and wrote scores of plays, many of which are themselves portraits of friends and of places. Two of her lectures in *Lectures in America* describe her aims in these kinds of work. She meditated long on the nature of narration and wrote the novel *Lucy Church Amiably*. This novel is a description of a landscape near Bilignin, her summer home in the south of France. Its subtitle and epigraph are: "A Novel of Romantic Beauty and Nature and which Looks Like an Engraving . . . 'and with a nod she turned her head toward the falling water. Amiably.' "

Those who had the opportunity of seeing Miss Stein in the daily life of her home will never forget an impressive realization of her practice of meditating. She set aside a certain part of every day for it. In Bilignin she would sit in her rocking chair facing the valley she has described so often, holding one or the other of her dogs on her lap. Following the practice of a lifetime, she would rigorously pursue some subject in thought, taking it up where she had left it on the previous day.

Her conversation would reveal the current preoccupation: it would be the nature of "money," or "masterpieces," or "superstition," or "the Republican party." She had always been an omnivorous reader. As a small girl she had sat for days at a time in a window seat in the Marine Institute Library in San Francisco, an endowed institution with few visitors, reading all Elizabethan literature, including its prose, reading all Swift, Burke, and Defoe. Later in life her reading remained as wide but was strangely non-selective. She read whatever books came her way. ("I have a great deal of inertia. I need things from outside to start me off.") The Church of England at Aix-les-Bains sold its Sunday-school library, the accumulation of seventy years, at a few francs for every ten volumes. They included some thirty minor English novels of the 'seventies, the stately lives of colonial governors, the lives of missionaries. She read them all. Any written thing had become sheer phenomenon; for the purposes of her reflections, absence of quality was as instructive as quality. Quality was sufficiently supplied by Shakespeare, whose works lay often at her hand. If there was any subject which drew her from her inertia and led her actually to seek out works, it was American history and particularly books about the Civil War.

And always with her great relish for human beings she was listening to people. She was listening with genial absorption to the matters in which they were involved.

> Everybody's life is full of stories; your life is full of stories; my life is full of stories. They are very occupying, but they are not really interesting. What is interesting is the way everyone tells their stories.

And at the same time she was listening to the tellers' revelation of their "basic nature."

> If you listen, really listen, you will hear people repeating themselves. You will hear their pleading nature or their attacking nature or their asserting nature. People who say that I repeat too much do not really listen; they cannot hear

that every moment of life is full of repeating. There is only
one repeating that is really dead and that is when a thing is
taught.

She even listened intently to dog nature. The often-ridiculed
statement is literally true that it was from listening to her
French poodle Basket lapping water that she discovered the
distinction between prose and poetry.

It can easily be understood that the questions she was asking
concerning personality and the nature of language and concerning "how you tell a thing" would inevitably lead to the
formulization of a metaphysics. In fact, I think it can be said
that the fundamental occupation of Miss Stein's life was not
the work of art but the shaping of a theory of knowledge, a
theory of time, and a theory of the passions. These theories
finally converged on the master question: What are the various
ways in which creativity works in everyone? That is the subject
of this book. It is a subject which she was to develop more
specifically in a book which of all her works is most closely
related to this one: *The Geographical History of America or The
Relation of Human Nature to the Human Mind.* It led also to a
reconsideration of all literature, reflected in the beautiful lecture "What Are Masterpieces and Why Are There So Few of
Them?"

Miss Stein held a doctrine which permeates this book, which
informs her theory of creativity, which plays a large part in her
demonstration of what an American is, and which helps to
explain some of the great difficulty which we feel in reading
her work. It is the Doctrine of Audience; its literary aspect is
considered in the Theory of the Moment of Recognition. In
The Geographical History of America it is made to illustrate a
Theory of Identity.

Let me enter into the subject by again quoting from her
words in a conversation:

Why is it that no preachers, no teachers, no orators, no parliamentary debaters ever have any ideas after the age of thirty-five? It is because when they talk they only hear what the audience is hearing. They get mixed up in their head and think that it is possible for one person to agree totally with another person; and when you think *that* you are lost and never have any ideas any more. Now what we know is formed in our head by thousands of small occasions in the daily life. By "what we know" I do not mean, of course, what we learn from books, because that is of no importance at all. I mean what we really know, like our assurance about how we know anything, and what we know about the validity of the sentiments, and things like that. All the thousands of occasions in the daily life go into our head to form our ideas about these things. Now if we write, we write; and these things we know flow down our arm and come out on the page. The moment before we wrote them we did not really know we knew them; if they are in our head in the shape of words then that is all wrong and they will come out dead; but if we did not know we knew them until the moment of writing, then they come to us with a shock of surprise. That is the Moment of Recognition. Like God on the Seventh Day we look at it and say it is good. That is the moment that some people call inspiration, but I do not like the word inspiration, because it suggests that someone else is blowing that knowledge into you. It is not being blown into you; it is very much your own and was acquired by you in thousands of tiny occasions in your daily life. Now, of course, there is no audience at that moment. There is no one whom you are instructing, or fighting, or improving, or pleasing, or provoking. To others it may appear that you are doing all those things to them, but of course you are not. At that moment you are totally alone at this recognition of what you know. And of that thing which you have written you are the first and last audience. This thing which you have written is bought by other people and read by them. It goes through their eyes into their heads and they say they agree with it. But, of course, they cannot agree with it. The things they know have been built up by thousands of small occasions which are different from yours. They *say* they agree with you; what they mean is that they are aware that your pages have the vitality of a thing which sounds to them like someone else's knowing; it is consistent to its own world of what one person has really known. That is a great pleasure and the highest compliment they can pay it is to say that they agree with it.

Now these preachers and orators may have had such moments of recognition when they were young; they may even have had them when they are addressing an audience—though that is very rare. After they have faced a great many audiences they begin to think that the audiences are literally understanding, literally agreeing with them, instead of merely being present at the vitality of these moments of recognition, at their surprising themselves with their own discovery of what they know. Then they gradually slip in more of the kind of ideas that people can agree with, ideas which are not really ideas at all, which are soothing but not exciting—oh, yes, they may be exciting as oratory, but they are not exciting as creation—and after a while they dry up and then they do not have any real ideas any more.

A portion of the ideas expressed above is found in the "Henry James" section of the present book:

> Mr. Owen Young made a mistake, he said the only thing he wished his son to have was the power of clearly expressing his ideas. Not at all. It is not clarity that is desirable but force.
>
> Clarity is of no importance because nobody listens and nobody knows what you mean no matter what you mean, nor how clearly you mean what you mean. But if you have vitality enough of knowing enough of what you mean, somebody and sometime and sometimes a great many will have to realise that you know what you mean and so they will agree that you mean what you know, what you know you mean, which is as near as anybody can come to understanding any one.

Miss Stein never claimed that these doctrines were new. She delighted in finding them in the great works of the past. She was never tired of saying that all real knowledge is common knowledge; it lies sleeping within us; it is awakened in us when we hear it expressed by a person who is speaking or writing in a state of recognition.

From consciousness of audience, then, come all the evils of thinking, writing, and creating. In *The Geographical History of America* she illustrates the idea by distinguishing between our human nature and our human mind. Our human nature is a serpents' nest, all directed to audience; from it proceed self-justification, jealousy, propaganda, individualism, moralizing, and edification. How comforting it is, and how ignobly pleased we are when we see it expressed in literature. The human mind, however, gazes at experience and without deflection by the insidious pressures from human nature tells what it sees and knows. Its subject matter is indeed human nature; to cite two of Miss Stein's favorites, *Hamlet* and *Pride and Prejudice* are about human nature, but not of it. The survival of masterpieces, and there are very few of them, is due to our astonishment that certain minds can occasionally report life without adulterating the report with the gratifying movements of their own self-assertion, their private quarrel with what it has been to be a human being.

Miss Stein pushed to its furthest extreme this position that at the moment of writing one rigorously excludes from the mind all thought of praise and blame, of persuasion or conciliation. In the early days she used to say: "I write for myself and strangers." Then she eliminated the strangers; then she had a great deal of trouble with the idea that one is an audience to oneself, which she solves in this book with the far-reaching concept: "I am not I when I see."

It has often seemed to me that Miss Stein was engaged in a series of spiritual exercises whose aim was to eliminate during the hours of writing all those whispers into the ear from the outside and inside world where audience dwells. She knew that she was the object of derision to many and to some extent the knowledge fortified her. Yet it is very moving to learn that on one occasion when a friend asked her what a writer most wanted, she replied, throwing up her hands and laughing, "Oh, praise, praise, praise!" Some of the devices that most exasperate readers—such as the capricious headings of subdivisions in her work, such sequences as Book IV, Book VII, Book VIII, Volume I—though in part they are there to make fun of pompous heads who pretend to an organic development and have no development, are at bottom merely attempts to nip in the bud by a drastic intrusion of apparent incoherence any ambition she may have felt within herself to woo for acceptance as a "respectable" philosopher. It should be noted that another philosopher who wrestled with the problem of restating the mind of man in the terms of our times and who has emerged as perhaps the most disturbing and stimulating voice of the nineteenth century—Søren Kierkegaard—delayed his recognition and "put off" his readers by many a mystification and by an occasional resort to almost Aristophanic buffoonery.

There is another evidence of Miss Stein's struggle to keep her audience out of her mind. *Four in America* is not a book which is the end and summary of her thoughts about the subjects she has chosen; it is the record of her thoughts, from the beginning, as she "closes in" on them. It is *being written* before our eyes; she does not, as other writers do, suppress and erase the hesitations, the recapitulations, the connectives, in order to give us the completed fine result of her meditations. She gives us the process. From time to time we hear her groping toward the next idea; we hear her cry of joy when she has found it; sometimes it seems to me that we hear her reiterating the already achieved idea and, as it were, pumping it in order to force out the next development that lies hidden within it. We hear her talking to herself about the book that is growing and glowing (to borrow her often irritating habit of rhyming) within her. Many readers will not like this, but at least it is evidence that she is ensuring the purity of her indifference as to whether her readers will like it or not. It is as though she were afraid that if she went back and weeded out all these signs of groping and shaping and reassembling, if she gave us only the completed thoughts in their last best order, the truth would have slipped away like water through a sieve because such a final marshaling of her thoughts would have been directed toward audience. Her description of existence would be, like so many hundreds of thousands of descriptions of existence, like most literature—dead.

Another spiritual exercise she practices is no less disconcerting. She introduces what I like to call "the irruption of the daily life." If her two dogs are playing at her feet while she is writing she puts them into the text. She may suddenly introduce some phrases she has just heard over the garden wall. This resembles a practice that her friends the Post-Impressionist painters occasionally resorted to. They pasted a subway ticket to the surface of their painting. The reality of a work of art is one reality; the reality of a "thing" is another reality; the juxtaposition of the two kinds of reality gives a bracing shock. It also insults the reader; but the reader is not present, nor even imagined. It refreshes in the writer the sense that the writer is all alone, alone with his thoughts and his struggle and even with his relation to the outside world that lies about him.

The fourth section of this book, by far the most difficult, seems to me to be full of these voices and irruptions. Miss Stein is sitting on the terrace of her villa at Bilignin toward the end of the day. The subject of George Washington comes toward her from a distance:

> Autumn scenery is warm if the fog has lifted.
> And the moon has set in the day-time in what may be drifting clouds. . . .
> George Washington was and is the father of his country. . . .

It should not be a disturbance if they can mistake a bird for
a bat or a bat for a bird and find it friendly.

At first view the plan of this book appears to furnish little
more than a witty diversion, a parlor game—What kind of
novels would George Washington have written? What kind of
military strategy would Henry James have devised? One soon
discovers, however, that it is a very earnest game indeed. It
asks about "how creativity works in any one," about the relations between personality and gifts, personality and genius.
No less searchingly, it asks another question: What is an
American and what makes him different from a citizen of any
other country?

Soon after Miss Stein settled in France for an almost unbroken residence of over forty years a very unusual thing
happened to her: she was really taken into a number of French
homes. She was told their secrets, told their finances, and told
their politics. That must seldom have happened to any American who was at once so loved, so tirelessly ready to listen to
details, and who had so consuming a passion to reduce the
multitudinous occasions of the daily life to psychological and
philosophical laws.

In addition, she spent some time in England during the
earlier part of the War of 1914–18. She spent a number of
summers in Spain and related what she saw to the characters of her three close friends, the Spanish painters Picasso,
Juan Gris, and Picabia. All the time, however, she was
meeting and "listening" to Americans and the contacts
with Europeans continued to sharpen her perception of
specific American nature. When after thirty years' absence
she returned to America and traveled it from coast to coast
her delight was not only in the experience itself; it was also
the delight of seeing her conclusions confirmed and extended.

The section on Ulysses S. Grant begins with a lively discussion of the relations between people and the Christian names they bear. Miss Stein relates it to superstition and to religion, as later she will relate it to the spell cast by novelists, the novelist Henry James and the hypothetical novelist George Washington.

She is tracking down certain irrational ways we have of knowing things, of believing things, and of being governed by these ways of believing. Even the strongest minds have been nonplussed and rendered angry by the extent to which they can be caught up into belief by imaginative narration. One remembers St. Augustine's anguished repudiation of the hold which theatrical performances had taken of him in Carthage. "Novels are true," says Miss Stein. Similarly, great minds have tried to revolt from the sway that superstition can exert over them—involuntarily downcast by omens, predictions, recurrences of certain numbers—just as lesser minds can be given courage by a palm-reading and can be crossed with fear by a broken mirror. There is no "truth" in these things, people say; but perhaps man knows nothing and will never know anything; the important thing is that he behaves as though he knew something and the irrational ways of knowing which are found in religion and superstition and in submission to a novel are among the more powerful driving forces toward how he behaves.

Miss Stein is talking about religion throughout this section and she is furnishing analogies to the kind of "knowing" that goes to make up religious belief. One of them is the haunting sense that your name is the right name for you.

Religion, as Miss Stein uses the term, has very little to do with cults and dogma, particularly in America. She makes a score of attempts to define it, but the attempts result in fragmentary analogies, straining the syntax of the English language to express flashes of insight. Religion is what a person knows—knows beyond knowing, knows beyond anyone's power to teach him—about his relation to the existence in which he finds himself. It is the tacit assumption that governs his "doing anything that he does do," his creativity. "Religion is what is alright if they have to have their ups and downs." "Religion is not a surprise but it is exciting." "There is no advice in American religion." "American religion is what they could not compare with themselves." "Nobody in America need be careful to be alone, not in American religion. . . ."

To illustrate what American religion is, she first chooses the figure of a camp meeting. There is no leader, or, to put it more exactly, there is a leader but the people are not led. Here is the first striking difference from European religion. It is in the open; there is even some deliberation as to whether the trees have to be there. Just as we hear that Americans have no home, just because their whole country is their home, so their church really has no house. The fact is Americans do not localize anything, not even themselves, as the whole book constantly reiterates. Here again we are a long way from European religion. Moreover, American religion is thanking, not supplication. Americans do not even wish. We shall see the extent to which they do not "wait"; they are not "ready," except in limited contingencies, they do not "prepare"—so little does an American believe that one forces circumstances to one's will. It is at the very heart of American religion that the majority of Americans "like what they have," and readers of *The Geographical History of America* will see how this relative absence of resenting the universe, despising the universe, try-ing to subjugate or reshape a "destiny" derives from the physi-cal constitution of our country and the problems our pioneers met. Now, in a camp meeting some walk up and down, some stand, some sing, some kneel, some wail; there is a leader but they are not led; and a congregation of four hundred is not four hundred, but it is one and one and one and one . . . up to four hundred.

The foregoing does not mean that Americans are passive.

The true passivity—that is, the true slavery and the true ineffectiveness—is to wish and to wait and to yearn and to conspire. Nor does the group that is one and one and one, and so on, mean that the American is an uncurbed individualist, for "they all go forward together." "They act as if they all go together one by one and so any one is not leading." "Go forward" has no moralizing sense; in Gertrude Stein it is hard to find a moralizing sense. Moralizing comes from that realm of belief which is acquired, learned, arrogated to oneself and promulgated; but which is not truly believed or lived by.

The passage to the effect that Americans cannot earn a living or be a success is likely to cause the bewildered astonishment that it first aroused in Miss Stein. ("Now, Lizzie, do you understand?") It is conceded that some Americans can make money, and that they can do what they have to do and that they can become "names which everyone knows," but that is not the same thing. Again Miss Stein is seeing Americans against her immense knowledge of French domestic life, compared to which the American relation to money is frivolous and the American relation to the whole practical side of life is without perseverance, foresight, or thorough application. The French would put it overwhelmingly that we are not *"sérieux."* In conversation Miss Stein went even further; she said that "Americans are really only happy when they are failures," and laughing deeply she would furnish a wealth of illustration. Again the reader should be warned against interpreting this passage in moralizing terms; this is not the sentimental commonplace that life's failures are the true successes nor does it mean that Americans are unworldly knights-errant. An American's inability to make a living is not a consequence of his "values" but of the way his mind works in him.

The portrait of an American is then beginning to assemble about the image of General Grant and his hypothetical alter ego, Hiram Grant, retired from the army and become very busily a failure in the harness store at Galena, Illinois. He did not wait for the great position that would someday fall to him, because Americans do not wait—that is, they do not live in the expectation that circumstance is coming toward them bearing gifts. There is no animism in American religion. The skies do not pity nor punish nor bring gifts. Nor does her American yearn, strain, or intrigue for the situations he may profit by; he is what he is, and what he *is,* not what he *wills,* is his expression. Some of the most exasperating of Miss Stein's phrases are employed to express this aspect of her subject. She seems to have a low opinion of the verb "sit," which to her expresses both the passivity and the expectancy which are not present in her Americans. Apparently, the word "there" and the verbs "come" and "go" all imply a degree of intention that is not in her Americans. So we get such upsetting combinations of these usages as: "Ulysses Simpson Grant was there as often as he came but he never came."

All this prepares us for the statement that Americans never die; they are killed or they go away, but they are not dead. This is in great contrast, of course, to the Europeans, who "wait for" their death, prepare, resist, foresee, bewail, or accept their death. This she puts down to the American sky, which is not really a sky but is just air; but it is obviously related to the other elements of the American religion, that all you have is in every moment of your consciousness (and that you like all that you have) and so self-contained is every moment of consciousness that there is nothing left over for expectation or memory. The American, then, who has lost that moment of consciousness is not that European thing called "dead"—so fraught with immemorial connotations—he has gone away. For this Miss Stein finds the striking image that every American is an only child—is *one,* has everything, and is the center of everything—is then naturally very solemn and cannot die.

This is followed by an apparently difficult passage which, however, yields us some light on a number of Miss Stein's

most characteristic locutions. General Grant was not "one of two" or "one of three"; for relief or guidance or comfort or support he did not ally himself with anyone else and even when he came to fill that high station for which he had not been waiting he was "not differently surrounded by himself" —surrounded, of course, he was, as we all are, but "surround does not mean surrender" (and surrender is here not the act of war but the loss of one's own knowing: "This is what I mean and this will I do").

So we begin to see what kind of a saint General Grant would have been if he had been a leader in religion. And now we see another reason why I went to some length to discuss Miss Stein's theory of Audience and her theory of the distinction between human nature and the human mind. It looks as though General Ulysses S. Grant and the saint he might have been had it in common that they did not listen to those seductive appeals from the Audience which keep crowding up from human nature. Neither Grant waited nor was anxious; neither came nor sat; both "knew what they knew at the moment of knowing it," a knowledge unsullied by expectation or memory. They did not let will or determination order them about; they did what they did, but they did not set about to do what they were to do.

One word hovers over the entire book and is never spoken. It is the word "abstract." American religion is presented as very abstract, and so are the mentalities of the Americans described here who are certainly prototypes of the generalized American. In *The Geographical History of America* Miss Stein goes on to explain that such minds are so formed by the physical character of the environment in which they live. "Everyone is as their land and water and sky are," and in America there is no sky—there is just air; there is just "up"; the majority of Americans, in addition, either know the straight line of the sea or the lake, or they know a land so devoid of natural features that "when they make the boundary of a State they

have to make it with a straight line." In European geography
there are no boundaries which are straight lines.

The section on Wilbur Wright begins with another teas-
ing play with Christian names. The reader can now share
Miss Stein's delighted consternation on receiving a letter
from a man named Ulysses Lee. "And there is nothing
more to be said is there. Names call to names as birds call
to birds." We have learned what a "Ulysses" nature is; a
nature of that degree of abstraction could conceivably be
born into a situation in which he would find himself called
Ulysses Lee.

In driving through Le Mans Miss Stein once came upon the
monument which the French had raised to Wilbur Wright.
She tells us that she was struck with the "funny feeling" that
Wilbur Wright was not there. France contains many monuments to its eminent dead and in a way she felt that their
eminent dead were there. As she has told us, Americans do not
die, they go away; but it was very clear that they do not go
away to their monuments. This set her brooding again about
American religion and American death and about Wilbur
Wright and how he made what he made. Presently she found
a relationship between aviation and painting and between
painting and acting.

Now a writer is not confronted by his past books. They are
not even there in his mind, staring at him. His past work is not
an audience to him. He is not his work and he is not connected
to his work, save at the moment of creation. All painters,
however, and particularly European painters, are surrounded
by their paintings, even if their paintings are distributed all
over the world. They are "extended" to their paintings. They
are not alone. And the paintings are not "left"—are not rele-
gated to a place outside consciousness. We are repeatedly told
that no painting can be "left."

This has something to do with seeing, and leads to a similar
situation in actors and in Wilbur Wright. Actors in a profound

sense see rather than hear what they say. (The words are but a small part of the creativity in their art and the words having been created in the "recognition" of the dramatist are resumed by the actor into his total creation, which is preponderantly visual. He "paints" a rôle employing the words of the dramatist as the raw material of his painting, just as his face, body, voice, and dress are raw material. It is in this sense that he "sees what he says.")

These creators who see their past work are eternally surrounded by it and are not alone. This is not urged as a reproach upon them; it is the character of their creativity; nor is their past work an audience to them in a bad sense, for they are their creativity, past and present. In the vocabulary of Miss Stein seeing always stands high. She enjoyed repeating that "seeing is believing." Readers will remark that among these thousands of references to creativity there is no reference to music. "Music is for adolescents," she used to say. The eye is closer to the human mind, the ear to human nature. She had passed through a phase of her life as an impassioned and informed music-lover and had put it behind her. Only once have I heard her concede that music—it was after a hearing of Beethoven's "Archduke" Trio—can occasionally issue from the human mind.

A reader having reached the middle point in the Wilbur Wright section is presumably becoming accustomed to Miss Stein's disregard for the first or generally received meanings of words and to her powerful compressions. (They have a relationship by contrast with her repetitions: a repetition is a small degree of progression by alteration and emphasis; a compression is a sweeping summary or a violent leap into new matter.) A reader is ready for such a passage as the following (the punctuation is impertinently mine):

> A painting is something seen after it has been done and—in this way—left alone; nobody can say: "he—or I—left it alone." No painting is left alone.

The airplane was that kind of creation and the man whose work it was to make the flying machine and to fly it saw himself moving; he was in his creation as a painter is in and of his painting.

There are many difficulties in this section for which I am not competent to furnish a gloss. The day will come when devoted readers of Miss Stein will furnish a lexicon of her locutions. There are hundreds of them which may strike a first reader as incoherent expressions thrown off at random; but they are found recurringly distributed throughout her work. The task of her future commentators will consist in tracing them to their earliest appearances embedded in a context which furnishes the meaning they held for her. Thereafter they became bricks in her building, implements in her meditation. To her their meaning is "self-evident"; she forgets that we have not participated in the systematic meditation which was her life.

I leave to the reader's contemplation also the spectacle of the extraordinary emotion which accumulates toward the end of each of these sections. Miss Stein loves, overwhelmingly loves, each of the heroes of this volume. "Who knows what Grant did. I do." "It is Ulysses S. Grant that is interesting, very interesting." "I cannot think of Ulysses Simpson Grant without tears." "Wilbur Wright is fine." "East and West. George Washington is best."

The Henry James section begins with Miss Stein's account of how she came to make an important discovery concerning writing. It is a curious thing to me that in each of her retellings of this story she has omitted a fact that throws further light on it. This fact is that when she wrote the poems called *Before the Flowers of Friendship Faded Friendship Faded* she began writing them as translations of a group of poems in French by her friend Georges Hugnet. They are far from being literal translations, even in the beginning, but they take their point of departure from his poems, and they remained, as her discussion shows, "the poems he would have written if he had written them."

Hence, she was not writing "what she wrote, but what she intended to write." A sort of ventriloquism had introduced itself into the process of writing, and she became aware that the words had a sort of smoothness which they did not have in the poems which she wrote "from herself alone." Suddenly this smoothness reminded her of a smoothness she had long noticed in Shakespeare's *Sonnets*. She says (in the fourth lecture on *Narration*):

> I concluded then that Shakespeare's sonnets were not written to express his own emotion I concluded that he put down what some one told him to do as their feeling which they definitely had each time for each sonnet as their feeling and that is the reason that the words in the sonnets come out with a smooth feeling with no vibration in them such as the words in all his plays have as they come out from them.

Many scholars have reached a similar conclusion as to Shakespeare's *Sonnets,* and not only in regard to the series written on the preposterous theme "Go, young man, and get married in order that you may leave a copy of your excellences to the afterworld."

Miss Stein was perhaps a little nettled to find also that the poems of *Before the Flowers of Friendship Faded* gave more pleasure to her friends than her earlier poems had given. This discovery led her straight to the problem of audience. There are two kinds of writing: the kind in which the words mean what they say and the kind in which the "meaning has to be meant as something [that] has been learned"—it has been written to satisfy a preconceived notion as to what it will be like when it is finished, or to satisfy someone else's expectation of it. It is surprising that at this stage of drawing up this distinction she expresses so little disapproval of the second type of writing. She appears to be reconciled to it, it is the way in which the majority of all books have been written.

Henry James, it appears, wrote in a combination of the two ways of writing. In this he resembled a general whose activity consists in doing what he has to do in a situation that has already been prepared. In a general's work for a while "nothing happens together and then all of a sudden it all happens together." For a general and for Henry James "everything that could happen or not happen would have had a preparation."

This treatment of Henry James does indeed awaken a feeling which one had had about his work. It does not mean that other novelists like Fielding, Jane Austen, and Anthony Trollope—to name three for whom she had the highest admiration —did not likewise follow a design and know well in advance the pattern their book was to take. Henry James went further; he finished the book before he wrote it; he wrote the book to resemble a book which he had completely envisaged. Like a general he arrived on a scene which had already been prepared or, as we are repeatedly told, had "been begun." He was to an unprecedented degree an audience to his own composition. We could wish that Miss Stein had helped us through these subtle distinctions by an occasional specific illustration. One is indebted to her, however, for two exquisite characterizations of Henry James's quality. She is speaking of a woman who lived in a *château* near Belley:

> She lived alone and in the country and so did Henry James. She was heavy set and seductive and so was Henry James. She was slow in movement and light in speech and could change her speech without changing her words so that at one time her speech was delicate and witty and at another time slow and troubling and so was that of Henry James.

And again:

He had no fortune and misfortune and nevertheless he had no distress and no relief from any pang. . . . He had no failure and no success and he had no relief from any failure and he had no relief from any distress.

There is an extended portion of this section in which Miss Stein gradually changes into a different style. It is the style of the "Portraits." In fact, when she alludes to this book in one of her *Narration* lectures, she calls it a book of portraits. In her lecture "Portraits and Repetition" she says:

And so I am trying to tell you what doing portraits meant to me, I had to find out what it was inside any one, and by any one I mean every one I had to find out inside every one what was in them that was intrinsically exciting and I had to find out not by what they said not by what they did not by how much or how little they resembled any other one but I had to find it out by the intensity of movement that there was inside in any one of them. . . .

In another place in the lecture she calls this work catching "the rhythm of personality." Opinions on this extreme style vary even among Miss Stein's greatest admirers. Some assure us that from the first reading they obtain a clear image of the personality so described; others acknowledge occasional flashes of insight but hold that Miss Stein was mistaken in thinking that she had been able to convey the "movement" of her sitters' personalities to anyone but herself. Readers who are indebted to her other writings for so wide a variety of pleasures—for the narrative brilliance of *The Autobiography of Alice B. Toklas,* the massive grasp of *The Making of Americans,* the critical insight and aphoristic skill of her lectures, the illumination and the trenchant thinking about fundamentals contained in the present book—such readers will return again and again to the most difficult pages not willingly conceding that these are forever closed to them.

The fourth section, "Scenery and George Washington," has the subtitle "A Novel or a Play." Its characters are "Scenery" and "George Washington." The section opens, as I have said, with an evocation of the valley below Miss Stein's villa at Bilignin toward which comes, as from a distance, the figure of Washington and the inquiry as to what kind of novels he would have written.

Now Miss Stein felt that the novel was threatened with extinction and she was much concerned with whether it could be saved. Her fears concerning it were not based, as those of many critics have been, on the fact that the assumption of omniscience on the part of the storyteller is untenable in our time. Her objection was that what happens "from outside" is no longer important to us, that we are aware of so much happening that the event is no longer exciting; and that we no longer feel that the sequence of events, the succession in time, is of much significance. As she says in the second *Narration* lecture:

> . . . there is at present not a sense of anything being succes-
> sively happening, moving is in every direction beginning and
> ending is not really exciting, anything is anything, anything is
> happening. . . . And this has come to be a natural thing in a
> perfectly natural way that the narrative of today is not a narra-
> tive of succession as all the writing for a good many hundreds
> of years has been.

And in the lecture "Portraits and Repetition" she says:

> A thing you all know is that in the three novels written in
> this generation that are the important things written in this
> generation, there is, in none of them a story. There is none in
> Proust in *The Making of Americans* or in *Ulysses.*

Miss Stein interrupts her discussion to give samples of the event novel, the succession novel, and she assures us that is not the kind of novel George Washington wrote. What he wrote was "the great American novel," an entirely new kind of novel and a thing which, if we can know it, will throw invaluable light on the American nature. With what she calls "Volume VI" begins a flood of definitions—that is, analogical definitions of what this novel is, just as the Grant section furnished a flood of descriptions of what "American religion" is.

In the first place, it has to do with the American time-sense. In the lecture "What Is English Literature" she shows how the English, living for centuries their "daily island life," made their literature out of it.

> They relied on it so completely that they did not describe it they just had it and told it. . . . In America . . . the daily everything was not the daily living and generally speaking there is not a daily everything. They do not live every day . . . and so they do not have this as something that they are telling.

We are back at the abstractedness of the American mind. It does not draw its assurance of knowing anything from an intense localization in time and place. The endless procession of phenomena separate themselves from their specific contingency and reform themselves as a generalized knowing.

> And so . . . Henry James just went on doing what American literature had always done, the form was always the form of the contemporary English one, but the disembodied way of disconnecting something from anything and anything from something was the American one. . . . Some say that it is repression, but no it is not repression it is a lack of connection, of there being no connection with living and daily living because there is none, that makes American writing what it always has been and what it will continue to become.

It should be unnecessary to say that this George Washington was not a novelist because he aesthetically composed his life or because he stood off at a distance and viewed his life. A novelist is sovereign over the elements of his imagined world;

but they have also an objective life (derived from the "knowing" that he has acquired); he may not force or wrench them, nor make them report a fairer world than he has experienced. We seem to be told by Miss Stein that George Washington moved among events like a novelist among his characters at the moment of their creation.

> (I am fond of talking about Napoleon but that has nothing to do with novel writing. Napoleon could not write a novel, not he. Washington could. And did.)

And because he was an American novelist, George Washington was disattached from the concrete and the specific. He could and did love concrete things. ("He was charmed with the dresses of the little baby"—how astonishing are Miss Stein's ways of enclosing the general in the specific! That is an example of the writing which she exalts in the Henry James section, where the "writing and the writer are alike," of a "sound heard by the eyes," and that "does not mean what it says because it just is"—that is, lands squarely on its truth and is only watered down by "preparation" and explanation, as I have watered it down here.) George Washington's love of the concrete in our human life and his pleasure in baby dresses was of the American order; it tended to transmute its experiences from things of human nature to things of the human mind. The human mind cannot be consoled by things nor rendered proud; it does not preach nor despise; it merely sees and tells what it sees. Such a novel George Washington was writing every day.

The pages begin to bristle with Miss Stein's most idiosyncratic expressions and we are again in the "portrait" style. This introduction is already too long to permit of an attempt to wrestle with them. The solution of many of them, however, can be found elsewhere in Miss Stein's work. For example, the long passage on Washington's youth beginning with the disconcerting phrases:

He could just smile if he was born already. . . . And he was
not born. Oh indeed no he was not born

has a history in her work. As early as *A Long Gay Book* Miss
Stein was observing that many people are rendered uneasy,
are even crippled, by the thought that they were once helpless
babies, passed about and tended by others. The dignity of
their human mind (which, of course, knows no age) is undermined by thoughts of themselves in infancy. It is this idea
which grows into fuller statement in *The Geographical History
of America* in the development of the astonishing question:

> What is the use of being a little boy if you are going to grow
> up to be a man?

The word "tears" occurs frequently in this book. What
things in our human lot seem to have moved Miss Stein to
tears? It was not the misfortunes of our human nature, though
she was a greatly sympathetic resource to her friends when
their griefs were real. What moved her deeply was the struggle of the human mind in its work, which is to know. It was
of Henry James's mind (and the phrase applies as beautifully
to those great heroines of his last novels who live not to assert
themselves but to understand) that she says "he had no relief
from any pang."

She said to me once:

> Everyone when they are young has a little bit of genius, that
> is they really do listen. They can listen and talk at the same
> time. Then they grow a little older and many of them get tired
> and they listen less and less. But some, a very few continue to
> listen. And finally they get very old and they do not listen any
> more. That is very sad; let us not talk about that.

This book is by an impassioned listener to life. Even up to her
last years she listened to all comers, to "how their knowing
came out of them." Hundreds of our soldiers, scoffing and
incredulous but urged on by their companions, came up to

Paris "to see the Eiffel Tower and Gertrude Stein." They called and found bent upon them those gay and challenging eyes and that attention that asked nothing less of them than their genius. Neither her company nor her books were for those who have grown tired of listening. It was an irony that she did her work in a world in which for many reasons and for many appalling reasons people have so tired.

TRIBUTES

FREDERICK J. E. WOODBRIDGE
1867–1940

To some, philosophy means a long discipline in abstract speculation; to the man in the street it means little more than resig-
nation; to Professor Woodbridge it was neither abstruse nor
passive. As writer, teacher, editor, and administrator he felt
philosophy to be in constant relation to every man's daily life.
Professor Woodbridge was not only a lover of wisdom himself, but he called forth the operation of the philosophic faculty in all who came in contact with him. He lived through the
years when the United States was producing a school of philosophy which arrested the attention of the whole thinking world
and he played a vital part in that movement, but he freely
acknowledged that he was more occupied with its extension
than with the formulation of its doctrines. He said of himself:

> The principle of realism seems so important to me for meta-
> physics and philosophy that I have been more busy with cham-
> pioning it than with developing it.

This championship was as remarkable for its diversity as for its
vigor.

Frederick James Eugene Woodbridge was born in Windsor,
Ontario, in 1867. His father was actively engaged at the time
in certain movements of political reform in the community,

Included in *Commemorative Tributes of the American Academy of Arts and Letters, 1905–
1941,* published in New York in 1942.

but, impatient with the conservatism of his fellow citizens, he presently crossed the border into this country and became the head of an institution of public health in Kalamazoo, Michigan. Frederick Woodbridge went from the schools of Kalamazoo to Amherst College, where he graduated in 1889, returning for the degree of Master of Arts in 1898. The thirty-four years of distinguished scholastic and administrative service which he gave to Columbia University did not prevent his serving his own alma mater with signal devotion: he was trustee of Amherst College for nineteen years; and twice he refused the presidency, believing, as he said, that "the final executive decision was not his forte" and that he could be more useful to both institutions as teacher and adviser.

For a time Frederick Woodbridge felt himself to be destined for the ministry and he accepted a scholarship at the Union Theological Seminary in this city, then a Presbyterian institution. Though philosophy was to regain its place as his primary interest, a religious emphasis reappears at intervals in his work, and in the last book, *An Essay on Nature,* his discussion of the teleological direction in nature derives from a religious point of view. In 1898 he made the first of many trips to Europe. He studied at the University of Berlin, where he was to return later as the Theodore Roosevelt Professor of Philosophy. After having taught two years at the University of Minnesota he was called in 1902 to be Professor of Philosophy at Columbia University. In 1895 he had married Miss Helena Belle Adams of Chicago, whose wide interests and sympathies found expression in an influential participation in various movements of social and civic betterment until her death in 1935. Professor and Mrs. Woodbridge are survived by four children.

When Professor Woodbridge first entered teaching, the temper of philosophical studies in this country may be described as reflecting a liberal idealism. What Santayana calls "the trade-winds of doctrine" were blowing from Kant,

Hegel, and the English rationalists. But the tide was gathering for the movement which, stemming from Charles Pierce's influence on William James and reinforced by a worldwide activity in experimental psychology, was to assume and outgrow the name of Pragmatism. William James published his *Principles of Psychology* in 1880, his *Will to Believe* in 1897; and in 1898 he delivered in Berkeley, California, his epoch-making lecture on "Philosophical Conceptions and Practical Results." Josiah Royce followed with his *Religious Aspects of Philosophy* and John Dewey with his *Studies in Logical Theory* in 1903. This tide was to make the tour of the world and to return to us from the University of Vienna as the logical positivism which is the prevailing "trade-wind of doctrine" that young philosophers are facing today.

It was this movement—"the shifting of emphasis in philosophy from pure intellect to perception," as it has been called —which Professor Woodbridge championed, and his gifts and energy opened up ever wider fields of activity. As an author he is best represented by his volumes *The Purpose of History, The Realm of the Mind,* and *An Essay on Nature,* the proofs of which he read during his last illness. On his seventieth birthday, in 1937, the philosophical faculties of Columbia, Minnesota, and Amherst combined in publishing and presenting to him a volume of his essays collected from periodicals and from his books. Professor Woodbridge's contribution to the movement as an editor was no less influential: in 1904 he founded *The Journal of Philosophy* and soon after *The Archives of Philosophy.* These journals served as vehicles for the increasingly adventurous declarations of the movement, and rereading them today one can recapture something of what Professor Woodbridge remembered as the "excitement" that surrounded their publication. A still more practical outlet was found, however, for his ideas; in 1912 he was appointed Dean of the Faculties of Political Science, Philosophy, Pure Science, and Fine Arts at Columbia University, an office he held until

1929. His annual reports to the President were widely read throughout the country; year after year they aroused fruitful controversy and have taken their place among the classical documents in the theory of higher education.

Professor Woodbridge felt, however, that the formation of those students who are now teaching philosophy in all parts of the world was his principal work, and neither editorial nor administrative duties caused any intermission in this task nor diminished the generous vitality he expended on it. His clarity and force as a writer were equally present in his conversation; he possessed to an unusual degree that art of discussion that is called the Socratic method, whereby ideas seem rather to be elicited than imposed and which combines informality with precision.

Professor Woodbridge became a member of the Academy in 1935. In his death we have lost not only the admired thinker and writer, but a wise associate and a valued friend.

CHRISTIAN BÉRARD

1902–1949

Christian Bérard was the foremost stage-designer of our time. He was, in addition, an admirable painter. He was known affectionately, and by his nickname, to a large number of persons in several countries. He was in possession, however, of another genius and another function which cannot be so briefly characterized.

His funeral took place in the church of St. Sulpice in Paris on the morning of the 16th of February. A visitor who might have strayed into the church to study the murals of Delacroix and who had refused to be swept out by the majestic beadles would have had some difficulty in determining the character and achievements of the man whose death had assembled so varied and so distinguished a company. The diplomatic corps was well represented; there were members of the government present; it was being whispered that a dozen duchesses had been counted; a general in full-dress uniform advanced bearing on a velvet cushion the decorations of the Legion of Honor; ribbons attached to the floral offerings were stamped with the words "The City of Lille," "The City of Aix-en-Provence," "The Municipality of Paris." Yet if these were the

Written in February 1949 shortly after the funeral of Bérard (who died on February 12), apparently for the Paris edition of the New York *Herald Tribune*, although its publication has not been traced. Printed from a typescript among the Wilder papers (YCAL).

obsequies of a statesman or a noble, how was one to explain
that a newsreel photographer had not been more promptly
removed from his crouching position on the shoulders of a
baroque statue? How explain that the music was of an austere
perfection, selected and supervised by Henri Sauguet?

Among the closest friends stood Jean Cocteau and Louis
Jouvet and Jean-Louis Barrault and Madeleine Renaud. Yet if
this was the funeral of a great actor or of a dramatist and
academician, how did one explain that a prominent place had
been accorded to garlands offered by the Union of Manicurists
of Paris, the Union of Hairdressers of Paris, the House of
Christian Dior, and the Restaurant Maxim?

This was indeed the funeral of one of the first citizens of
Paris. The wide variety of tributes was his due. The grief was
sincere and was not without an apprehension that he might be
for a time irreplaceable. Christian Bérard, in addition to his
other gifts and activities, was the arbiter of elegance and the
north star of mode.

There are several reasons why mode tends to depend upon
an extremely small group of arbiters and why, in times when
a great deal of attention is being paid to it, it has frequently
been guided by a single person. Many have the discriminating
taste which can adapt its dictates; many have the courage to try
to impose a novelty; but very few in addition to taste and
courage have the imagination to foresee where the next ac-
ceptable innovation lies waiting to be discovered.

In America the word "mode" is often thought to imply
servility. In France, on the contrary, it carries a sense of enter-
prise and independence. To a Parisian a disregard for mode
would indicate both timidity and servility, for the refusal of
mode is merely a retreat into the mode of yesterday. Many
Americans think of mode as something one follows; the
French think of it as something on which one rides. Mode is
the element of innovation without which dress, ornament, and
habitation lose their individuality. Both the Americans and the

French, however, are aware that mode is exciting because, forever exploring novelty, it moves constantly at the verge of risk and danger. It is a very real humiliation to have attempted to achieve a beauty by means of audacity and to have failed. Mode constantly and knowingly skirts the absurd.

The world of mode, then, is continually haunted by a sense of insecurity. Each of its innumerable manifestations must have in some degree an element of surprise; but the surprise must be pleasing. For the purveyors a large investment is at stake; for the purchasers, their dignity—or at least their assurance. The arbiter is one whose instinct is so right and whose confidence is so unshakable that he is able both to divine—as though from an unfolding logic within beauty—where the next innovation lies and at the same time to express it in such a way that it has an air of self-evident fitness. Such an arbiter was Christian Bérard. He did not seem to impose novelty; he merely opened people's eyes to a novelty of which they were already half aware. There are many houses of couture in Paris which have consummate taste; he was allied to the two or three which have genius. Their assurance and their inventiveness were ultimately dependent on his suggestion and criticism.

He did not have the air of an arbiter nor was he in himself a figure of elegance. His clothes were a pleasant and rueful accommodation to his bulk and to the permanent presence of the dog Jacynthe lodged under his arm. The nickname of Bébé happily expressed the childlike way in which he both enjoyed and deprecated the admiration and affection that were showered upon him. Compliments seemed to cause him a barely supportable pain; his hand would start waving in protest, his eyes would roll to the ceiling for protection, and from behind the famous red beard would come a long, murmurous denial of any accomplishment whatever. He gave at first the impression of being one of those artists who never quite get around to painting, and Louis Jouvet has indeed described the difficulties of extracting the completed masterpieces from him. Each collaboration between them was a drama of procrastination and revolt, of cajolement and threats. In the fine arts, however, the malingerers are not necessarily the unendowed. From the moment that the image was finally clear in his mind he worked consumedly and with the costing demands upon himself which were to hasten his early death.

On the third evening after the day of his funeral a farce, *Les Fourberies de Scapin,* opened in Paris. It was written by Molière and directed by Louis Jouvet; the leading rôle was played by Jean-Louis Barrault, and the scenery and costumes were by Christian Bérard. It was an overwhelming success and more than a success; it was a sunburst of French genius. And again Bérard in his contribution had achieved a triumph out of audacity. The play is laid in a Mediterranean seaport, and the characters are close to the grotesque figures of the Italian *commedia dell'arte;* yet Bérard's picture was all in gray occasionally relieved by rose and yellow. A riotous farce played against gray? The magician had achieved a gray that was neither doleful nor negative. Visually, the production threw the emphasis on the actors' faces; psychologically, it threw the emphasis on the mind of Molière, which was reporting the Italian exuberance in a very French way. The cooler North was laughing at the agitated South.

Bérard's last work—together with the two other productions he had created within the year, Molière's *Don Juan* and the ballet *La Rencontre d'Oedipe et le Sphinx*—illustrated a quality which has not always been restricted to the French but which remains their characteristic gift: they achieve a richness through simplification and a maximum of effect by an economy of means. Prior to the emergence of Christian Bérard the French contribution in the fields where he was to be a leader had been unsettled. The French genius is susceptible to influences from without and requires a considerable amount of time to assimilate them, to make them French. It had suffered two powerful shocks: the sensual violence of the Russian Ballet and the intellectual violence of the Spanish Post-Impressionist painters. The work of Christian Bérard from his first *décor* for Cocteau's *La Machine infernale* has been a demonstration of how such disparate foreign elements can be integrated into a French expression. With his great design for Molière's *L'École des femmes* Paris returned to its highroad; the production was unmistakably modern, yet it took its place in that line which descends from the ornaments of the cathedrals and the miniatures of the medieval manuscripts. His stage designs, in addition, exhibited the deep French sense of the practical. These were not easel paintings imposed upon a stage, but fields for action. They were designed from above as well as from before. They combined at once magnificent design and color, a rich culture, and a sense of the dynamic character of drama. It is characteristic of him, moreover, that he was at his greatest when he was serving masterpieces and that on only one occasion did he furnish designs for a play that was of less than the highest literary quality.

The church of St. Sulpice was full and the square before it. An artist had died; one who through the years of the Occupation and the years of anxiety had exemplified those characteristic qualities of French beauty which are order and *mésure* and clarity, and he was receiving the thanks of the capital and of Lille and of Aix-en-Provence and of the Union of the Manicurists of Paris and of a dozen duchesses and of the Restaurant Maxim.

JOHN MARIN
1870–1953

John Marin was born in Rutherford, New Jersey, on the 23rd of December 1870 and lived the greater part of his life at a short distance from his birthplace. He died at the age of eighty-two at Cape Split, Addison, Maine, on 1 October 1953. His paternal great-grandfather, Jean-Baptiste Marin, came to this country from France, but he was of Spanish origin. John Marin's mother, who died when he was nine days old, was of English and Dutch stock.

John Marin was slow in coming to an assured realization of his calling, though he used to say that he had been drawing since the age of three. After having attended the public schools at Weehawken he enrolled at Stevens Institute in Hoboken, where he prepared himself to be an architect. Indeed, he followed the profession of architect-contractor for a time, but was—as he put it—"no first-rate man." He began painting and from 1899 to 1901 his father supported him, first as a student at the Pennsylvania Academy of Fine Arts, then at the Art Students' League in New York, where he worked principally under Frank Vincent Du Mond. "I must say," he wrote, "I derived very little from that period." In 1905 he went to Paris, but after two months he ceased attendance at the atelier which he had selected. He tells us that he took

From the *Proceedings of the American Academy of Arts and Letters and the National Institute of Arts and Letters,* published in New York in 1955.

walks in the country; he played billiards; he made several visits
to the Louvre. Slowly, however, a confidence in painting land-
scapes "in his own way" began to assert itself. He exhibited
ten water colors in the Autumn Salon of 1910. He was forty
years old. Alfred Stieglitz had seen his work the year before
and had returned to America to exhibit it in his now historic
Photo-Secession Gallery at 291 Fifth Avenue. After six years
in Paris, Marin returned to this country. His comment on the
Paris years was that

> in the water colors I had been making even before Stieglitz
> first saw my work, I had already begun to let go in complete
> freedom.

We ourselves can see in the work to what extent this "complete freedom" was self-won. During those years in Paris he
could have seen the painting of Cézanne, Van Gogh, and
Picasso, but he assures us that he did not. He was searching
for his freedom within; it was only later, and to a limited
extent, that his curiosities turned outward toward the work of
other artists, discovering elements which he could assimilate
to himself.

The forty-two years that followed on his return were devoted to confident and even joyous painting. Only occasionally do we find him under strain as he sought to break through
into some new expansion of vision and expression. All his
work he brought to Alfred Stieglitz and it was shown in the
successive galleries wherein Stieglitz carried through to triumph his remarkable powers as a discoverer, inciter, and cru-
sader of the new movement in American painting. Stieglitz
shielded Marin from practical cares and distractions and
opened his way to a life dedicated to painting alone. In 1912
Marin married Marie Jane Hughes, a neighbor in New Jersey;
a son, John Marin, Junior, was born to them in 1914. Thereafter he spent all his winters in a house he had bought in
Cliffside, New Jersey; his summers in the Berkshires, the Adi-

rondacks, the White Mountains, but with increasing frequency on the lower coast of Maine. In 1929 and 1930 he visited the Taos Valley in New Mexico.

Freedom is the name that every artist must give to his creation. It is a subjective attitude and in the cases of many greatly admired artists it is scarcely perceptible to us, so consistently and effortlessly does the work—that of a Vermeer, a Chardin, even a Raphael—seem to emerge from that of the contemporaries. It is apparent to all, however, that the freedom of Marin was hard-won. He takes his place in the line of authentic American autodidacts. The bolder the individual vision, the more slowly it is formed. Self-knowledge comes first through an uneasy repudiation of the contemporary performance; there is no precocious brilliance; each step must be taken in alternations of courage and self-doubt. Such was the early progress of Whitman and Melville and Thoreau. In their accounts of their development it is precisely the word "courage" which returns most frequently, and it is often accompanied by a smiling and unfrightened allusion to their work as "crazy." The statements which Marin furnished for the catalogues of his exhibitions were, like his letters, written in the ebullient American idiom:

> So there now [he writes in 1922], this is how I try to paint a picture, using to the best of my ability color and lines in their identity places. And there is the fellow up there in the sky who laughs, he who sheds tears, and the fellow who shouts at the top of his lungs, Courage! he the loudest of all.

Three years before, he had written from Maine to Stieglitz:

> Today I am an apostle of the crazy, but Damit, it's got to be a caged crazy, otherwise it would butt into another crazy.

This jubilation is reflected in many of the paintings. There is little that is somber or gloomy in the work of Marin, though he could seize the brooding majesty of the Indians' sacred mountain that rises above Taos or the menacing grandeur of a storm descending, in violent purple light, upon a forested height above Lake Champlain. It is in quickening energy that we must seek what Marin meant by "complete freedom."

The freedom that he won consisted, first, in releasing an inner compulsion to present a single subject, or a single aspect of the scene before him—what the eye sees in one deep gaze, not what the eye sees as it roams about the subject in ever shifting focus. He was accustomed to say to younger artists who brought their work to him: "But you have there, on one canvas, three (or four or ten) pictures." As early as 1908 we see that Marin's instinct had prompted him to draw lines enclosing the central subject of his picture, painting an irregular frame well within the boundaries of his margin. This he called "bringing it forward." Later he was to do more: he isolated the central subject by setting it on an oblique plane, further cutting it off from its immediate surroundings. The effect is one of passionate appropriation of the thing seen. He seems to be saying: "What you see with an unwavering gaze has a reality which is lost when you permit your eye to rove over the scene and receive the succession of scores and hundreds of glances."

But this delight in devouring a single object had to be reconciled with a second urgency of his nature—a joy in orienting the object toward a total universe of light and space and air and forms. Particularly is this true when the chosen subject is not primarily an object or a form but one passage of color (Marin on his knees before one epiphany of color); for a color declares itself pre-eminently through a juxtaposition with color. The single gaze is not all-sufficient; we are not only Eye; we are aware of the universe by other organs, by the sense of balance and gravity. And for these ends the self-taught master evolved his own ways of indicating depth and luminosity and movement. There are pictures, for example, of a schooner dancing on the waves of a harbor in Maine. The ship is enclosed in a sort of parallelogram. Below it, in what is at first a disconcerting play of tilted planes, are suggestions of shore, fir trees, of white houses, and a church steeple. And above the ship, in a rectangle, is a *fragment only* of the intense blue of the sky. These offer, indeed, the sum of several glances, but their separateness is stated with great candor; they are not merged, and the result is that the schooner, "brought forward," rides in our quickened imagination, sun-drunk and sea-borne, *sub specie aeternitatis.*

Marin was once asked why some of his paintings were more "literal" than others. "Well, you see," he replied, "when I come into a new territory I paint what I see; when I've been there a while I paint what I know." It is well to remember that Marin painted "in series," making eight to a dozen paintings of the subject before him—a wind-twisted fir growing from between two ledges of rock; a row of yellowing cottonwood trees beside an *arroyo* in New Mexico; the Telephone and Telegraph Building seen from New York Harbor. It was his custom to keep his paintings by him for a year before he permitted them to be shown. During this year he gradually destroyed a number in each series. Perhaps no painter of his stature ever destroyed so many completed pictures.

Throughout his life Marin felt that painting in oil was as authentic an expression of his vision as painting in water color. The fact that he is generally known as a water-colorist is largely due to a particular intention on the part of Alfred Stieglitz. In the Western world water color has been widely associated with the preparatory sketch and the informal notation, whereas in the Orient it has served for centuries as the vehicle of the highest inspiration. Stieglitz wished to enlist Marin in his campaign to rehabilitate the water color as a major medium and Marin for a time permitted Stieglitz to focus this emphasis upon his work.

The great artist teaches us a new entrance into the visible world, a new homage, and a new knowledge. Each of the

master landscapists has informed our eyes: Turner taught us
to see opalescence; Constable, the war of sun and cloud and
wind and the white light that falls on tower and treetop; Pous-
sin, the sovereign equalized light of noon or evening; Ko-
koschka, the geography, the geology, the history of the earth
that lies behind the surface of city and valley; the Chinese
masters, the landscape as background for a philosopher's meditation, itself fraught with the metaphysical implication of
being and non-being; Hiroshige, a world accorded to the
measure of man, lovingly, whisperingly, often drolly returning the love which he showers upon it. What is the overruling
communication of John Marin?

Surely, we are still too near him to gather it from amid the
rich diversity of his work. Yet one seems to be learning from
him that the visible world is constantly speaking, is prompted
by mind and energy; and this he conveys in the twentieth-
century spirit, without the least resort to animism or anthropo-
morphism, without any imposing of our human "moods"
upon the scene—by selfless gazing. From Marin's lyrical series
of the flowering fruit trees of New Jersey to the oil paintings
of sea surge and tumult, nature seems to have been caught
surprised, in a world where no men are, eternally fulfilling
itself in energy and beauty.

The New World is only beginning to receive that patina
which generations of artists have conferred upon the Old, that
of being greatly pictured, that ultimate reconciliation of man
and his physical environment; and our gratitude to John Marin
is doubled by this indebtedness to him as poet-painter of our
land.

THOMAS MANN
1875–1955

Thomas Mann was born on 6 June 1875, of a prosperous and influential family in the Hanseatic free city of Lübeck. His mother, however, was from Brazil and was of mixed German and Portuguese stock. He frequently called attention to this mingling in him of the North and the South. From the North came his appearance and his manner of life. He had the air of a thoughtful and somewhat severe lawyer or businessman. He was methodical in work and of great industry, furnishing constant occupation to two secretaries; and even the upheaval in Germany and his voluntary exile did not alter his pleasure in a patriarchal form of family life. From the South came the luxuriance and range of his fancy, which included a preoccupation with the irrational and even morbid sources of artistic creation.

His father—senator and twice mayor of Lübeck—died when Thomas Mann was fifteen and the century-old family firm went into bankruptcy. His mother moved with her large family to Munich, where for a time he worked in an insurance office. He had been interested in writing, however, from his early years and at the age of twenty-two he published a first volume of short stories. With his brother Heinrich, who was also to become a distinguished novelist, he took a trip to Italy,

From the *Proceedings of the American Academy of Arts and Letters and the National Institute of Arts and Letters,* published in New York in 1957.

where he began the composition of a long novel about the decline of a patrician family like his own in an unnamed Hanseatic city. *Buddenbrooks* was published at the end of 1900. At first it aroused little interest, but, reissued the following year, it suddenly attracted wide attention and the author at twenty-six found himself famous. This work is unlike those long family novels to which we are accustomed in English and American literature, as it is unlike any apparently similar works in German literature. It seems—particularly in translation—to bring not only an element of irony to the description of persons and place but one of outright derision. Referring to it obliquely in another work, Thomas Mann describes it as "passion preserved in ice." That is to say: the South not merged with the North, not annihilated by the North, but dominated by it. It is without hero or heroine. Of the three characters who most engage our attention one is a woman of no exceptional or even pleasing qualities; her brother, inadequate in business, to his elevated social station, and to his family relationships; and a suffering boy, whose death is described, to our consternation, in the transcription from a medical manual of the successive stages of typhoid fever. This objectivity is not characteristic of German literature, yet the success of the book was enormous. Within less than a generation a million copies had been sold in the original language alone, which, in view of the book's high distinction and the number of German readers in the world, is without precedent.

In 1905 Thomas Mann married Fraülein Katja Pringsheim of Munich, and six children were born to them, growing up, for a time, in the leisured and richly cultured society of the Bavarian capital. For twenty-four years after the appearance of *Buddenbrooks* Mann published only essays and short novels, including *Tristan, Tonio Kröger* (generally regarded as his finest work in that form), and *Death in Venice.* Many of these deal with what he called "the inveterate dilemma of the creative artist in this world"—the gulf between those who "simply live" and those who strive to capture and preserve reality through the imposition of form. During the First World War he wrote a series of essays which were published in 1918 as *Reflections of an Unpolitical Man.* These contain many statements and points of view which he was later to repudiate strenuously. They exalted war; they affirmed that Germany had nobler tasks to perform than could be expressed within the framework of democratic institutions; he ridiculed an excessive resort to "reason." His shift of position came rapidly, however; within four years he was warning his readers against the "obscurantism" which he had so lately recommended.

Thomas Mann's next book was profoundly enriched precisely by this revolution within his thought. In 1924 he published his great novel *The Magic Mountain.* Modern civilization is there presented to us under the figure of life in a tuberculosis sanatorium. The successive points of view through which he had passed, and others which he had observed about him, are distributed among the various doctors and patients in the institution, and developed with dialectical force as well as dramatized in striking characterizations. Thomas Mann described it as "the philosophical renunciation of much that I once loved, of many a dangerous sympathy . . . to which the soul of Europe has been and still is prone . . . a book of leave-taking and pedagogical self-discipline."

He was now the most eminent German man of letters and the award to him of the Nobel Prize for Literature in 1929 raised him to world renown. He viewed with alarm the dangerous tendencies that were beginning to emerge in German public life, but unlike his brother he refrained for a while from polemics. He felt that his distinguished position might yet enable him to be useful as an advocate of reason and reconciliation. Under strong provocation, however, in 1933 he spoke out in sharp warning. It became evident that he would not long remain undisturbed and he removed with his family to Switzerland. There he completed in 1934 the first volume of his tetralogy *Joseph and His Brothers.* There, too, with the intention of preserving all that was best in the continuity of German intellectual life, he edited a review characteristically entitled *Measure and Value.* In 1938 he accepted a call to join the faculty of Princeton University and brought his family to this country, where he was to reside—finally as a citizen of the United States—for fourteen years. In 1939 the Rector of Bonn University informed him that the honorary doctorate that had been conferred upon him was rescinded. His famous letter in reply was but one of many publications, addresses, and broadcasts in which he invoked the conscience of Germany and clarified the issues of the war. It was to this activity that our then Secretary, Van Wyck Brooks, referred in proposing Thomas Mann for honorary membership in this Academy. "He is defending," wrote Mr. Brooks, "the basic ideas of our civilization perhaps more powerfully than any other writer." In addition to this political writing Thomas Mann completed two more volumes of the Joseph cycle. This enormous work was begun, he said, as an attempt "by means of a mythical psychology to present a psychology of the myth"—that is, not only with immense learning and narrative skill to analyze the motivations within so ancient a story, but to show us the ways in which such stories arise from the dreaming soul of the race and are molded by constant retelling.

In his last major novel, *Doctor Faustus,* he resumed on a vast scale many of the themes that had recurred so often in his earlier work. Here, under the symbol of a pact with the devil, he shows a great composer consciously employing toward the making of masterpieces those elements of unreason which are inseparable from all artistic creation, and he identifies them with the demonic forces which in and through Germany had wrought such havoc in our times.

To the two formulations we have found for characterizing Thomas Mann's work—the mingling of North and South, and the "passion preserved in ice"—should be added a third: the application to literature of musical forms. As early as *Tonio Kröger,* of 1903, he began consciously to build his narratives upon systems of recurrent themes and symbols, of contrasting sections with their developments and resolutions. The organization of the longer novels is of an extraordinarily refined complexity which even includes a calculated play with numbers—such as the omnipresent employment of seven and the sevenfold in *The Magic Mountain.* This is the rigor and order of the North; this is the ice which impresses form upon the passion. The South is in the exuberance of his imagination and in the dazzling resourcefulness of his style. Through sheer virtuosity Thomas Mann constantly exercised his gift in what might be called a higher form of parody. The greater part of *Doctor Faustus* is written in imitation of a clerkly early-nineteenth-century Biedermeier narrative; yet there are three chapters in the style of Martin Luther's contemporaries. The short novel *The Holy Fool*—with its now famous opening page describing the bells of Rome—is in the spirit of a very early Saint's legend. In *Lotte in Weimar* there is an extraordinary chapter in what we have come to call the stream-of-consciousness technique, reproducing the thoughts of the aged Goethe as he awakes to a new day. His last published work, *The Confessions of Felix Krull, Confidence Man,* which he had begun forty years earlier, is one long droll recapture of the false elegance of an uneducated impostor. Yet he could write with utter simplicity, as in the tender story about his youngest daughter, published here under the title *Early Sorrow.*

Thomas Mann was first elected to Honorary Membership in our Academy, but after his adoption of American citizenship he became, in 1951, a regular member.

Four years after the close of the war he accepted Germany's greatest honor, the Goethe Prize of the city of Frankfurt am Main—an occasion fraught, for speaker and listeners, with profound and painful emotion. In 1952 he returned to Europe for the last time and made his home in Zürich, where he died on 12 August 1955, in his eighty-first year.

CHAUNCEY BREWSTER TINKER

1876–1963

Chauncey Brewster Tinker was born in Auburn, Maine, on
22 October 1876, and died in Wethersfield, Connecticut, on
17 March 1963, at the age of eighty-six. All his life he retained the characteristics of a Maine man: the deliberate
pause before replying to a question, the refusal to be impressed by any honor which the world may confer, and the
practice of invoking moral considerations prior to social and
practical ones. He was the son of the Reverend Anson
Phelps Tinker, a Yale graduate of the class of 1863, and
Martha Jane White Tinker. In his youth his father took the
family to Colorado, where Chauncey Tinker attended the
East Denver High School. He graduated from Yale University with honors in English in the class of 1899 and received
from the same university the degrees of Master of Arts and
Doctor of Philosophy in the following three years. Later he
was to receive honorary degrees from Yale, Princeton, the
College of Wooster, Hobart College, and the University of
Rochester. Except for the year 1903, when he served as Associate Professor of English at Bryn Mawr, and the year
1937, when he assumed the Charles Eliot Norton Professor-
ship at Harvard, his entire academic life was spent at Yale.
In New Haven he was appointed a full professor in 1913
and the Sterling Professor of English Literature in 1923. He

From the *Proceedings of the American Academy of Arts and Letters and the National Institute of Arts and Letters,* published in New York in 1964.

retired in 1945 after almost a half-century of active teaching.
Mr. Tinker was one of the foremost bibliophiles in the
country. He assembled a notable private collection, which he
bequeathed to the Yale University Library. He owned many
works by William Blake of the greatest rarity; all Anthony
Trollope; and pristine copies of the masterpieces of the century with which he is mainly identified: Dr. Johnson's *Dictionary,* Boswell's *Life of Samuel Johnson, Gulliver's Travels, Tristram Shandy,* and many more.

Throughout his long life as a teacher Mr. Tinker conducted
classes covering a wide range of English literature from *Beo-
wulf* to Keats, Byron, and Shelley, but from early in his career
his interest centered on the eighteenth century and particularly on Dr. Johnson and his circle. Above all, he was bent on
rehabilitating James Boswell from the sneering depreciations
of Macaulay's famous essay. He was convinced that Boswell
was not only a highly idiosyncratic individual but a distinguished writer. He published first a *Young Boswell,* for general
readers, and, in 1924, a *Letters of James Boswell,* in two volumes.
He had long suspected that there were many Boswell papers
in existence that had not come to the attention of scholars. In
1925 he inserted a few lines in *The* (London) *Times* requesting
information and assistance. He received two replies—one almost totally illegible, the other a postal card, unsigned, bearing the words "Try Malahide." Malahide Castle is in the vicinity of Dublin. By adroit maneuvering he obtained an
invitation to tea with Lord and Lady Talbot de Malahide. Lord
Talbot was a descendant of James Boswell. From there one
clue led to another and the flow of Boswell papers has since
grown from a trickle to a large stream. They have emerged
from ebony caskets and croquet boxes, from attics and stables.
The results of these exhumations have delighted and astonished and occasionally shocked a large public. Mr. Tinker's
days continued to be filled with his devotion to teaching and
with his wide bibliographical interests. We may assume that he

did not long suffer under the disappointment of not having been assigned the editorship of this enormous treasure. It was enough that, like Moses, he had struck the rock and that the copious spring had been released.

President Lowell of Harvard once said, "There are not enough great teachers in this country to fill the faculty of one small college." Mr. Tinker was an admirable writer and a distinguished bibliophile; he was a great teacher. When we remember that at one time or another almost ten thousand men were enrolled in his courses, we must take into account also that in his most famous course, "The Age of Johnson," the number of listeners was generally doubled by undergraduates who attended—as the academic phrase goes—as "visitors." There are certain forms of genius of which no concrete record may be transmitted to aftertime, not even with the aid of the highest refinements of camera and sound-recorder. Among them is that of the born teacher. Its essence lies not primarily in the imparting of knowledge and wisdom but in a relationship. At one and the same time it gives and it receives. Mr. Tinker could be richly and vividly informative; he could be extremely funny; but the lasting impression of his lectures was of an extraordinary gravity. He made vibrate the chords of awe and wonder. He not only aroused admiration for the writers of the eighteenth century but for life itself and for great literature, which he never failed to relate to life. His lectures were composed with the greatest care and were annually redigested and reshaped. Their very length was so artfully adjusted that they concluded with an effect that would have appeared theatrical in a lesser man. In the few seconds that followed his last words the bells of Battell Chapel—or, in his last years, of "Harkness"—would sound the hour. "That will be all for today, gentlemen," he would say. For a moment the intellectual integrity of Edmund Burke or the wisdom of Samuel Johnson would hover above the classroom like a spell, like a summons.

One of the saddest phrases in English literature is that with which John Milton condemned the clergy of his time: "The sheep look up and are not fed." It applies to the majority of lecture halls. The most nourishing food for young men and women—at that time when they are still uncertain of values, still hesitant before the choices that lie open before them—is to hear great things greatly praised. Mr. Tinker's power was moral; it derived from his deeply religious life. Without ever being "preachy" or even didactic in the smaller sense of the word, he pictured the stern disciplines of the intellect and of art and of life as attractive and rewarding.

Many are the students who remember him with a deep indebtedness. They include such distinguished scholars as Frederick Pottle and Wilmarth Sheldon Lewis, editors, respectively, of the Boswell *Journals* and of Horace Walpole's *Correspondence;* and a host of writers—many of them members of our Institute and Academy: Sinclair Lewis, Stephen Vincent Benét, Archibald MacLeish, Philip Barry, John Hersey, the writer of these lines, and many others.

Mr. Tinker was elected a member of the Academy in 1937, joining two colleagues of his own faculty, Wilbur Cross and William Lyon Phelps, and he served as our Chancellor from 1949 to 1951.

SIR PHILIP SASSOON'S

THE THIRD ROUTE

SIR PHILIP SASSOON'S
THE THIRD ROUTE

"Life will be beautiful two or three hundred years from now,"
Chekhov used to say as he bent over his garden, coughing in
far-off Yalta, his "sunny Siberia." And it is of that future that
the pages of this book set one thinking. It is the property of
these pages—for all their author's poised understatement—to
furnish endless material for wonder and for reverie. Sir Philip
is as effortlessly at home in the future as he is in the remote
past and as he most strikingly is in the present. It is this inter-
mingling of prevision, of archeology, and of present duty that
gives his account its overtones of poetry. Nothing, it seems to
me, would be more likely to move a poet to the composition
of an ode than the experience of reading this book, where
one minute we are considering the civilizations of antiquity
and

> What the gold Chaldee or silver Persian saw;

and the next minute contemplating the future day when the
skies will be darkened with transportation, and apostrophizing
the voyager that

> Wilt anon in thy loose-reined careere
> At Tagus, Po, Sene, Thames and Danow dine.

The introduction to Sir Philip Sassoon's *The Third Route,* published in Garden City,
New York, by Doubleday & Company, Inc., in 1929.

Science in her vulgarer moments and fiction in her more pretentious have offered us a number of imaginative pictures of that great age; but our minds are chilled by them. These bald people, dressed in togas (unlikely enough on a race that will dress for velocity and altitude), with numerals for names or with names ending in -ion; these children brought up in incubators and in schools like incubators, and all this food to be purchased at pharmacies—these repel us. I grudge the improvements that will be made upon the pianoforte, the magic lantern, and the family. To be sure, diseases will be reduced to a handful, and a domesticated death will arrive either very suddenly or very late; love will be assigned by the state, and its anxieties will be statistical. I am driven to thinking of an even remoter future: of a time when the English and Chinese languages will be mixed, as oil and water mix; when scholars will deny that *Lear* and *Twelfth Night* are by the same hand; when it will be said of our war that "no doubt there was a struggle of some kind"; and when the works of Beethoven will be hesitantly reconstructed and played upon aerial microchromatic instruments. It was not of these activities that we were recommended "to greet the unseen with a cheer."

But to deplore the future is one of the subtler gratifications of self-pity. Life will be beautiful two or three hundred years from now, and it is ignoble in us to wish it to be beautiful with the same kind of beauty to which we are accustomed. The love of beauty is an admiration for the slight deviations from a proportion to which the eyes and ears have become accustomed. We shall not see the new proportions and their deviations: Sophocles also did not live to revile Shakespeare, nor Raphael, Cézanne.

But from reading this book I see that we can be reconciled to this unfamiliar activity by the thought that it will all be permeated by influences derived from living in the air. All the liberating power and breadth that we feel from life on the sea, however brief our participation, will be multiplied for those who daily submit themselves to the currents of the sky.

Our position [Sir Philip writes], when we had left the last faint
outline of Italy behind and sea and sky met in an unbroken
horizon all around us, was quite wonderful. We found ourselves suspended in utter isolation between an unflecked sky
and an unflecked sea, blue reflecting and intensifying blue. We
spun along as though cupped between two azure cymbals,
resonant with sound which seemed of deeper meaning than
the roaring of man-made engines.

It is not without application here that we remember that all the
words denoting the qualities we admire most and strive for are
based on images of altitude.

The Third Route turns one's mind as persuasively toward the
past as it does toward the future. Here is much to disturb the
pitying condescension which we bear the earlier civilizations
and which will someday be visited upon us. As we bend over
Thebes, over Ur, over Babylon, even over Athens, there floats
up to us that murmur made up of cries of war, cruelty, pleasure, and ever of religious terror. Even as our civilization will
someday exhale to its observers the same cries of soldiers,
slaves, revelers, and suppliants. It is Sir Philip's extraordinary
photographs that help us to see this past. Who does not know
in the usual travel book the photographs intended to complete
the magic of the text and to transport us to the very spot?
Those graceless ruins or portals serving as background to
some conscious native; such views as are forever associated
with the controlled desperation of a lecturer's wand, signaling
for another slide; those Colosseums on a schoolroom wall; the
Acropolis in the manuals to which we must bring faith to
believe that the hill is impressive. But the elevation of the
camera has given two new dimensions to these photographs.
One can well spare some details from the façades in order to
gain this power to see the setting of the building and to feel
its depth and to realize its plan. For me the Sphinx is less
puzzling than it was.

But there are a number of other trains of thought set in
motion by this book. For example, it is not so much a saving

in time that will be gained through foreign travel by air as it is a clearer idea of the setting of cities. Our first impressions of Rome and Florence, of Paris and Nanking hitherto have been of the industrial suburbs that surround them, the warehouses and the sordid railway stations. Only a long stay can remove the attitude that such cities are a collection of monuments in a waste of ugliness. But approach them from the air; we see them lying beside their rivers or cupped in their hills, and all later acquaintance with their stations and factories cannot rob us of the all but unconscious realization of their natural setting. Again, how moving is the fact that aviation has been so useful to archeology, that the outlines invisible even to those who passed over them hundreds of times on foot have become apparent first only to watchers from a great height. But the mind from aviation goes on continually following new implications and new hopes. . . .

It seemed best to you, Sir Philip, to welcome a layman's introduction to your book, and these are the thoughts that you have stirred up in one who knows all too little about your great subject. But borne on the tide of your enthusiasm and your humanistic view of the life of all times on the planet beneath your machines, I too can exclaim that life will be beautiful two or three hundred years from now, beautiful as the curve of a homing plane, beautiful as your gardens at Lympne.

APPENDIX:

THREE RESEARCH

PAPERS

NEW AIDS TOWARD
DATING THE EARLY PLAYS
OF LOPE DE VEGA

Attempts at determining a chronology of Lope de Vega's vast dramatic output are at last making progress. The most recent advance was the publication in 1940 of *The Chronology of Lope de Vega's Comedias* by Professors Morley and Bruerton, together with the "Addenda" to that volume published in 1947.[1] This work demonstrated that it was possible to assign a fairly accurate date for any *comedia* through a statistical tabulation of the poet's metrical practice throughout the successive stages of his life. It was received with certain skepticism in some quarters, but was strikingly vindicated in 1945 through the discovery and publication by the distinguished *Lopista* Dr. Agustín de Amezúa of Madrid, of transcriptions from Lope's autograph of thirty-two *comedias,* each furnishing the date on which the poet finished writing the play.[2] Of seventeen hitherto undated plays, Professors Morley and Bruerton had correctly arrived at the date of composition of thirteen. Within the chronological framework afforded by their work, it now becomes possible to concentrate a close attention on small

A paper contributed to *Varia Variorum: Festgabe für Karl Reinhardt,* published in Münster and Cologne by the Böhlau Verlag in 1952.
    [1]Published by the Modern Language Association of America, New York, and the Oxford University Press, London. The "Addenda" are in *The Hispanic Review,* Vol. XV, No. 1, January 1947.
    [2]*Una Colección Manuscrita y Desconocida de Comedias de Lope de Vega Carpio,* por Agustín G. de Amezúa, Centro de Estudios sobre Lope de Vega, Madrid, 1945.

groups of approximately contemporaneous plays, and so attempt to arrive at a still more precise chronology. The present paper aims to afford an example of such a procedure, showing how we may now avail ourselves of the considerable body of information which has been assembled concerning the organization of the theatrical companies to whom Lope sold his plays and of a new use to which we may put the so-called *Peregrino* lists.

In the introduction to his novel *El Peregrino en Su Patria,* first published in Seville and Barcelona in 1604 but completed at the close of 1603, Lope de Vega listed the titles of 219 *comedias* which he had written up to that time. When he reissued the novel in Madrid in 1618 he added 228 titles, a number of which we now know to have been written even before 1604. These lists are in neither alphabetical nor chronological order, and scholars finding no reason for leaving them in their apparently planless sequence have consistently reprinted them in alphabetical order. A closer inspection, however, has revealed that Lope or his publisher arranged the titles according to a general intention or association (though with many a puzzling variation in the design): they are grouped according to the *autores*—actor-managers—to whom the poet sold the plays. The *Peregrino* list of 1618 is arranged according to a different plan which will be the subject of a later paper. In the 1604 list, for example (and naturally disclaiming any account of the many lost plays), it may be affirmed that P-134 *El Verdadero Amante* to P-148 *El Ingrato Arrepentido* (with the exception of P-143 *El Perseguido,* which was produced by Cisneros) were sold to Nicolás de los Ríos; P-205 *La Serrana de la Vera* to P-213 *La Pobreza de Reinaldos* were sold to Pinedo—and were hence written after 1598, when Pinedo first assumed management of a company; P-98 *El Cuerdo Loco* to P-104 *Pedro Carbonero* were sold to Antonio Granados; of the sequence P-106 *El Favor Agradecido* to P-119 *Los Fajardos* we can identify ten as having been produced by Luis de Vergara. For the purpose of this paper we will examine the long list of plays which give evidence of having been sold to the famous manager, Lope's close friend, Gaspar de Porras, adding to it a number of plays which we know to have been sold to him prior to 1604 or very near to that time and which Lope apparently forgot when drawing up the 1604 *Peregrino* list. The sequence we are considering extends from P-152 *Las Ferias de Madrid* to P-195 *Los Torneos de Aragón*. Within this sequence twenty-two plays have been lost or are still unavailable to us; P-158 *El Príncipe Inocente* and P-170 *El Amor Desatinado* are in the collection discovered by Dr. Amezúa; they have not yet been published, but a study of their *licencias* shows that they were produced by Porras. For purposes of brevity we shall omit consideration of plays which we know to have been before 1596 or which Professors Morley and Bruerton assign to those years. Of the nineteen plays thus isolated for our study we have independent evidence (furnished below) that at least twelve were owned by Porras; of four of them we know the very day on which Lope finished writing them; of another we can be fairly certain of the year. In the case of two of them, we have the very *repartos*—the names of the actors appended to the rôles they were to play.[3] With the help of this material we now invoke certain further aids toward determining an ever more precise date of composition by searching for the answers to several questions: What were the personal characteristics of the leading male player in Porras's company? On what performers in the company did Lope rely for comic effect? And in what year did Porras obtain the services of a qualified *gracioso*—low comedian?

Every play of the period closes with a *despedida*—the direct address to the audience by one of the actors announcing that the play is at an end and stating its title. Generally, this function is undertaken by the actor-manager himself, especially in

---

[3]These *repartos* are in the recently discovered *Colección* but have not yet been published. The present writer is greatly indebted to the kindness of Dr. Amezúa for permission to see them during a visit to Madrid.

the years prior to 1610. The plays produced by Porras, however, exhibit an exception; we see that he has asked Lope to give the *despedida* to the actor playing the *primer galán*—leading man. Porras was born in 1550 and in the *repartos* of *Los Torneos de Aragón* and *El Tirano Castigado* we see that he has assigned himself the rôles of dignified old men.

From Lent 1595 to Lent 1597 Porras's *primer galán* was probably Agustín Solano, of whom Lope said:

> *en la figura del galán, por la blandura, talle y aseo de su persona nadie ha igualado.*[4]

But Solano was no longer young; in the *reparto* of *El Tirano Castigado,* of July 1599, he is not even playing *tercer galán* but an old king. He was succeeded in Porras's company by Baltasar de Pinedo, one of the greatest actors of his time, himself soon to become a manager. Lope, Tirso de Molina, and Ruiz de Alarcón were to write many plays for him. In May 1598 the theaters of Spain were closed for eleven months, through the action of censors and later during the months of mourning for the death of Philip II. During this time Pinedo left the company of Porras and was succeeded by Pedro de Morales, the friend of Cervantes. This furnishes us with a chronological line of demarcation: Morales was young and handsome, and each rôle that Lope wrote for the *primer galán* during his incumbency abounds with allusion to these characteristics: he is of *"tierna edad"* and *"más bello que Apolo";* those written for Pinedo are filled with opportunities for tragic power, but are accompanied by no words of praise for his person; at the most, he receives an occasional lukewarm *"buen talle."*

Students of the problem of the *gracioso* have long been bewildered by Lope's statement that in the rôle of Tristán in

---

[4]Solano's contract for these years is in Pérez Pastor, *Nuevos Datos acerca del Histrionismo Espagnol,* 1ª serie, *sub* 19 March 1595. A passage in Rojas's *El Viaje Entretenido* seems to place him in Cisneros's company in 1594; he went to that of Ríos in 1597, and returned to Porras in 1599.

La Francesilla (which we now know to have been finished by Lope on 6 April 1596) he created the first *gracioso,* the first of so many thousands, in Spanish drama. An adequate treatment of the subject would require an entire book; for the purpose of our present study it is merely necessary to ask in what year a given manager was able to engage an actor capable of filling this highly specialized type of rôle. Porras was not able to find such an actor until 1600. Previous to that year the plays he staged contained comic characters—ridiculous rustics, boastful *villanos* and *bobos,* eccentric aged *escuderos* and *guardadamas,* even short rôles for cynical *criados*—but the test of a *gracioso* is not merely that he have the traits which we associate with the type, but that he appear in every act, that he be introduced at the finale, and that he be *felt by the audience to be of equal importance with the leading characters.*

It is well known that in 1599 Lope began to introduce the figure of his beloved Micaela de Luján into his plays under the name of Lucinda. The first dated play containing a Lucinda is *El Amigo por Fuerza,* finished by him on 14 October of that year, but it seems increasingly likely that he fell in love with Micaela in August (on the eve of the Feast of the Assumption). We now know for the first time to which company she belonged; her name and that of her husband, Diego Diaz, appear in the *reparto* of *El Blason de los Chaves de Villalba,* furnished by Lope on 20 August for the manager Melchor de Villalba; for her Lope wrote the part of Dorotea, an actress playing a man.

In *El Argel Fingido,* which we know Lope wrote for Luis de Vergara in late 1599 or early 1600, occur the words:

> *Mejor es que el pelo enlaces (con aquestos alfileres)*
> *que usan en la corte agora.*

The vogue of these *alfileres*—pins worn by women in their hair —must have been sudden and intense. The plays begin to abound with allusions to them. In earlier plays the only allusion I have found to them[5] is as an article of men's dress associated with horsemanship. It is highly probable that Margarita of Austria brought the fashion into Spain at the time of her marriage to Philip III in May 1599. Just as abruptly the vogue of the *chacona* as a dance-song seems to have arisen a little later. Dr. Amezúa has found an allusion to it in a book whose *aprobación* is as early as 1 January 1598.[6] Its first appearance in a dated play is in *Los Amantes sin Amor* of 1601.

In the following list the dates adjudged for each play by Professors Morley and Bruerton are given preceded by the initials "M-B." "Parte IV" was a collection of Lope's plays published in 1614 by Porras with the declaration that he had bought them from the poet. When in 1617 Lope began publishing his plays himself, he frequently gives the name of the manager to whom he sold them preceded by the word *"Representóla."* In a few cases the word, however, indicates the principal actor or actress, and not the manager.

Prior to Lent 1597

P-166   *Jorje Toledano.* M-B 1595–1597. Lope in Parte XVII specifically declares that the play was produced by Porras and that the principal rôle was played by Solano. As has been stated above, this would almost certainly be in 1595 or 1596, and, as the rôle of Jorje is a very youthful one, as early as possible.

P-183   *La Vida y Muerte del Rey Bamba.* M-B 1597–1598. There is no evidence other than its presence in the Porras sequence within the *Peregrino* list that this play was produced by that manager. It is probable that this is also a Solano rôle. This "saintly fool" does not resemble any rôle written for Pinedo or Morales, but suggests the naïveté which is reflected in the first act of *Jorje Toledano.* (The great actor of "saintly fools"—Salvador Ochoa—does not enter Porras's

---

[5]Apart, that is, from the idiomatic use of the word to express an opposite idea, a thing of no value, not worth *dos alfileres.*

[6]His edition of Cervantes' *El Casamiento Engañoso y el Coloquio de los Perros,* Madrid, 1912, p. 486.

company until 1603.) Moreover, there is here only one considerable rôle for a woman player; of the three other women none has more than five verses and one is mute. An edict issued on 5 September 1596 (but soon rescinded) forbade the appearance of women on the stage. It is likely that Lope was bearing this contingency in mind. The comic interest in the play is entrusted to *villanos*.

1597 and 1598. Pinedo as *Primer Galán*

P-190 *La Hermosa Alfreda.* M-B 1596–1603, "probably 1598–1600." Pérez Pastor, *sub* 20 March 1601, prints a document wherein Porras expressly warns Pinedo against performing it under the latter's independent management. *Despedida* by the *viejo* because the *primer galán* Conde Godolfe is dead. There is no word of praise for the Conde's appearance. A passage on the misfortune of kings who are unable to marry of their own choice would tend to date the play well before the royal marriage of 1599.

P-195 *Los Torneos de Aragón.* M-B 1596–1598, "probably 1598." The recently discovered transcript of Lope's autograph shows that he finished it on 14 November 1597. Parte IV. The *reparto* shows that the *primer galán,* with *despedida,* was played by Pinedo. There is no word in the text expressing admiration for his appearance. The comic element is furnished by *labradores*—peasants —and by the *primera dama,* who, dressed as a man, plays a *truhán* —clown.

1599. Morales as *Primer Galán.* Absence of *Gracioso,* but Presence of Strong Elderly Comic Player. First Appearance (after 14 August?) of References to Lucinda. Vogue of *Alfileres.*

P-173 *Los Horacios—El Honrado Hermano—.* M-B 1596–1603, "probably 1598–1600." No independent indication that this play was sold to Porras. *Despedida* by *viejo* because the first, Curiacio— *"tierna edad," "tantas gracias encierra"*—is dead. No comic element.

P-185 *El Mayorazgo Dudoso.* M-B 1598–1603. No independent

evidence that this play was bought by Porras. *Primer galán* is of "*tierna edad*" and is "*bello . . . hermoso.*" Comic element by shepherds.

P-186   *El Tirano Castigado.* M-B 1598–1603. Now known that Lope finished it on 17 July 1599. Parte IV. Porras's ownership confirmed by *licencias. Primer galán* specifically assigned to Morales in the *reparto;* he is "*el hombre más gallardo que ha nacido.*" Comic element afforded by rustics, particularly an elderly village *alcalde.*

P-188   *La Fé Rompida.* M-B 1599–1603. Parte IV. *Primer galán:* "*Mas bello que Apolo,*" "*gracia, ingenio y hermosura.*" *Primera dama* is called Lucinda. Comic elements: Lucinda, dressed as a man, has extended passages of *gracioso* color. Allusion to *alfileres.*

P-187   *El Amigo por Fuerza.* M-B 1599–1603. Now known that Lope finished it on 14 October 1599. Parte IV. *Primer galán: "más mirado que un espejo"* and of "*tierna edad.*" *Primera dama* is called Lucinda. Comic element by *viejo escudero.* The *criados*—servants—begin to have light touches of *gracioso* color.

P-189   *La Resistencia Honrada de la Condesa Matilde.* (This appears in *El Peregrino* as "Amatilde." Passages in *Los Tres Diamantes* show that Lope used the names Matilde and Amatilde interchangeably.) M-B 1596–1599?–1603. There is no independent evidence that this play was produced by Porras, but note the sequence of *Peregrino* numbers. *Despedida* by *viejo,* because the *primer galán—"como un sol," "galán, discreto y hermoso"*—has died. Comic element: a *viejo escudero* as in *El Amigo por Fuerza.* Reference to *alfileres.*

P-167   *Los Tres Diamantes.* M-B 1599–1603. No independent evidence that this play was produced by Porras. *Primer galán: "bravo mancebo.*" *Primera dama* is called Lucinda. Comic element: in Act I Belardo, a near *bobo;* in Act III, by Hermano Crispin with elaborate low-comedy treatment allied to rustic *bobo* type rather than to *gracioso.*

1600–1603. First Appearances of Developed *Gracioso.* Likewise First Appearance (in Porras's Company) of a Soubrette or *Criada* as Feminine Counterpart of the *Gracioso. Morales (or Ochoa) as *Primer Galán.*

P-191 *Los Enredos* (Embustes) *de Celauro.* M-B 1599–1603. Now known to have been finished by Lope on 25 January 1600. Parte IV. *Primer galán: "espejo de hombres en talle."* Lucinda referred to. Comic element: *villanos* in Act III; three *criados* all touched with *gracioso* color, one considerably developed. No soubrette.

P-56 *La Viuda Valenciana.* M-B 1595–1603. Lope, publishing it, says, *"Representóla* Mariana Vaca." She was the wife of Pedro de Morales (here as *primer galán:* never *"hombre más bello y galán"*) and both were in Porras's company in 1600, the date of this play, as the several references to the Jubilee Year show. Completely developed *gracioso* and a soubrette. Reference to *alfileres.*

P-234 *La Boda entre Dos Maridos.* M-B 1596?–1603? Parte IV. *Primer galán* is a student at Salamanca. The Court is at Madrid—*i.e.,* before or after its removal to Valladolid 1601–1606. The play is certainly pre-1606 and the tentative development of the two quasi-*graciosos* suggests 1600. The heroine's sister is almost a soubrette.

P-174 *La Probreza Estimada.* M-B 1597–1603. No independent evidence that this play was owned by Porras. *Primer galán: "más bello quē Apolo"* and of *"tierna edad."* *Gracioso* and soubrette. Reference to *alfileres.*

P-88 *Los Amantes sin Amor.* M-B 1601–1603. Lope, publishing this play, says: *"Representóla* Pedro de Morales." Morales did not separate from Porras's company before mid-1602. The play refers to the removal of the Court to Valladolid as having taken place five or six months before—*i.e.,* late spring 1601. There are two fully developed *graciosos* and a soubrette; and allusions to *alfileres* and to the *chacona.*

Three Plays Presenting Peculiar Difficulties

P-233 *El Genovés Liberal.* M-B 1599–1608, "probably 1599–1603." Parte IV. The *segundo galán* receives the praise. He is called upon to sing during the action, which tends to suggest that he is played by Salvador Ochoa, who may have entered the company as *segundo* in 1603. He sings in *El Hermano Francisco,* which is almost certainly 1604. (Porras's company played before the Queen in the fall; note in that play the marked reminiscences of the royal wedding and the allusions to the Queen's journeys.) There is a fully developed *gracioso*, the rôle being entirely written in crude Italian, and a soubrette. The play's political and humanitarian implications ally it to some later plays.

P-157 *El Galán* (Rufián) *Castrucho.* M-B *"circa* 1598." Parte IV. This is very unlike any other play of the Porras repertory, but appears to have been written for Nicolás de los Ríos. The title rôle with *despedida* brilliantly exemplifies the gifts for which he was famous. It contains a magnificent "Celestina" part; there is not a single rôle for an older woman in any play written for Porras during the years we are studying, but they are frequent in the Ríos repertory. The *primera dama* is very young—"sixteen"—another Ríos and not a Porras characteristic. In the late spring of 1600 Ríos was banished from the Court for a year and a half for having offended the French ambassador. It seems probable that Porras bought the play from him at that time. There are two references to *alfileres* and one to the *chacona.*

P-184 *El Nuevo Mundo.* M-B 1596–1603, "probably 1598–1603." Parte IV. The rôle of Columbus would appear to be a Pinedo rather than a Morales part, hence 1597–1598. There is a comic savage, however, which resembles the rôles written for the strong character actor in the company in 1599; and a scornful reference to the vogue of *alfileres.*

---

*EDITOR'S NOTE: Thornton Wilder's concluding paragraph to this essay is substantially the same as the final paragraph in the essay following. To avoid repetition, the conclusion is omitted here and appears only at the end of the second essay.

LOPE, PINEDO,
SOME CHILD ACTORS,
AND A LION

Bad times had fallen on the theater. In November 1597 the playhouses of Madrid were closed while the Court went into mourning for the death of the King's sister; in May 1598 a council of theologians prevailed upon the King to close them throughout all Spain; then Philip II himself died in September of that year. Actors and dramatists were starving. Porras took his company to Lisbon; other managers betook themselves to Valencia and Barcelona and to the remoter regions, where the edicts were less strictly enforced. Lope de Vega turned to writing narrative poems. Finally, however, there was news in the air that the royal double wedding was to take place in Valencia in the spring of 1599, and there was promise that the theaters would be reopened.

Baltasar de Pinedo and his wife, Juana de Villalba, were among the most admired actors of Spain. They had long held the *primeros papeles*—leading rôles—in the company of Gaspar de Porras, Lope's old friend. Pinedo was no longer sufficiently young and dashing to play the type rôle of *primer galán,* but he was very fine at mad scenes and frantic laments, and Lope obligingly provided him with such opportunities in many a

Reprinted from *Romance Philology* for August 1953. (Thornton Wilder used the editions of Lope de Vega's works published by the Royal Spanish Academy: *Obras,* 15 volumes, Madrid, 1890–1913, and *Obras . . . (Nueva edición) Obras Dramaticas,* 13 volumes, Madrid, 1916–1930, cited, respectively, as "Acad." and "Acad. N.")

play. Juana de Villalba was a *mujer varonil,* a *Diana cazadora,* an *Hércules,* a *"gigante hecho de nieve y de rosas."* She frequently bestrode the stage in man's armor and overcame all contestants in tourneys at a play's finale. From the moment the theaters were closed this couple broke away from Porras's company and prepared to launch one of their own, and they called upon Lope to furnish them with the greater part of their repertory. The first play that Lope wrote for them for which we have an exact date is *La Varona Castellana,* completed by the poet on 2 November 1599. He had probably furnished them several during the preceding months, but I think it can be said with considerable assurance that no "Pinedo play" was written before 1599. This paper represents an effort to establish a chronology for a number—though not all—of the plays which Lope wrote for this new company between 1599 and 1606.

Pinedo had neither the money, the company, nor the texts to launch out at once. He first joined forces with his brother-in-law Melchor de Villalba. Villalba was held in such high esteem that he was the only *autor*—actor-manager—who was invited to perform at the wedding celebration in Valencia. Pinedo remained with him, and together they furnished the Corpus Christi festival in Madrid, 1600. Thereafter Villalba disappears from our records, and it is safe to assume that Pinedo took over the strength and direction of his company. This company included a number of figures who were to play an important part in the theater of the *Siglo de Oro* and in Lope's life, but none more remarkable than Micaela de Luján, Lope's Lucinda. Writers on the period have long affirmed that Micaela de Luján was in Pinedo's company during the first few years of its existence, but no document has been found to confirm the fact. Strength is lent to the conjecture, however, by the recent discovery that she was, at least, a member of Villalba's company in the fall of 1599[1] and therefore probably

---

[1] In the still unpublished *reparto* of the text of *El Blasón de los Chaves de Villalba* furnished by Lope on 20 August 1599. A transcription of Lope's manuscript is

continued in it when it passed into the hands of Pinedo. Lope's movements in the next two years will be related to the peregrinations of Pinedo's company, in which Micaela was playing *tercera dama* to the *primera* and *segunda* of Juana de Villalba and Ana Martínez (*ossia* de los Reyes *ossia* la Baltasara).

There are four ways in which we can determine which plays were sold to Pinedo. In 1616 Pinedo drew up a document listing the titles of twelve *comedias* which he affirmed had been sold to him by the poet. Secondly, when Lope finally undertook the publication of his plays himself, he frequently furnished the names of the *autor* who had first produced them. Thirdly, the licenses for performance attached to the manuscripts often permit us to establish the company producing them; and, finally, the position of the title in the so-called *Peregrino* lists. In "New Aids Toward Dating the Early Plays of Lope de Vega" I was able to show that the apparently incoherent list of titles of his plays which Lope printed at the beginning of his novel *El Peregrino en Su Patria,* 1604 (licensed 25 November 1603), is not so haphazard as it first seems. The titles there are listed—although with many a puzzling exception—according to the manager to whom Lope sold them. The plays from P-205 *La Serrana de la Vera,* through P-216 *El Catalán Valeroso*—twelve plays which include four lost plays about which we know nothing—are indubitably "Pinedo plays," written before the end of November 1603. The order of the titles in the second *Peregrino* list of 1618 does not tell us much relative to *autor;* Lope is (in the earlier part of this list) merely copying down the titles in the order in which they appear in the table of contents of the pirated *Partes.*

In these ways we arrive at the titles of some nineteen *comedias* of which we can feel fairly certain that they were written for Pinedo by Lope between 1599 and 1606. In at-

described by the editor in *Una Colección Manuscrita y Desconocida de Comedias de Lope de Vega Carpio.* The present writer is greatly indebted to Dr. Amezúa for permission to transcribe this *reparto* during a visit to Madrid.

tempting to arrange them in chronological order I am going
to omit a discussion of several whose dating would unduly
lengthen this paper.

The first thing that we notice about many of these plays
which Lope wrote for Pinedo in the earlier years (he was still
writing for him as late as 1617—*Lo Que Pasa en Una Tarde*)
is that they call for the services of first one, then two, highly
accomplished child actors. This requirement becomes of such
importance that by 1603 an entire play, *El Niño Inocente de la
Guardia,* turns upon the child as central figure rather than (as
usually) a character appearing in one act only. Children occasionally make their appearance in other companies; but it
should be noted that in the twenty-seven plays which we know
to have been sold to Porras there is no child who is assigned
more than twelve verses. In the eighteen plays which are
certainly or probably from the repertory of Nicolás de los Ríos
there is only one child (the *muchacho Pelayo* in *El Sol Parado*)
and he is fourteen years old and is an expectant father. So little
did the companies lean on child actors that when Lope dramatized Boccaccio's great story of the falcon for Riquelme (*El
Halcón de Federico, ca.* 1605), he robbed the story of much of
its poignancy and force by making a sick child a young man
of sixteen already in search of a wife.

All the more striking, then, is the recurrent use of children
in the Pinedo repertory. These rôles might have been played
by girls or women (we remember Lope's admiration for
Jusepa Vaca's performance in *Los Mocedades de Roldán*); but
two observations support our feeling that Pinedo's child players were indeed boys. There are two boy rôles in plays for
other companies where Lope inserts into the dialogue an express explanation or apology for the fact that the boys have
disconcertingly long hair. Young Adonis *("es tan niño")*
in *Adonis y Venus (autor:* Luis de Vergara) says (Acad. VI,
26b):

> *Si mi rostro y mi cabello*
> *Señas feminiles son,*
> *Mira que un hombre, si es bello,*
> *Tiene más obligación. . . .*
> *De no parecello.*

Similarly, in *El Rey sin Reino,* written for an undetermined *autor,* two courtiers exclaim in the presence of the boy King (Acad. VI, 591*a*):

> *¡Qué hermoso cabello cría! . . .*
> *Casi hasta el hombro le llega.*

Moreover, it seems likely that the principal boy player in Pinedo's company was Pinedo's own son. When this child plays a rôle which is the son of the character played by Pinedo (and Pinedo rôles are easily recognizable), Lope expatiates on the resemblance of the child to his father. This is particularly noticeable in *Las Pobrezas de Reinaldos* and in *La Fuerza Lastimosa.* Such family resemblance would be more striking in a son than in a daughter.

The increasing age of this child actor (even though the age is "stage age") will help us toward dating some of the plays. In a play whose date we know—*Los Benavides,* June 1600—the child is specifically said to be six years old. In a play which gives evidence of being 1604–1605, *Los Porceles de Murcia,* the plot requires that the child be nine; in *Las Paces de los Reyes,* which I have other reasons for thinking to be about 1605, the action of the play turns on the fact that the boy King is just under ten years of age. Hence when in *La Fuerza Lastimosa* we hear that a child was born at the end of the first year of a marriage which took place (six times affirmed) six years before, we can state that the child is five years old and that the play is among the earliest that Lope wrote for Pinedo—a supposition confirmed by the position of the title in the *Peregrino* list. This growth in the boy's years will be accompanied by an increase in the number of lines which he will be given to memorize and the increase of responsibility accorded to him as actor. *El Niño Inocente* is the only play in which he appears in all three acts; it is a little surprising to feel that the play is even as early as 1603.

For a year or two Pinedo was in possession of a lion or a costume made from a lion-skin. It figures in three plays, one of them the dated play *La Varona Castellana,* 2 November 1599. It is in *La Serrana de la Vera,* and *two* lions appear briefly in a sort of pageant at the close of *Los Palacios de Galiana.* I am inclined to think that Pinedo enjoyed the services of a poor aged and edentate beast, simply because the lion is always called upon to do the same thing—to come to the feet of a leading player and lie down. Were it an actor in a skin, the lion would certainly have been given more varied and more thrilling things to do. The appearances of this lion are not necessary to the plot, and the scenes can easily be cut out. I suspect that Pinedo called upon Lope to introduce them and for a short time they furnished a considerable theatrical sensation for the Pinedo season. It confirms for us the fact that all three plays belong to Pinedo's first and second years. Similarly, the manager Vergara had a lion or a lion-skin some five years earlier, and Lope wrote several plays for its appearance, including one on the subject of Androcles and the lion *(El Esclavo de Roma);* there too the animal is required merely to subside at Androcles's feet with a show of affection and gratitude. In Bernard Shaw's play on the same subject the actor in the lion-skin is given a wide variety of actions to perform.

Another incidental aid in assigning dates to these plays is to remark the gradual decline of the rôle of the *autora* Juana de Villalba; from *primera dama* she dwindles to brief, though impressive, appearances in the last acts only. Ambitious rising actresses would not join a company in which the manager's wife enjoyed all the big rôles. We have contracts in which actresses demand assurance that they will play half the *primeros papeles* and that they will never be assigned less than the *segundos*.

Now to consider the plays. Note the sequence of many of the *Peregrino* numbers. In counting the verses assigned to the child players I have counted any part of a verse as a full verse. On a number of occasions I have altered the assignment of a speech to a given character where a corruption in the printing of the text seems to have mistaken the speaker.

P-205 *La Serrana de la Vera.* Acad. XII. M-B 1595–1598. The lion. No child. This is probably the first play Lope wrote for the new company. The Juana de Villalba rôle *in excelsis.* She slays scores of men; is *amazona* and a *fiera.* M-B places this play before 1599 because it seems to be alluded to in *El Galán Escarmentado* and THAT play, in turn, seems to have been written before the death of Philip II. This antedating is unnecessary. Philip III and his Court do not seem to have been offended by hearing the King's father referred to as *"Filipo sin segundo";* the expression even more strongly phrased occurs in a play which we know to have been finished by Lope on 15 February 1600—*La Contienda de García,* etc. (Acad. XI, 493a):

> *El príncipe Filipo, aunque segundo,*
> *Para ser sin segundo vino al mundo.*

Both plays give other evidence of having been written after 1598. The second act of *El Galán Escarmentado* closes with an allusion to a popular song which was all the rage in 1601 and for many years thereafter, *"Hey, hey, hey"* (see a *loa* in *El Viaje Entretenido,* and the *baile* preceding *El Ejemplo de Casadas*).

P-206 *La Fuerza Lastimosa.* Acad. XIV. M-B "1595–1603 (probably 1599–1600)." Child: aged five (Lope contradicts himself on the time-scheme in Act II). Child has 129 verses. The Juana de Villalba rôle is *segunda.* The heroine is Isabella, model of conjugal love. Lope's wife, Isabel de Urbina, died in 1594. This tribute tends to date the play before his attachment to Micaela de Luján in the summer of 1599, and the additional factors confirm it.

P-207 *Los Palacios de Galiana.* Acad. XIII. M-B 1597–1602. No child. Two lions! Juana de Villalba *prima.*

P-209 *La Santa Liga (La Batalla Naval).* Acad. XII. M-B "1598–1603, probably 1598–1600." Child: *"soy muy chico"*— 44 verses. Juana de Villalba *prima.*

P-85 *La Varona Castellana.* Acad. VIII. Autograph: 2 November 1599. Lion. Child: *"apenas ocupo la Real silla"*—364 verses. Big rôle for Juana de Villalba: *"nací con inlinación / a las armas y al ser hombre."* Fights all night with Alfonso el Batallador of Aragón and overcomes him. Note the large number of verses assigned to the child at this early date. This appears to be the last play in which Juana de Villalba overwhelmingly out-tops all the women's rôles.

P-213 *Las Pobrezas de Reinaldos.* Acad. XIII. M-B 1599. Child: *"ser tan niño no es falta"*—138 verses. Probably the first Lucinda play written for Pinedo (the first dated Lucinda play was *El Amigo por Fuerza,* finished for Porras on 14 October 1599).

P-210 *Los Benavides.* Acad. VII. Autograph: 15 June 1600. Child: aged six—55 verses. He is carried *"en brazos."* Juana de Villalba enters in Act III, *"gran cazadora . . . Diana debe de ser."*

We now pass on to plays furnished a few years later, though several plays written by Lope for Pinedo fall within the years 1600–1602: P-212 *La Ocasión Perdida,* P-216 *El Valeroso Catalán,* and P-224 *El Castigo del Discreto.*

P-276 *El Niño Inocente de la Guardia.* Acad. V. M-B "1598–1608, probably 1604–1606." This powerful but horrifying play was surely finished before the birth of the future Philip IV on 8 April 1605. St. Dominic's prophecy that the Inquisition would be carried on by Philip III and the two Infantas would certainly have been extended to an Infante, heir apparent, if he had been born. Who then are the Infantas? Ana Mauricia de Austria, born 22 September 1601, and María de Austria, born 1 February 1603. Little María lived only a month, despaired of daily, but I do not think that there can be any doubt that the play was written between 1 February and 1 March, when she died. The fact that the child player *("ya es grande para los brazos")* has only 170 verses gives a misleading impression of his participation; the demands upon his performance are enormous.

P-227   *Los Porceles de Murcia.* Acad. XI. M-B "1599–1608 (probably 1604–1608)." Two boys: Don Luis, aged ten—112 verses; Don Pedro, aged nine—132 verses. A passing allusion tends to assign this play to the years 1604–1605. Apparently a ghost story was gaining wide circulation in Madrid and perhaps throughout the whole country. A student named Osorio claimed to have seen the dismembered body of a man descending some stairs at midnight. In *La Prueba de los Amigos,* which Lope finished for Granados on 12 September 1604, we read (Acad. N. XI, 122*a*):

> *Mas que ha de darse el cuitado*
> *como los cuartos de Osorio.*

In *Los Porceles de Murcia* (XI, 579*a*) a character urges another to show no surprise even if he were to see before him *"las sombras que vió Osorio el estudiante";* the other replies that he would control himself even

> *Si viese descender del propio modo*
> *Los cuartos de aquel hombre á media noche.*

As there is no other mention of this episode in all the discursive conversation of scores of *graciosos* in the plays throughout those years, we may assume that the story was "hot" toward the latter half of 1604.

P-225   *El Gran Duque de Moscovia.* Acad. XI. M-B 1606 (later information admits the possibility that details of the story of Boris Godunov and the "False Demetrius" may have reached Spain at an earlier date). Two boys of the same age, *"tan niño"*—Demetrio, 146 verses; César, 18.

P-226   *Las Paces de los Reyes.* Acad. VIII. M-B "1604–1612, probably 1610–1612." Here is the only time I must diverge from the preferred recommendation of the *Chronology*. The child actor is presented in Act I as just under ten years of age (in Act II he is full-grown and played by another actor). He has 240 verses. A boy actor who was six in 1600 is approximately ten in 1604, but there is a more persuasive reason for ascribing this play to late 1605. In September of that year Lope writes the Duke of Sessa that he has just sent off his epic poem *La Jerusalén Conquistada* to the censors in Valladolid. The events of the second and third acts of this play are also treated in that poem. In the epic a large company of nobles, incited by the Queen, crosses the Tajo to kill Raquel, the King's mistress. In the play four nobles plan the murder without any intervention of the Queen. All have reason to fear the King's wrath and vengeance, and in the epic, Book IX, they advance *"caminando delante la hidalguía/y detrás la lisonja y cobardía."* Lope remembered this, and in the play Garcerán Manrique advances, saying (p. 553*a*):

> *El que se quedare atrás,*
> *Ó es villano ó lisonjero.*

The speech is suitable as applied to a throng; it is insulting as addressed to three resolute patriots. Had a considerable time elapsed between the writing of the epic and the play, Lope's imagination would have prevented his memory from obtruding itself thus inappropriately. It is highly likely that the epic was written first and the play very soon after.

Such work as this, inevitably involving a great deal of supposition, would not have been possible prior to the publication of *The Chronology of Lope de Vega's Comedias* by Professors Morley and Bruerton, a work which has been confirmed as so notable a landmark in Lope studies. By its aid we are at last able to isolate within Lope's immense dramatic *oeuvre* small groups of approximately contemporaneous plays in the hope of establishing an ever more precise chronology. [In the light of such a chronology it will be possible to attempt an entirely new appraisal of his art, his ideas, and the autobiographical details which he continually poured into his plays.] The work is difficult and detailed; it involves combining conjecture with conjecture until their sheer multiplicity affords sufficient grounds for confidence. Each clarification, however, expands our admiration for the poet's variety, for the unfailing felicity of his versification, for his dramatic resourcefulness, [for his profound knowledge of human nature,] and for the fascinating complexity of his personal character.*

---

*EDITOR'S NOTE: This concluding paragraph substantially repeats the final paragraph originally printed with the preceding essay. A sentence and a phrase which appear only in the conclusion to the first essay are here printed within square brackets.

GIORDANO BRUNO'S LAST MEAL
IN *FINNEGANS WAKE*

On any page of *Finnegans Wake* the reader finds a number of interwoven themes and to the difficulty of deciphering and isolating any one of them is added that of furnishing an explanation for their juxtaposition. I am about to show that pages 404 through 407 are largely concerned with Giordano Bruno's trial and torture and with his death at the stake, which took place on 17 February 1600 in the Campo dei Fiori at Rome. Interwoven with this material are at least five other themes: the seven colors of the spectrum; the entrance of Shaun the Post in the first act of Boucicault's play *Arrah-na-Pogue;* the composition of a pack of playing cards; some events of the last days of Christ's life, together with the liturgical offices which commemorate them; and the account of a barrel of Guinness stout rolling down the Liffey to Dublin Bay. I shall consider here only the first four of these.

To readers who have not the volume before them I must emphasize that all these varied themes are being pursued simultaneously. By startling feats of ingenuity Joyce forces a phrase or a single word into service for two or more purposes at the same time. A "wheel" is at once a form of torture employed by the Inquisition and a playing card in the Tarot pack. The "blessings of . . . Haggispatrick and Huggisbrigid"

An article printed in the *Hudson Review* for Spring 1963.

(404.35) are not only an allusion to this prodigious meal, to Shaun the Post's preferred saints, to a chorus in the distance singing the Trisagion, but to the fact that Bruno was a Dominican condemned by Dominicans. Because of their black-and-white habit the order was popularly identified with magpies; in Old English dialects the magpie was called a "haggis." The bird was also called a "margaret" (the French called *la pie* "*la margot*") and we find that at this meal there is a "bulby onion (Margareter)" (406.7). We shall presently see what associations are set in motion by such words, not found in any dictionary, as "Juhn" and "lightbreakfastbringer." The style of *Finnegans Wake* may be called that of the "collocation of disparates." In the principal passages studied in this paper Joyce employs it for effects of grinding horror; but the novel is of wide diversity. Elsewhere by superimposing on one page a pubkeeper's wife, Homer's Hera, and a song by Robert Burns; or on another page Melville's Billy Budd, Eamon de Valera, and the Buddha, he obtains effects of lyrical beauty or of savage satire. It can be said that this style is something new in literature and that by extending in various ways the function of metaphor it moves largely in the realm of poetry. The first impression one receives is that it is a work of comic intention, for verbal distortions always appear to us as proceeding from wit, even when they arise from the unconscious; but though there are innumerable puns in the novel, Joyce's interest is not primarily in the puns but in the simultaneous multiple-level associations which they permit him to pursue. *Finnegans Wake* appears to me as an immense poem whose subject is the continuity of what is Living, viewed under the guise of a resurrection myth. This poem is conducted under the utmost formal rigor controlling every word and in a style that enables the author through apparently preposterous incongruities to arrive at an ultimate unification and harmony.

Now to return to the four themes in the passage we are studying:

I suspect that the colors of the rainbow are here to remind us of another heroic person burned at the stake, Jeanne d'Arc. Her name like Shaun's is derived from John, and by one of those coincidences that so often gave support to Joyce's propensity toward superstition her name recalls the rainbow; she was indeed an *arc-en-ciel.* Moreover, both Bruno and Jeanne illustrate one of the most frequently recurring symbols in the book, the phoenix. Like the "bird of Arabia" they were consumed by fire and are continually reborn in the mind and spirit of aftertime. At the close of this paper I shall show that Joyce elsewhere associates Ste. Jeanne with Bruno.

The spectrum appears as "red" (404.25, with the Russian "krasnapoppsky," papal red); "orange" (405.33); yellow, "guilbey" (German *gelb, gelbe*) (406.33); green, "pease, rice, and yeggyyolk" (the colors of the Irish Free State, giving us another yellow) (404.29–30); blue, "starspangled zephyr" (star . . . sapphire) (404.27); "indigo" (404.18); and purple, "mauveport" (407.21).

The appearance of Shaun the Post from Boucicault's play introduces the heroine, "arrah" (404.4); Shaun himself (404.7); and Beamish (MacCool) (405.16). Page 404 gives us a general description of his costume as we see it in the theatrical documents and the name of the actor who played it for years on both sides of the Atlantic. The name of Chauncey Olcott appears elsewhere in the novel—where it is also associated with Shaun—as "my chancey oldcoat" (451.2). Here we glimpse "a classy . . . o'coat" (404.17). Other theatrical references are "suparior" (404.18, *sipario,* Italian, a theater curtain) and "hand prop . . . prompt side to the pros" (404.16). Behind "indigo braw" (404.18) we can hear Chauncey Olcott bringing down the house with the ancient Irish war-cry "Erin go bragh"—"Ireland forever."

One event from this play furnishes a beautiful symbolic idea recurrent in the novel. Arrah frees a man from prison by transferring the "key" to him by way of a kiss through the bars. The image is present in the last words in the volume. It is not Shaun, however, who is liberated, though he is her lover. Beyond the fact that Shaun is a bringer of messages it is hard to see why the figure of the simple-minded postman is superimposed upon that of Bruno. But this is the principle of collocation. Just as in a moment we are to see an agonizing death presented under the image of an enormous banquet in a city bright with flowers and riotous with card-playing, so it may be for contrast we are here shown a rural Irish scene, a merry-hearted youth, and a naïve theatrical performance.

The pack of cards is displayed as follows:

On page 405, spades, "spadefuls"; clubs, "leave your clubs in the hall"; hearts, "knives of hearts"; diamonds, "the diamond bone" (406.16). The following are all on page 405: ace, "prime card"; king, "No mistaking"; queen, "the once queen of Balrothy"; jack, "his knives of heart"; ten, "up Dacent Street"—with Dublin accent, *decem;* nine, "nunch"; eight, "would aight through the months"; seven, "this even's"; six, "hundred and sixty"; five, "a pint" (Greek, *pente*); four, "fourpart"; three, "threepartite"; two, "twice." The joker is on the preceding page, "his popular choker" (404.25–26). In addition we are given "the Wheel of Fortune" (405.24), which is the tenth card in the Tarot pack. Readers may also find references to whist, whisk, tricks, trumps, and so on. Bruno was burned in a Jubilee year, 1600. Rome was filled with pilgrims from all over Europe. *Autos-da-fé* were part of the general "jubilation."

There are hundreds of allusions to Bruno in *Finnegans Wake,* and in general Joyce identifies Bruno with himself as Shem—speculative, rebellious against authority, and—in his own eyes—persecuted. On many pages, however, he is an aspect of Shaun; yet Shem and Shaun are ultimately one, just as the stationery partners on Nassau Street, Browne and Nolan, become one: Bruno of Nola. (Another astonishing coincidence.) The passage before us occurs in the first of the

Four Watches of Shaun. Bruno's name is constantly appearing in all of them, though it is not explicitly present in these pages unless we pick up the "brown" of 406.25. But the circumstances of his last days are given: the Pope was present at a session of the trial: the Russian papal red of 404.24–25; *tu es Petrus* (407.15); and his stake was "peatrefired" (405.35). There were several bishops, "evectuals" (405.36), *"avic"* (406.14), *"avec"* (406.22). Here is his vicar, Paolo di Mirandola, "merendally" (406.1, *merenda,* Spanish for "lunch"). The stake was set up in the Flower Market, "aflowering" (406.24) and "floreal" (406.36). The witness beholds the occasion with the "hundred and sixty odds rods and cones" of his retina—yes, the number is "odd" for he has lost a zero to give the year 1600. The Papal Nuncio ("nunch," 405.17) had had much difficulty in extraditing Bruno from the Republic of Venice.

We have no record that Bruno was tortured, for the records have mysteriously disappeared from the archives; but we know that Campanella, author of *The City of the Sun,* a similar case, was put to the torture many times, once for twenty-four hours. Here we have already found the "wheel"; there is also the "grid" (406.5) and even a St. Lawrence, "Saint Lawzenge" (405.24), who is so often represented holding the gridiron of his martyrdom in his hand. One of the tortures of the Inquisition, particularly favored in Scotland, was the "boot," a construction of spiked iron enclosing the foot and leg. Remembering that "sparable" is a small nail used by cobblers, we are now ready to read 404.20–21 and .30–33. He had "thick welted brogues" (perhaps one hears "Maxwelton's braes") "on him hammered to suit the scotsmost public . . . iron heels and sparable soles . . . breaking over the ankle and hugging the shoeheel." Much later in the novel, H.C.E. will give his bride "pattens for her trilbies that know she might the tortuours of the boots" (548.29–30). Another torment was the "cangue"—a wooden frame like the stocks but carried on the shoulder and not attached to the ground. The Dominicans were particularly engaged in the ferreting out of heretics and by a pre-Joycean pun were known throughout Europe as *Domini Canes,* "Hounds of the Lord." Bruno was himself a Dominican and the General of the Order sat on his court. We are told elsewhere (424.3–4) that Shaun had thought to "join the clericy as a demonican sky terrier." Here we read that he has "an Irish ferrier collar, freeswinging . . . from his shoulthern" (404.19–20). We are told that on the way to the stake Bruno's tongue had been tied; here we shall see that during the meal he will have some trouble in "getting his tongue arount it" (406.13). Victims were subjected to the "water" torture. Shaun was served "a clister of peas, soppositorily petty" (406.19)—the water was imposed in the form of an enema.

The execution itself is presented as one extended horrifying pun upon the words "stake" and "steak," together with allusions to frying and roasting and other forms of cooking. Of the steak-stakes we have, on page 405, "prime," "No mistaking," "round," "top," "porterhouse," "clubs," "chucks," "rump" (in "frumped," 405.28), "cold forsoaken steak," and on page 406, "round steak, very rare"; "Braten's," "saddlebag steak," "steak . . . pepper the diamond bone." He even had a grubstake ("he grubbed his tuck all right," 407.2).

The joke is so appalling and Joyce's relish in his own ingenuities so evident that the tone seems to be one of mere savage derision. I turn some seventy pages to find a mitigation. Shaun has finished his sermon to the leap-year girls. He takes his leave. He will be missed, but will return. "Dearest Haun of all, you of the boots . . . lampaddyfair . . . our rommanychiel!" (472.20–22). Bruno was the author of a *De lampade;* we shall see in a moment why he is identified with the gypsies. Until his return, however, time will be ". . . rived by darby's chilldays embers, spatched fun Juhn . . ." (473.9).

Here are Darby and Joan, and the span between December

and June. Here are two dialogues by Bruno: *La cena de la ceneri,* The Ashwednesday Dinner and its embers (elsewhere, also with the phoenix: "when the fiery bird disembers" (24.11); and the *Spaccio de la bestia trionfante,* the driving out of what was interpreted as the Pope. Seeing Darby and Joan and the age-levels implied by the months, we now read: by that time even the children ("childer" is a favorite expression of Joyce) of those now aged will have turned to dust, their fun over; just as Bruno and Joan of Arc will have become ashes. Joyce has compressed three allusions into the word "Juhn"— the proverbial aged spouse, the month of June, and St. Joan. I suspect that the spelling is to remind us of Schiller's Johanna, "Die Jungfrau von Orleans."

Bruno was for Joyce the type of the phoenix, symbol of immortality, and by two more coincidences Joyce in his Paris apartment watched over two small date-palms (botanically, *Phoenix*) reminding him of Dublin's handsome Phoenix Park. To understand the continuation of this passage, the following information is necessary: the Egyptian word for the phoenix bird was *Benu;* Bruno was born in the environs of Naples under Spanish rule; and here Joyce alludes to two powerful arias in Verdi's *Il Trovatore.* In *Stride la vampa* the Gypsy Azucena contemplates her imminent death at the stake and that of her mother before her; and in *Di quella pira* her supposed son Manrico sings of the same death. (Joyce has earlier invoked the first of these arias: "O murder mere . . . Thrubedore I did . . . striding on the vampire . . ." (411.25–31).) We continue:

> Shoot up on that, bright Bennu bird. . . . Eftsoon so too will our own [that is: Joyce's] sphoenix spark spirt his spyre and sunward stride the rampante flambe. Ay, already the somber opacities of the gloom are sphanished. Brave footsore Haun! Work your progress! . . . The silent cock shall crow at last. The west shall shake the east awake. Walk while ye have the night for morn, lightbreakfastbringer. . . . Amain.

We know why he is "footsore." "The silent cock shall crow at last"—when those who have denied their Lord will be confronted with their betrayal. "Light . . . bringer," "How art thou fallen from heaven, O Lucifer, son of the morning!" "Break fast"—Lent is over!

Bruno wrote a *De progressu.* "Work your progress!" What higher homage could Joyce extend than to identify Bruno's book with *Finnegans Wake,* which, when those lines were written, was still entitled *Work in Progress?*

INDEX

COPYRIGHT ACKNOWLEDGMENTS

297